JOURNEYING INTO GOD

# Egypt and Palestine

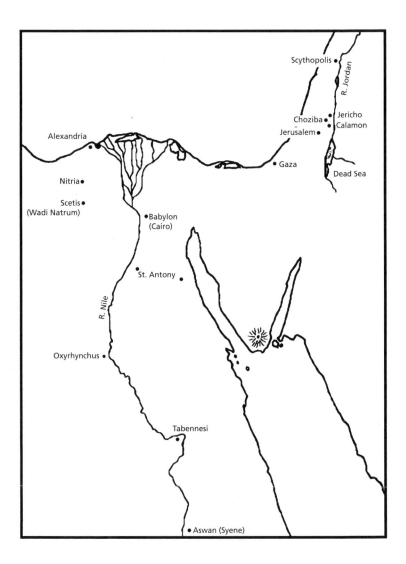

# JOURNEYING INTO GOD

SEVEN
EARLY
MONASTIC
LIVES

Translated, with Introductions, by
Tim Vivian

Fortress Press
Minneapolis

JOURNEYING INTO GOD

Scripture quotations from the Revised Standard Version of the Bible are copyright © 1946, 1952, 1971 by the Division of Christian Education of the National Council of Churches of Christ in the U.S.A. and are used by permission. Scripture quotations from the New Revised Standard Version of the Bible are copyright © 1989 by the Division of Christian Education of the National Council of Churches of Christ in the U.S.A. and are used by permission.

Cover and text designed by Joseph Bonyata.

Cover photo: "Monk's Ladder;" George Peer; Meteora, Greece; from "Pilgrimage Series;" Pinhole camera contact silverprint; Copyright © 1994 George Peer. Used by permission.

Library of Congress Cataloging-in-Publication Data

Journeying into God : seven early monastic lives / translated, with
   introductions by Tim Vivian.
      p.    cm.
   Includes bibliographical references and indexes.
   ISBN 0-8006-2855-1 (alk. paper)
      1. Christian saints—Rome—Biography. 2. Christian Saints—
Byzantine Empire—Biography. 3. Monks—Rome—Biography 4. Monks—
Byzantine Empire—Biography 5. Nuns—Rome—Biography 6. Nuns—
Byzantine Empire—Biography 7. Monasticism and religious orders—
History—Early church, ca. 30-600—Sources. 8. Monastic and
religious life—History—Early church, ca. 30-600—Sources.
   I. Vivian, Tim
BR 1710.J65   1996
271'.0092'2—dc20
[B]                                                              96-1109
                                                                 CIP

The paper used in this publication meets the minimum requirements of American National Standard for Information Science—Permanence of Paper for Printed Library Materials, ANSI z329.48-1984.

Manufactured in the U.S.A.                                    AF I-2855

00   99   98   97   96   I   2   3   4   5   6   7   8   9   10

# CONTENTS

Preface                                                          ix

Introduction                                                      1

1. Hearing God's Call: Saint Antony of Egypt                      7
   Introduction                                                   7
   *The Coptic Life of Antony* 1–15                              12

2. Journeying into God: Abba Pambo                               25
   Introduction                                                  25
   "The Story of Abba Pambo"                                     30

3. A Woman in the Desert: Syncletica of Palestine               37
   Introduction                                                  37
   *A Narrative about Syncletica who Lived in the*               46
   *Jordanian Desert*

4. What Is Spiritual Is Local: Saint George of Choziba          53
   Introduction                                                  53
   *The Life of Saint George of Choziba* 1–42, 57–60            71

5. The Monk as Holy Man: Abba Aaron                             106
   Introduction                                                 106
   "The Life of Abba Aaron"                                     113

6. Holy Example and Heavenly Intercessor: Saint Theognius        134
   Introduction                                                  134
   *An Encomium on the Life of Saint Theognius*                  145

7. Paradise Regained: Saint Onnophrius                           166
   Introduction                                                  166
   *The Life of Onnophrius*                                      172

Bibliography                                                     188

Suggestions for Further Reading                                  193

Scripture Index                                                  197

Index of Names and Subjects                                     201

*The longest journey is the inward journey that we all make.*
—Dag Hammarskjöld

*The geographical pilgrimage is the symbolic acting out of an interior journey.*
—Thomas Merton
*Mystics and Zen Masters*

*Our real journey in life is interior: it is a matter of growth, of deepening and of an ever greater surrender to the creative action of love and grace in our hearts.*
—Thomas Merton
*The Road to Joy*

*A long journey must follow: an anguished and sometimes perilous exploration. Of all Christians the monk is, or at least should be, the most professional of such explorers. His journey takes him through deserts and paradises for which no maps exist. He lives in strange areas of solitude, of emptiness, of joy, of perplexity and of admiration.*
—Thomas Merton
*A Thomas Merton Reader*

*A brother, seized by sadness, asked an elder, saying, "What should I do, for I have thoughts that assail me, saying, 'You renounced the world in vain, for you will not be saved'?" The old man said to him, "You know, brother, even if we are unable to enter the promised land, it is better for our bones to fall in the desert than for us to turn back to Egypt."*
—John Moschus
*Pratum Spirituale* 208 (PG 87.3: 3100D)

*What does this narrative give us in order that we may survive?*
—Walter Brueggemann
*Interpretation and Obedience*

*You don't have anything if you don't have stories.*
—Leslie Silko

*To*
*Miriam*
*Meredith, John, David*
*beloved*

*to Maggie*
*August 5, 1952–April 19, 1994*
*dear friend, classmate, priest*

*and to*
*Jim, Mike, Benjamin,*
*dead of AIDS yet alive in Christ*

# PREFACE

PORTIONS OF THIS BOOK ORIGINALLY APPEARED, IN DIFFERENT form, in the following publications, to which grateful acknowledgment is made:

Chapter 1: "The Coptic *Life of Antony*" (complete Coptic *Life*), *Coptic Church Review* 15; nos. 1–2 (Spring and Summer 1994). The translation in Chapter 1 was also published, with different notes, as part of the complete *Coptic Life of Antony* (San Francisco and London: International Scholars Publications, 1995). Used by permission.

Chapter 2: "Journeying into God: The Story of Abba Pambo," *Cistercian Studies Quarterly* 26; no. 2 (1991): 95–106. Used by permission.

Chapter 3: "Syncletica: A Sixth-Century Female Anchorite," *Vox Benedictina* 10; no. 1 (Summer 1993): 9–37. Used by permission.

Chapter 4: The complete *Life of Saint George of Choziba*, with expanded introduction and notes, was published as part of *The Life of Saint George of Choziba and The Miracles of the Most Holy Mother of God at Choziba* (San Francisco and London: International Scholars Publications, 1994). Used by permission.

Chapter 5: The "Life of Abba Aaron," part III of the *Histories of the Monks of Upper Egypt*, was published as part of *Paphnutius: Histories of the Monks of Upper Egypt and the Life of Onnophrius* (Kalamazoo, Mich.: Cistercian Publications, 1993). Used by permission.

Chapter 6: "An Encomium on the Life of Saint Theognius," co-authored with William Morison, appeared in *Cistercian Studies Quarterly* 30:1 (1995): 59–89. Used by permission.

Chapter 7: "The Life of Onnophrius: A New Translation," *Coptic Church Review* 12; no. 4 (Winter 1991): 99–111. The translation is based on the unpublished text of Codex Pierpont Morgan M. 580, folios 1v–19v, found in the Coptic manuscript collection of the J. Pierpont Morgan Library in New York. I wish to thank the Morgan Library for permission to publish this translation. Used by permission.

Unless otherwise indicated, scripture is quoted according to the Revised Standard Version (RSV) or New Revised Standard Version (NRSV) of the Bible, altered to conform to the Greek and Coptic texts.

I wish to thank Apostolos Athanassakis, Rowan Greer, Rick Kennedy, and Jeffrey Russell for reading portions of the book in manuscript; their comments, suggestions, and criticism allowed me to make many valuable changes. I wish to thank Mark Gardner for reading the completed manuscript and offering his suggestions as a parish priest; Mark, thank you even more for giving me a parish home in exile.

I am grateful to Apostolos Athanassakis and Birger Pearson for their help with my inquiries about Greek and Coptic.

Prof. Athanassakis and I together translated the *Life of Saint George of Choziba* (chapter 4), and William Morison and I worked together on the *Encomium on the Life of Saint Theognius* (chapter 6).

I wish also to thank Bill Morison for his ungrudging bibliographical help. Finally, I wish to thank Cynthia Thompson, Beth Gaede, and Joe Bonyata at Fortress Press for making many suggestions for improving this work.

This book is intended primarily for a non-scholarly audience; therefore, I have omitted from these pieces as they originally appeared many footnotes and details from footnotes that will be of interest mostly to scholars. Interested readers are referred to the original publications.

Since this book went to press several good books in English have appeared on early monasticism that I was unable to use. I wish to note them here, and in the bibliography, for interested readers: John Binns, *Ascetics and Ambassadors of Christ* (Oxford: Clarendon Press, 1994); David Brakke, *Athanasius and the Politics of Asceticism* (Oxford: Clarendon Press, 1995); Robert Doran, *The Lives of Simeon Stylites* (Kalamazoo: Cistercian, 1992); Susanna Elm, *"Virgins of God": The Making of Asceticism in Late Antiquity* (Oxford: Clarendon Press, 1994); Joseph Patrich, *Sabas, Leader of Palestinian Monasticism* (Washington, D.C.: Dumbarton Oaks, 1995).

—TIM VIVIAN

# INTRODUCTION

JESUS WAS THE FIRST MONK—AT LEAST ACCORDING TO SAINT
Euthymius, one of the founders of monasticism in Judea in the fifth
century. Each year on the Epiphany, in the East the feast day of
Christ's baptism, Euthymius would follow his Lord's example (Mt.
4:1–11) and go off into the far reaches of the desert, where he would
remain until Palm Sunday. Then, also like his Lord, he would leave the
desert to come up to Jerusalem.[1] For Euthymius, and thousands of
other Christians in the fourth through seventh centuries, monasticism
was, literally, the following of Jesus Christ.

Following requires journeying. Jesus' first disciples followed him
through Judea and Samaria, but most of them (the men, anyway) exited
short of the crucifixion. After their Lord's death and resurrection,
some of them journeyed throughout the Roman Empire with the good
news—to Arabia, Greece, Asia Minor, Italy, Egypt. Journeying is so
central to early Christianity that legend had the apostles traveling even
to India and England.

Each of the stories in this collection involves journeying, into the
desert and into the desert of the human heart where, the early monks
believed, you most fully encounter God. Antony (chapter 1) is archetypal: the first part of the Christian journey, the *Life of Antony* tells us,
is evangelical—hearing and heeding God's call to live a gospel life. The
second stage is leave-taking, separating yourself from those things that

---

1. Cyril of Scythopolis, *Life of Euthymius* 7, trans. R. M. Price, *Cyril of Scythopolis: The
Lives of the Monks of Palestine* (Kalamazoo, Mich.: Cistercian Publications, 1991), 10.

I

pull you away from God—in Antony's case, family, possessions, property. Journeying then becomes geographical, where geography is both literal and the outward and visible sign of the interior, evangelical journey. Antony leaves his village and goes farther and farther into the desert until he comes to the outer mountain, which he always returned to "like someone heading home."

Pambo's journeying (chapter 2) is almost entirely interior, into himself, into mystery and God. The landscape both he and Paphnutius (in the *Life of Onnophrius*, chapter 7) traverse is almost mythical, archetypal, symbolic, a palimpsest of the spirit where the map of the spiritual journey has been written over the terrestrial map. A few details of the latter are visible, but so primary is the former that it almost—but not completely—effaces earthly landmarks.

The desert is more palpable in Paphnutius's report of the "Life of Abba Aaron" (chapter 5). In this story Abba Isaac is the journeyer, the one who goes out into the desert to find the holy man Abba Aaron. Isaac finds, at least initially, more than he has bargained for: the desert is hot, severe, and peopled with demons. Readers who have ventured before into early monasticism know that heat, sand, and demons are props and property of the literature, so common that sometimes they seem clichés, scenery to be dragged from one stage to the next; after successive scenes they become more and more tattered and threadbare. New readers may welcome the exotic locations; if early monasticism is merely exotic, however, we become simply spiritual tourists. Exoticism is not lived daily, and, as the stories in this collection make clear, these deserts were lived.

What is most striking, though, about the "Life of Abba Aaron" is that after Isaac settles with Aaron, the focus shifts from geography to people, from the struggle of the soul in its desert to the struggles of ordinary people in their daily lives: camel herders, fishermen, farmers, fruit-pickers, villagers, rich men, loan sharks, childless husbands and wives. With these people come the attendant accidents and terrors of the everyday: drownings, stillbirths, loss of crops, sudden death, dying children. The desert of the ordinary, we learn, can be just as terrifying as the desert of the demons. At the still point of these horrors, however—that is, at the still point and center of the daily—Abba Aaron sits, praying—and healing, healing through faith in the name of Christ. Resplendent in his asceticism, Aaron is a striking witness—striking, but by no means unique or bound solely to the past—to the continuing incarnation of Christ in the world, an incarnation that transfigures and transforms all geographies.

Syncletica, George, and Theognius (chapters 3, 4, and 6, respectively) are firmly grounded in the rocky terrain and holy landscape of Palestine. Syncletica and Theognius come to the Holy Land as pilgrims, and thus their footsteps join those of thousands of other Holy Land pilgrims in late antiquity. But the emphasis in these three stories is not on the sanctity of place but on the holiness of people. As George says, it is not the place (*topos*) that makes one holy but the way of life (*tropos*). "Way of life" in these monastic texts does not mean "standard of living"; it means "dedication to God," a definition that, if we are at all spiritually awake, should make us in the West uncomfortable.

Syncletica overthrows the conventions of Constantinopolitan society, including the twin gods wealth and security, in order to sit quietly with God; Theognius prays so long and so fervently that even when asleep he holds the words of the psalms on his lips; George eats other people's leftovers, wears rags from the garbage dump, and reads the human heart. Sojourners themselves, because of their holiness, they become objects of pilgrimage and veneration. Syncletica flees adoration, George takes on a disciple, and Theognius founds a monastery to house his followers. What did the ancient pilgrims to these pilgrims see in them? What made these monks, whose lives are chronicled here, so holy?

Modern scholars, in their attempt to recover "the world behind the text," have sought to answer this question with a number of socio-economic and historical measuring sticks, many of them accurate (as far as their devices measure). But as Walter Brueggemann has pointed out with regard to biblical narratives, the authors of the stories translated here are not much interested in "the world behind the text": "They are not interested in knowledge that records, controls, and chronicles. They are interested rather in the world 'in front of the text.' They ask, What does this narrative give us in order that we may survive?"[2] The answer, stripped to essentials—like the lives of the monks—is prayer. Lived prayer. That answer, of course, is neither simple nor easy to live out, as the lives of these monks testify, as anyone knows who has tried to pray without ceasing, that is, to make one's life *into* prayer. That living

2. Walter Brueggemann, *Interpretation and Obedience: From Faithful Reading to Faithful Living* (Minneapolis: Fortress Press, 1991), 31.

out, though, *is* the desert, the *real* desert. The false desert, the one that really kills, is the illusions we manufacture—and believe—about ourselves, and the world and weapons crafted to work that deception. We imagine this illusionary desert to be a garden, and so we prefer to live there, in fear of the real desert, real life, life stripped of illusions and close to God. The desert of the monks, however, is the real garden, as the *Life of Onnophrius* reveals to us. When Jesus went out into the desert after his baptism, he confronted the devil and thereby smashed the illusions of power, control, and self-centeredness. But he could smash them only for himself, not for these monks, nor for us. The desert is where, in profound and deepest silence, and only there, you hear the breaking of idols.

The desert of the Lord, at least in its first full geographical and spiritual flowering, bore fruit for Christianity for about four hundred years. The desert of the Lord included the desert that Euthymius disappeared into for the greatest of Lents, and in which he reappeared each year in obedience to resurrection; the desert that Antony, Pambo, and Paphnutius journeyed into; the desert that Aaron, Onnophrius, Syncletica, George, and Theognius settled as homesteaders for the gospel, where they temporarily resided on their way to God. Their manner of living was as diverse as their lives, but each sought out God and sought God in solitude. Lack of holy solitude, *hesychia*, is the modern Western world's greatest deprivation. The monasticism of the monks in this collection is solitary, what we commonly call anchoritic or eremitic monasticism. Although each of them attracts followers, Antony, Aaron, Onnophrius, and Syncletica live alone. Pambo, it is true, returns to the monastic settlement at Scetis, but we hear nothing of his life there. George lives attached to a cenobium, a community of monks dwelling together, but he himself is part of a laura, a group of monks who each lived alone, scattered in cells or caves, and who came to the monastery for worship, supplies, and fellowship. Theognius became a bishop, but even as bishop he returned often to his monastery where he, too, probably lived in a cave.

Antony left home for his spiritual home on the outer mountain late in the third century, before the Roman Empire was officially Christian; Aaron lived at the end of the fourth century when Christianity, seemingly triumphant, had begun its continuous compromise with the state, a compromise yet unfinished, and still resisted. Theognius died in 525; at 97 years of age he had lived most of the fifth century, a period of ongoing and enervating theological warfare. Syncletica probably belongs to the sixth century, and George of Choziba died, "as someone might change his pace as he walks," around 630, just a few years before Jerusalem and the Holy Land fell to the Muslims, and when the monasteries seemed—seemed—silent.

By this time, however, the spiritual descendants of these early monks had carried monasticism in the West to Italy, Gaul, and the British Isles, where Cassian, Benedict, and the Celtic monks would carry on the traditions of both the Lord and the desert. Much that is good in modern Western Christian spirituality looks back appreciatively to desert forebears.[3] In the East, hesychastic monasticism would spread to Greece, the Balkans, and Russia. It survived when Byzantium fell and Hagia Sophia was turned into a museum, and now it has outlasted the Soviet Union. And now the desert monasteries in Egypt and Palestine have themselves undergone a renaissance; some monasteries have been revived, while others have been in continual existence for over fifteen hundred years.[4] The monks of Mount Athos in Greece still refer to their way of life as that of the desert; they very deliberately look back—perhaps too much—to the mothers and fathers of the first desert.[5]

That desert is and is not our own, can and will never be our own. It is, after all, a place and a time, both distant, both subject to the glories and infirmities of all time and every place, our own included. That time and place in the early desert must not be idealized. The desert was, conspicuously, inhabited more by demons than angels. Perhaps finally that is what this desert still offers us, and what we most need: to see our demons (which are there whether we see them or not), to confront them, and finally through love, prayer, humility, and self-sacrifice, to overcome them. The desert offers us the chance to live out the Gospel, if not perfectly, then concretely and, as much as humanly possible, fully.

I once heard a bishop say with regard to social justice that it is good for us to rescue the drowning; eventually, though, we will have to go

---

3. See the "Suggestions for Further Reading," p. 194.

4. See Alaine and Evelyne Chevillat, *Moines du Désert D'Égypte* (Lyon: Terre du Ciel, 1990), which has wonderful pictures of modern-day monks. For a heartfelt appreciation of what the desert monasteries can offer Western Christians, see Alan Jones, *Soul Making: The Desert Way of Spirituality* (San Francisco: Harper & Row, 1985), 12–16.

5. See Archimandrite Cherubim, *Contemporary Ascetics of Mount Athos* (Platina, Calif.: St. Herman of Alaska Brotherhood, 1991).

upstream to see who's throwing all these people in the water. The monks in this collection lived by that stream, and all streams, and as the reports of their miracles and the examples of their charity in these stories demonstrate, they rescued their share of the drowning. More importantly, they would also go searching upstream, daily, hourly, without ceasing, on foot and in their prayers: they offer us another form of journeying.

"The whole point of history," Jeffrey Burton Russell has observed, "and its great joy, is to encounter people in the past as real people, to rescue them from oblivion, to restore them as living, whole human beings."[6] The saints gathered here—despite the conventions of hagiography, the accidents of memory, and the differences that time and custom create—are real people. The whole point of spirituality, it seems to me, is to encounter ourselves as living, whole human beings in the presence of God.[7] These saints are both parent and child of that encounter. My intention when I began this collection was indeed to rescue these saints.[8] As I have lived with them these past five years, however, they have outgrown my intentions: I now hope they can rescue us.[9]

6. Quoted from an unpublished paper presented at the University of California, Santa Barbara.

7. Three recent and admirable studies of how ancient ascetic spirituality mattered in people's lives are Douglas Burton-Christie, *The Word in the Desert: Scripture and the Quest for Holiness in Early Christian Monasticism* (New York and Oxford: Oxford University Press, 1993); Graham Gould, *The Desert Fathers on Monastic Community* (Oxford: Clarendon, 1993); and Susan Ashbrook Harvey, *Asceticism and Society in Crisis: John of Ephesus and the Lives of the Eastern Saints* (Berkeley: University of California, 1990).

8. Of the Coptic monks, Paphnutius and Onnophrius, and of course Antony, articles appear in *The Coptic Encyclopedia*; articles about Isaac, Pambo, and Aaron do not. The Palestinians fare worse: *The Oxford Dictionary of Byzantium* does not include George, Theognius, or Syncletica. Of the monks in this collection, the *Encyclopedia of Early Christianity* and *The Oxford Dictionary of the Christian Church*, 2nd ed., give space only to Antony. Only Antony, Onnophrius, and Paphnutius are represented in the two-volume *Encyclopedia of the Early Church*.

9. I maintain, against much current scholarly opinion, that real people lie within and behind these stories. Yes, the stories have typological and hagiographical elements, but they also contain a wealth of lived detail. Most importantly, I believe—in opposition to a certain academic pretense of disinterest and disinvolvement—that these stories, like the Gospels they spring from, seriously involve us, as they did those for whom they were originally told and written.

# 1

# HEARING GOD'S CALL: SAINT ANTONY OF EGYPT

## Introduction

HEARING GOD'S CALL, MONKS GIVE UP EVERYTHING—PROPERTY, possessions, family, friends—to live a life devoted to Christ. They are Christianity's true "fundamentalists": fundamentalists because they take the gospel literally, at its word; "true" because their *intention*—they are, after all, human—is to practice in love the fundamentals of the Christian faith (prayer, hospitality, charity). The fundamental virtues of monasticism are love, compassion, and humility, all gospel virtues, all made flesh most completely by Christ, the first monk.

The *Life of Antony* offers us a vision of monasticism made flesh in Antony. It presents, to be sure, an ideal vision and an idealized monk,[1] as though in the United States George Washington had been chosen by a contemporary to represent not only the beginnings of American democracy, but also its consummation and highest achievements, before democracy even had much of a history or had shown its staying power. Though idealized, the *Life of Antony* is, nevertheless, true— both to the wider history of early monasticism and, more importantly, to the self-understanding of the early monks.[2] Antony was not the first

---

1. See James E. Goehring, "The Origins of Monasticism," in Harold W. Attridge and Gohei Hata, eds., *Eusebius, Judaism and Christianity* (Detroit: Wayne State University Press, 1992), 235–55; and Goehring, "The Encroaching Desert: Literary Production and Ascetic Space in Early Christian Egypt," *Journal of Early Christian Studies* 1, no. 3 (Fall 1993): 281–96.

2. See Diarmuid O. Murchu, "St. Antony of Egypt: The Man and the Myth," *Cistercian Studies* 20, no. 2 (1985): 88–97.

7

monk. The *Life* itself tells us that: when Antony embraced the ascetical life, monks were already practicing asceticism "a little way" outside
their villages; an old man in Antony's own village "had practiced
asceticism from his youth"; Antony entrusted his sister "to some faithful women . . . so that she would live in virginity" (all described in
chapter 3).[3]

Antony's importance is not so much that he was the first monk—he
was not—but that he defined the nature of monastic spirituality for
his own generation and for succeeding generations of Christians, not
just for monks. Recent studies have shown that this definition given to
us in the *Life of Antony* cannot be written off as "mere" hagiography or
dismissed as just an implausible glorification of an ideal. Walter
Brueggemann, with regard to the stories about Elisha, has spoken of
"narratives of amazement," "told not to preserve past miracles but to
generate present awe and to anticipate future astonishment. . . . The
narrative does not just remember a world that was. It creates a world
that could be. . . ."[4] Antony's story, and the story of each monk gathered
in this collection, is a "narrative of amazement" (words of amazement
and wonder occur at least thirty times in the *Life of Antony*),[5] offering
the world as it could be, as it *can* be, in Christ, embraced by God.

The Antony who lives and breathes in these pages is true—demons
and all—to the way these early monks lived, thought, and believed. He
is also true to the way the monks saw and understood their vocation,
both as a calling (*vocatio*) and as a way of life (*politeia*).[6] Central to
Antony's calling to the monastic life is scripture. The beginning of the
*Life* does present Antony too neatly, a child-adult, too serious to play
like the other children (chapter 1). But after his parents' death, the
story becomes more realistic: left in charge of his home and younger

---

3. On village ascetics, see E. A. Judge, "The Earliest Use of Monachos for 'Monk'" (P.
Coll. Youtie 77) and the Origins of Monasticism," *Jahrbuch für Antike und Christentum* 20
(1977): 72–89. On earliest monasticism, see Goehring, and J. C. O'Neill, "The Origins of
Monasticism," in *The Making of Orthodoxy: Essays in Honour of Henry Chadwick*, ed. Rowan
Williams (Cambridge: Cambridge University Press, 1989), 270–87.

4. Brueggemann, 31.

5. "Amaze," "amazed," "amazement," "astonish," "astonished," "marvel," "marvelous,"
"wonder," "wonders." See the Word Index in Tim Vivian, trans., *The Coptic Life of Antony*
(San Francisco and London: International Scholars Publications, 1995), 139–52.

6. See Samuel Rubenson, *The Letters of St. Antony: Origenist Theology, Monastic Tradition
and the Making of a Saint* (Lund: Lund University Press, 1990); and Douglas Burton-
Christie, *The Word in the Desert: Scripture and the Quest for Holiness in Early Christian
Monasticism* (New York and Oxford: Oxford University Press, 1993), 47.

sister, Antony one day is walking to church. "While he was walking, he considered how the apostles gave up everything and followed the Savior" (see Mt 4:20, Lk 14:33) (paragraph 2). This thought leads him to think of the Christian community depicted in Acts, where everyone gave up their possessions and gave to those in need (Acts 4:34–35). "Pondering these things in his heart, he went into church and it happened that the Gospel was being read; he heard the Lord saying to the [rich man], 'If you want to be perfect, go and sell all your possessions and give them to the poor, and come and follow me, and you will have treasure in heaven'" (Mt 19:21). Antony does as the gospel asks: he gives up everything to follow Christ.

Such renunciation *and* embracing certainly had a wider social context than the *Life* presents. But Antony's central motivation in the passage *is* simple: he obeyed, literally, the words of Christ. As Armand Veilleux has pointed out: "All the motivations that [the monks] themselves revealed to us in their writings came from scripture. Do we have a right to pretend we know their secret motivations better than they did?"[7] Hearing the gospel, really hearing it, prompts Antony to *act*: "All his desire and all his attention he directed to the great effort of asceticism" (chapter 3).

The rest of the *Life of Antony* is really a telling of this single-mindedness: Antony's goal is to be a "lover of God" (chapter 4); in order to do this, he must not allow himself to be distracted—drawn away—from God.[8] The myriad demons are distractors: they draw us away from God. Whether they are "physical" or "psychological" is irrelevant; they are real. Sometimes the whole purpose of our modern era—whether expressed in communism, capitalism, materialism, consumerism, scientism—seems to be to draw us away from God. Television has only exacerbated the situation observed so acutely by Aldous Huxley fifty years ago:

> But it is upon fashions, cars and gadgets, upon news and the advertising for which news exists, that our present industrial and economic system depends for its proper functioning. For . . . this system cannot work unless the demand for non-necessaries is not merely kept

7. Armand Veilleux, "Monasticism and Gnosis in Egypt," in Birger A. Pearson and James E. Goehring, eds., *The Roots of Egyptian Christianity* (Philadelphia: Fortress, 1986), 306.

8. For a sympathetic discussion of Antony's desire for "cleanness of heart," purged of worldly distractions, see Colm Luibhéid, "Antony and the Renunciation of Society," *Irish Theological Quarterly* 52 (1986): 304–14.

up, but continually expanded; and of course it cannot be kept up and expanded except by incessant appeals to greed, competitiveness and love of aimless stimulation. Men have always been a prey to distractions, which are the original sin of the mind; but never before today has an attempt been made to organize and exploit distractions, to make of them, because of their economic importance, the core and vital center of human life. . . .[9]

In the *Life of Antony*, Antony confronts the demons of distraction, as real then as now. One scene, an enacted parable, gives this theological and spiritual confrontation a concrete setting. Because Antony is literally on his way to God, on the road to the mountain where he will live with the holy, the scene becomes both incident and metaphor, biographical detail and universal symbol. One day Antony

> set out for the mountain, but the enemy saw his eagerness and, wishing to trip him up on the way, cast onto the road the apparition of a large silver dish. [But Antony] recognized the wiles of the hater of goodness, and he stood and looked at the dish. He knew that it was a work of the devil and said, "How did this dish get here in the desert? No path has been worn here before now, nor is there any traveler's footprint. If someone had dropped it, he would have known it because it is large, and whoever lost it would have returned and looked for it and found it because this place is a desert. What has happened here is the work of the devil. You will not trip me up by doing this, devil! Instead, this will go with you to destruction!" [See Acts 8:20.] When Antony said these things, it vanished like smoke.
>
> Afterwards, while he was walking on his way, he saw some gold, not in a fantasy, but truly. Whether it was the enemy who showed it to him or whether a mighty power was training the [athlete] and showing the devil that he was not tormented by money, he did not tell us, nor do we know what happened—only, it was truly gold that he saw. Now Antony marvelled at the quantity of gold, but he passed it by, fleeing as one flees fire; as a result, he did not take one step toward it.
>
> He advanced closer and closer to the mountain. (chapters 11–12)

Early monasticism, represented well by the *Life of Antony*, offers a striking and uncompromising opposition to the "greed, competitiveness and love of aimless stimulation" that Huxley so presciently

9. Aldous Huxley, "Distractions—I," in *Vedanta for the Western World*, ed. Christopher Isherwood (Hollywood: Vedanta Press, 1946), 129.

warned us about: asceticism. But today asceticism often conjures up images of dirty and emaciated men wearing hair-shirts and flogging themselves. The monks themselves, however, defined asceticism very differently (chapter 3).[10] For them asceticism was really very simple: working and spending—something even *The Wall Street Journal* would approve! But it was working and spending as defined by the gospel, not by Wall Street: Antony worked with his hands, and "he would spend what he earned from his handiwork rightly: he would spend part on bread and part on those in need." Monasticism directs the monk inward *and* outward. Most importantly, Antony "prayed all the time, having learned that it is necessary to pray without ceasing (1 Thess 5:17)." The action of the monastic life, then, is prayer, prayer without ceasing, prayer not divorced or cordoned off from work and the rest of life, prayer *as* life and life as prayer. Some monks prayed even while seemingly asleep.[11] Others, in obedience to the gospel, had others pray in their stead while they slept.

The monks valued such single-mindedness. Antony, like many others, was a model of monastic determination. The *Apophthegmata*, or *Sayings* of the desert fathers and mothers, preserve a saying by Antony in which he teaches a young monk in an unforgettable way about the seriousness of his calling:

> A brother renounced the world and gave his goods to the poor, but he kept back a little for his personal expenses. He went to see Abba Antony. When he told him this, the old man said to him, "If you want to be a monk, go into the village, buy some meat, cover your naked body with it and come here like that." The brother did so, and the dogs and birds tore at his flesh. When he came back the old man asked him whether he had followed his advice. He showed him his wounded body, and Saint Antony said, "Those who renounce the world but want to keep something for themselves are torn in this way by the demons who make war on them."[12]

The demons did—and do—wage war, silently and noisily, quietly and violently, relentlessly. As Huxley pointed out, and as we can read in the newspaper each morning and witness in our homes and neigh-

---

10. For an excellent discussion, see Burton-Christie, 181–296.

11. See the *Life of Theognius*, p. 160 below.

12. *Apophthegmata* Antony 20, trans. Benedicta Ward, *The Sayings of the Desert Fathers: The Alphabetical Collection*, rev. ed. (Kalamazoo, Mich.: Cistercian Publications, 1984), 5.

borhoods each day, the demons have only intensified their efforts in the modern era. But the *Life of Antony* offers a vision of the demons defeated, the community and its citizens at peace (chapter 4). This vision, based as it is on Luke's depiction of the early Christian community in Acts 4:32, *is* an idealization, but it is an idealization with its roots planted deeply in the desert earth, where nothing grows. That earthly paradox lies at the heart of the *Life of Antony*: this work—and the lives of the first desert monks that it portrays—envisions the desert "filled with monks" (chapter 4). Only those filled with the love of God could imagine—and live—such an impossibility. They continue to offer possibility to us.

# THE COPTIC LIFE OF ANTONY 1–15[1]

## Antony's Origins

1. Antony was an Egyptian by race. His parents were well-born, for they had many possessions and, since they were Christians, from his childhood Antony advanced also in the Christian life. He was raised by his parents and so knew nothing besides them and life at home. When he grew and advanced in age, he did not wish to continue his writing lessons, wishing to stand apart from the ordinary activities of children. His whole desire was, as it is written,[2] to remain in his home without deceit.[3] He would join his parents in church, and he was never recklessly playful like a child, nor was he contemptuous while growing up; instead, he obeyed his parents and observed their wishes, and he would keep in his heart what was profitable from them. Moreover, although he had many possessions as a child, he did not pester his parents for all kinds of food, nor did he look for the pleasures associated with them. He was content with what he had and he never looked for anything more.

---

1. The translation is based on the Sahidic Coptic text edited by G. Garitte, *S. Antonii Vitae Versio Sahidica*, CSCO, Scriptores Coptici Series Quarta, Tomus I (Paris: 1949). Paragraphing follows that of the Coptic text, although chapter headings are the translator's.

2. Gen 25:27.

3. Coptic *krof*, "guile, deceit." *Sa nkrof*, "deceiver," is a common designation for the devil.

## Antony's Call to the Ascetic Life

2. After his parents' death, Antony was left behind with his little sister, and at eighteen or twenty years of age had to take good care of his home and his sister. Six months had not passed since the death of his parents when, as was his custom, he left the house and went to church. He was reflecting on their wishes and gave his full attention to them. While he was walking, he considered how the apostles gave up everything and followed the Savior.[4] There were those who sold their possessions, as it is written in Acts: "They brought them and laid them at the feet of the apostles so they could give them to those in need."[5] And he reflected on what sort or what kind of hope there is for them in heaven.[6] Pondering these things in his heart, he went into church and it happened that the Gospel was being read; he heard the Lord saying to the [rich man],[7] "If you want to be perfect, go and sell all your possessions and give them to the poor, and come and follow me, and you will have treasure in heaven."[8]

Now Antony, when he received the remembrances of the saints[9] from God and reckoned in his heart how that passage had been read for his sake, immediately left that church, and the possessions that his parents had left him (there were three hundred very prosperous acres), these he freely gave away to the people of his village, so they would not bother him or his sister about anything. All the rest of his lesser possessions he sold and, collecting a great amount of money, gave it to the poor. He kept a few things for his sister.

## Antony Embraces the Ascetic Life

3. When he entered the church again and heard in the Gospel the Lord saying, "Do not be concerned about tomorrow,"[10] he could no longer bear it; he immediately went out and gave his remaining things to the

---

4. Mt 4:20.

5. See Acts 4:34.

6. Col 1:5; see Mt 19:21.

7. Coptic "neighbor." The translator read *tō plousiō*, "neighbor," instead of *tō plēsiō*, "rich man," which the Greek text has.

8. Mt 19:21.

9. That is, in the scriptures; Papias (second century) uses the phrase "the memoirs of the apostles."

10. Mt 6:34.

poor. His sister he entrusted to some faithful women, knowing that they were virgins, so that she would live in virginity.[11] He for his part left his household and devoted himself from then on to ascetic practice, disciplining and strengthening himself. For there were not yet many monasteries at all in Egypt, and no monks knew yet the farther desert, but each one who wished to would attend to himself, going outside of his village a little ways, and he would practice ascetic discipline by himself.

Now there was an old man in that village who had practiced asceticism from his youth, living the life of a monk. When Antony saw this man, he emulated him in goodness and he began also by at first remaining there outside his village. And if he heard about anyone who was serious about following good practices, he would go and search out that man like a wise honeybee and would not return to his own place unless he had seen that man. He was like someone who had received from that man provisions for traveling the road to virtue.

Living at first in that place, he resolved that he would not return to see the things of his parents, nor would he think of his relatives. All his desire and all his attention he directed to the great efforts of asceticism. He worked with his hands, for he had heard the scriptures say, "He who does not work, let him not eat."[12] And he would spend what he earned from his handiwork rightly: he would spend part on bread and part on those in need. He prayed all the time, having learned that it is necessary to pray without ceasing.[13] Indeed, he paid such close attention to what was read in church that nothing in the scriptures escaped his notice. He kept everything in his heart, with the result that in his heart, memory took the place of books.

4. Thus Antony conducted himself, and he was loved by everyone. He was obedient in a sober and serious way to those who devoted themselves to ascetic discipline; going to them, he would consider in his heart the ascetic practice of each one and the good spiritual formation and devotion of each. He saw that one was filled with grace[14] and that another was strong in ascetic discipline; another he saw powerful in prayer, while another was never angry, and another loved all of humanity. One would pass the night in prayerful vigil, and another would

---

11. Coptic *parthenia*; Greek *parthenōna*, "in a convent."
12. 2 Thess 3:10.
13. 1 Thess 5:17.
14. "One . . . grace": literally, "person of grace," *remncharis*, Greek *philanthrōpos*.

read well. He marveled at one's patient endurance and another's fasting and sleeping on the ground. He watched closely the gentleness of one and observed the patience of another. With one accord they all scrupulously held on to their godly worship of Christ and their love for one another.[15]

He considered all these things in his heart and, filled with all these things, returned home to his own ascetic practice for God. He embraced in his heart all the things he had seen in each one and strove to manifest all of them in himself. He was not one to quarrel with those of his own age except that he would not be inferior to them in good works but would manifest in himself what was better. And he would do this without causing them sadness; rather, he would cause them to rejoice all the more for him. Everyone, then, in the village, and all the conscientious people with whom he associated, would call him "God-loving" when they saw his example. Some would greet him as "son," and others as "brother."

## The Devil's First Attack on Antony

5. The devil, who hates and envies what is good, could not bear to see such zeal in this young man, so he now undertook to do to him those things that he customarily concerns himself with doing. First, he attempted to lead him away from his ascetic practice, casting into him memories of his possessions and his guardianship of his sister, longing for family and kin, love of money, boasting, the pleasure in eating many kinds of food, and the other satisfactions of life. Finally, he cast into his heart the difficulty of virtuous living, how great its hardship and manifold its sufferings, and he displayed for him the body's weakness and the many years required to attain perfection, and he raised up in him a great dustcloud of thoughts for him to consider, wishing to separate him from his righteous thoughts.

When the enemy saw him, and saw that he himself was powerless before Antony's will, and that he was being badly defeated by the strength of that man, and that he was being thrown to the ground because of Antony's unceasing prayers, he then armed himself with the weapons upon his navel.[16] Armed with these, and gloating over them

---

15. See Acts 4:32.

16. Job 40:16 (Septuagint: LXX): Behemoth's "strength is in its loins, and its power in the navel of its belly."

(for these are the arrows he prefers to cast first against the young), he advanced to fight against Antony, disturbing him at night and bothering him so much that [even those who were watching][17] could see that there was a fight being waged between the two of them.

The enemy hurled foul thoughts at Antony, but he drove them back through prayer; the enemy raised up pleasurable desires in him, but Antony, ashamed of them, fortified his body with faith and fasting. And the devil took on the form of a woman at night and imitated all of a woman's ways in order to deceive Antony. But thinking about Christ in his heart and the intellectual vision[18] of his soul, he extinguished the devil's coals. But the enemy once again cast into him the desire for pleasure, but Antony, as though he were angry and grieving, considered in his heart the threat of fire and the worm that works his devices there.[19]

All these things happened to the shame of the enemy, for he who thought "I will be able to fight against God" was mocked by Antony. For working with him was the Lord who bore flesh for us and gave victory to his chosen ones against the devil so that each of those who struggle can say, "It is not I but the grace of God that is in me."[20]

6. Finally, then, when the dragon was unable to cast Antony down, he became angry at himself and gnashed his teeth at Antony.[21] Becoming deranged, he appeared to him in the illusory form of a young black boy. He became like one mad and, using a human voice, said to Antony, "I have deceived many like you, and I have brought down a multitude. Just now I did my utmost against you, as I have done to others." Antony asked, "Who are you saying these words to me?"

Immediately the devil cried out in a powerful voice, "I am the friend of fornication. I am the one who possesses its traps and desires, waging war against the young. They call me 'the spirit of fornication.' How many wanted to live wisely, and I deceived them! How many were quietly patient, and I deceived them by casting into them daily preoccupations! I am the one whom the prophet accuses on account of

---

17. Greek; Coptic lacks this phrase. Translations of the Greek text are quoted from *Athanasius: The Life of Antony and the Letter to Marcellinus*, trans. Robert C. Gregg (New York: Paulist Press, 1980).

18. Coptic *peiōrh nnoēron*: Greek *to noeron*, what is intellectual/rational *and* spiritual.

19. See Mk 9:48.

20. 1 Cor 15:10.

21. See Acts 7:54.

those who have fallen: 'They have been led astray by a spirit of fornication.'[22] I am the one who led them astray. On account of me they fell. I am the one who harassed you so often, but up to now you have defeated me."

Antony gave thanks to the Lord and, summoning up his courage, he said, "You will succeed all the more in becoming despised, for you are black of mind and you are like a small child, without power. From now on, I will have no anxiety about you. 'The Lord is my helper, and I shall look upon my enemies.'"[23] When he heard these words, the enemy immediately fled, trembling before them, and he was afraid to approach Antony at all.

## Antony's First Ascetic Practices

7. This was Antony's first contest with the devil—or, rather, it was the Savior's victory in Antony. For he who took on flesh from the virgin Mary condemned sin in the flesh in order that the justification of the Law might be made manifest in us who walk not according to the flesh but according to the Spirit.[24] Antony, however, did not become neglectful or arrogant, as though the devil had fallen beneath his feet. Nor did the enemy, when defeated, stop setting traps but, like a lion, was prowling around looking for an opportunity to attack Antony.[25]

Antony learned from the scriptures that the tricks of the enemy are numerous, so he practiced his asceticism even more, thinking in his heart that although the enemy had not been able to trap him in any way with bodily pleasures, he would not stop tempting him but would try to trap him by means of some other pretext. For the devil is a lover of sin, especially against the saints.[26] Antony subdued his body, making it a slave,[27] so that he would not, after conquering some temptations, be drawn into others and be deceived by them. He made plans to enter into an even more difficult and demanding regimen of ascetical practice, and many marvelled at him, but he endured the pain and hardship with ease.

22. See Hos 4:12.
23. See Ps 118:7.
24. See Rom 8:3–4.
25. Ps 17:12; 1 Pet 5:8.
26. See 1 Jn 3:8.
27. See 1 Cor 9:27.

The eagerness within his soul endured for such a long time that it created in him a good disposition so that when he received even small suggestions from others, he showed great enthusiasm for [them]. He would often pass the night in vigil without sleeping, and he would do this not once or twice but many times, and people would marvel greatly at him. Now he would not eat each day until after the sun had set, but oftentimes he would eat every second or fourth day. His food was bread and salt and water. It is not necessary even to speak of meat and wine, for nothing of this sort is found among those who are zealous. A mat would suffice for him to sleep on, and often he would just sleep on the floor.

He took care not to anoint himself with oil, saying that it was more fitting for young people to bring forth in themselves ascesis with eagerness and not to seek after those things that the body relies on, but to [accustom] it to difficulties, thinking[28] about what the apostle said: "When I am weak, then I am strong."[29] For Antony used to say, "The mind of the soul is strong when the pleasures of the body are weak." And truly people used to marvel at this other principle of his: he did not wish to measure the path to virtuous thought by time, nor withdrawal from the world[30] for its own sake, but by one's love and intention. So he did not count time that had passed, but each day, as though beginning his asceticism anew, he produced in himself great progress, meditating continually on what the apostle says: "We are forgetting what lies behind and straining forward to what lies ahead."[31] He would also remember the voice of Elijah the Tishbite, who said, "The Lord lives, the one before whom I stand today."[32] He observed that in saying "today," he was not counting time that has passed but was always laying a foundation, endeavoring each day to stand before God and to attain an acceptable form in order to appear before God pure in heart and prepared to obey his will alone, and no other. And he used to tell himself from the way of life of the great Elijah that it was necessary for ascetics at all times to know their own lives, as in a mirror.

---

28. The Coptic participle *efmeeue* is also ambiguous.
29. 2 Cor 12:10.
30. "Withdrawal from the world": *anachōrēsis.*
31. Phil 3:13.
32. 1 Kings 18:15.

## Antony, Living in the Tombs,
## Is Assaulted by the Devil

8. In this way Antony armed himself and went into the tombs that lay at a distance from the village. He remained there, asking one [of his friends] to bring him bread after a number of days. He went into one of the tombs, and the monk[33] remained there alone, having closed the door on himself. The enemy could not stand him being there; he was afraid that little by little Antony would fill the other deserted places with ascetics. So he came out one night with a crowd of demons and beat Antony with so many blows that he remained lying on the ground, unable to speak because of the torturous blows. Indeed, Antony said with certainty that the pain from the blows was so great [that one would say] the blows came from powerful men inflicting tortures.

But by the providence of God—for the Lord does not [forget] those who trust in him—the next day his friend came with a little bread for him. When he opened the door, he saw Antony lying on the ground as though he were dead. Immediately he lifted him up and took him to the church in the village and laid him there. Now many of his relatives and people from the village were sitting and standing around Antony as though he were dead. But at midnight, when he regained consciousness and sat up, he saw that all of those around him were asleep and only that one fellow whom he knew was awake. He beckoned to him to come near and asked him to lift him and carry him once again to the tombs, and he woke no one.

9. So his friend took him and closed the door, and Antony remained inside by himself. He was unable to stand because of the blows from the demons, but he prayed while lying on the ground. And after his prayer he cried out, saying, "Look, here I am—Antony! I will not run from your blows; even if you do worse things to me, nothing will separate me from the love of Christ Jesus my Lord.[34] For it is written in the psalms: 'Though war should rise up against me, my heart will not be afraid.'"[35] These were the things the ascetic thought and said, but the enemy, who hates everything good, was amazed that after all these blows Antony was still strong in heart and had returned again to that place.

---

33. Or "solitary one": *monachos.*
34. See Rom 8:35.
35. Ps 27:3.

The enemy gathered together his dogs and, so angry he was about to burst, said to them, "You see that neither with the spirit of fornication nor with beatings have we been able to stop this man! Even worse, he has stubbornly opposed us! Let us, then, approach him by some other way." (Now these ways of the devil are evil things.) That night, then, he worked such deceit that that place was shaken as by an earthquake that seemed to tear everything apart. The demons came inside, taking the shape of wild beasts and reptiles in a nightmare. Suddenly the place was filled with the illusory shapes of lions and bears and leopards and bulls and male and female serpents and wolves, and each one came toward him with a loud roar and hissing,[36] according to its kind. The roaring lions wanted to leap upon him; the bull acted as though it would gore him; the snake struck but did not reach him; and the wolf stalked towards him. All of these appeared together, and the sound of their roars and hissings was very fearful.

Antony, wounded by them, suffered terribly in his body, but in his soul he was even more vigilant and, while still lying on the ground, was strong and unafraid. He groaned because of the pain in his body, but he was in control of his thoughts and, as though he were mocking them, said to the demons, "If you had any power over me, just one of you would be enough against me, but because the Lord has destroyed your power, you attempt to terrify me with a mob. But you show your weakness because you imitate the forms of animals." Again he was courageous and said, "If you are able[37] and have authority over me, don't stop but attack right now. If you are not able, why do you bother me in vain? For our seal and purity and wall of protection is our faith in our Lord Jesus Christ." So they tried to do many things to him, and they gnashed their teeth against him.

10. He looked up and saw that the ceiling appeared to be opening, and he saw what seemed to be a beam of light descending toward him. And suddenly the demons vanished and the pain in his body immediately ceased and the place where he was was restored to its former condition. Now Antony recognized that the Lord had saved him, and when he took a breath he realized that he had been relieved from his suffering. He entreated the one who had appeared to him, saying,

---

36. "Roar and hissing": literally "voice" (*smē*). And immediately below.

37. Coptic *ounsōm mmotn*. *Sōm* also means "power, strength," as has been translated above.

"Where are you?" and "Why didn't you appear to me from the beginning so you could heal me?" A voice then came to him, saying, "I was here, but I waited to see your struggle. And now, since you persevered and were not defeated, I will be a helper to you forever, and I will make you famous everywhere." When Antony heard these things, he stood and prayed, and he was so strengthened that he felt the strength return to his body. Now he was about thirty-five years old at that time.

## Antony Leaves for the Mountain

11. The next day he went outside, joyfully worshiping God. He went to the old man, the monk[38] mentioned earlier, and asked him to go with him to worship the Lord in the desert. But that old man declined, saying it was both on account of his age and also because he had never practiced anything of this sort. Antony, however, immediately set out for the mountain,[39] but the enemy saw his eagerness and, wishing to trip him up on the way, cast onto the road the apparition of a large silver dish. [But Antony][40] recognized the wiles of the hater of goodness, and he stood and looked at the dish. He knew that it was a work of the devil and said, "How did this dish get here in the desert? No path has been worn here before now, nor is there any traveler's footprint. If someone had dropped it, he would have known it because it is large, and whoever lost it would have returned and looked for it and found it because this place is a desert. What has happened here is the work of the devil. You will not trip me up by doing this, devil! Instead, this will go with you to destruction!"[41] When Antony said these things, it vanished like smoke.

12. Afterwards, while he was walking on his way, he saw some gold, not in a fantasy, but truly. Whether it was the enemy who showed it to him or whether a mighty power was training the [athlete] and showing the devil that he was not tormented by money, he did not tell us, nor do we know what happened—only, it was truly gold that he saw. Now Antony marvelled at the quantity of gold, but he passed it by, fleeing as one flees fire; as a result, he did not take one step toward it.

---

38. Or "the solitary," as above.

39. Coptic *ptoou*. For a discussion of mountain and desert in early Egyptian monasticism, see Tim Vivian, "Mountain and Desert: The Geographies of Early Coptic Monasticism," *Coptic Church Review* 12, no.1 (Spring 1991): 15–21.

40. Coptic "he."

41. See Acts 8:20.

He advanced closer and closer to the mountain. He saw a deserted [fortress] on the far side of the river, deserted so long that it was full of reptiles, and he made his home there. Now the reptiles there fled as though they were being chased out, and they moved away. Antony closed the door and laid away enough bread for six months (the Egyptians do this, keeping the bread with them for a whole year, and no harm at all comes to it). He shut himself in[42] and had water with him, and he remained inside there alone; he did not go out, nor did he see those who came to see him. He did this a long time, living ascetically this way, twice a year lowering his bread down to himself from the rooftop.

13. Since those who came to see him knew that he would not allow them to come inside, they would [often] remain outside, spending days and nights at his doorstep. They heard what sounded like mobs inside creating a disturbance and making noise, raising their feeble [voices], crying out and saying, "Get away from what belongs to us! Why are you living here in the desert? You will not be able to endure our treachery!" Now those who were outside at first thought that there were some men in there who had gotten inside to see him by means of ladders; then they looked inside through some holes, but did not see anyone. At that point they realized that those men were actually demons [and, becoming afraid, they were calling to Antony].[43] He heard them, but he was not concerned about them.[44] Antony came to the door and asked the men to go away and not be afraid, saying, "This is the way demons act, creating apparitions of this sort for those who are fearful. Protect yourselves with the sign of the cross, and depart strengthened and encouraged, and leave them to mock themselves." So they went away, protected[45] by the sign of the cross.

Now Antony remained alone, and the demons could not harm him at all as he competed against them all the more. The [visions that continued] to come into his mind every day, and the weakness of the enemy who fought against him, gave him great relief from his sufferings and encouraged him towards even greater zeal. For indeed those

42. Coptic lacks Greek "as in a shrine."
43. Coptic lacks this clause (which the Greek has), but the next sentence requires it.
44. The pronoun, ambiguous in Coptic, could refer to those outside, or to the demons.
45. Both the Greek *teteichismenoi* (*teichos*: "wall") and the Coptic *ktēu* (*kōt*: "build, edify; building") retain the image of being protected by surrounding strong walls.

who knew him would often go there, thinking that they would find him dead, and they heard him singing, "Let God arise, and let his enemies be scattered; and let those that hate him flee from before him. Let them vanish as smoke vanishes; as wax melts before the fire, so let sinners perish from before the face of God."[46] And "All nations surrounded me; I drove them off in the name of the Lord."[47]

## Antony Emerges and Inspires Others to the Ascetic Life

14. Antony spent almost twenty years practicing asceticism alone in this way; he did not go outside, nor was he often seen by anyone. After a while, the consciences of many were pricked, and they wished to imitate him, and they forcefully tore down his door. Antony came out, and God was with him.[48] This was the first time that he came out of the fortress and appeared to those who came to see him. And when they saw his body, they marvelled at his sweetness, for he had not exercised yet he was not weak as though he had come out from fasting and fighting with demons; they found him just as they had known him before he withdrew.[49] They saw that the thought of his soul was pure, and he was not sorrowful and suffering; he had neither been disturbed by pleasures, nor had laughter or sadness ruled over him. Moreover, when he saw the crowd, he was not disturbed, nor was he delighted when they greeted him. Rather, he maintained complete equilibrium because reason[50] was guiding him.[51]

Now many of those there were sick. The Lord healed them through him because the Lord gave grace to Antony in his words. And he comforted the many who mourned, while he reconciled others at enmity and made them brothers. He would tell everyone to honor nothing among the things of the world more than love for Christ Jesus. He taught each person about the good things that will come and about God's love for humankind, which has come to us because God did not spare his own son, but gave him for all of us.[52] So he persuaded many

46. Ps 68:1–2.
47. Ps 118:11.
48. "And God was with him": Greek, "as though from some shrine, having been led into divine mysteries and inspired by God" (Gregg).
49. Coptic *anachōrei*.
50. Coptic/Greek *logos*.
51. Coptic lacks Greek "steadfast in that which accords with nature" (Gregg).
52. See Rom 8:32.

to choose the monastic way of life, and in this way monasteries[53] came into being in the mountains, and the desert filled with monks,[54] and they lived there, having left their homes. They registered themselves for citizenship in heaven.[55]

## Antony the Good Father

15. Afterwards, he needed to go visit the brothers in [Arsinoë]. He crossed the Nile,[56] and the river there was full of crocodiles. But he prayed and forded the river along with those who were with him, and none of them were harmed. When he returned to his cell,[57] he embraced holy labors that were full of all power. Speaking often to those who had become monks, he increased their zeal even more, and he stirred most of the brothers to a love of asceticism. His speech[58] attracted multitudes to him, and many monastic cells[59] came into being, and he guided them all like a good father.

53. Or "monastic cells": Coptic/Greek *monasterion*.

54. "Filled with monks": Greek "was made a city by monks" (Gregg). The Coptic text conspicuously omits the idea of "civilizing" or making a city of the desert, an idea appreciated, and borrowed, by later Greek monastic writers such as Cyril of Scythopolis. See his *Life of Sabas* 37, trans. R. M. Price, *Cyril of Scythopolis: The Lives of the Monks of Palestine* (Kalamazoo, Mich.: Cistercian, 1991), 135.

55. See Heb 12:23.

56. Literally "the river."

57. Coptic/Greek *monasterion*.

58. Coptic/Greek *logos*.

59. Coptic/Greek *monasterion*.

# 2

# JOURNEYING INTO GOD: ABBA PAMBO

## Introduction

THE STORY OF ABBA PAMBO PUTS US IN THE PRESENCE OF ANGELS and archetypes. This narrative comes from the Coptic monastic tradition and was written down sometime between the fifth and tenth centuries.[1] Stories such as this in the Coptic tradition are very difficult to date with precision, and it is almost impossible to have historical certainty about the events described.[2] But the very problems these stories present to the historian turn into virtues for the reader interested in theology and spirituality. The tale of Abba Pambo was never meant to be read as a historical document; it was written for those seeking a

---

1. Pambo's story was first published as "The Life of Apa Cyrus" by E. A. Wallis Budge (see p. 30 n. 1 below). Abba Cyrus is the last of three monks whom Pambo visits, and this visit is the most important part of the text. However, the story is not so much about the life of Cyrus as it is a narrative of the spiritual journey made by Pambo.

2. From the history of Egyptian monasticism, we know of two monks named Pambo. The famous Pambo of Nitria was a priest and died in 374. Another Pambo, an old man and a monk of Scetis, is mentioned in a story about a visit made to Scetis by Theophilus, bishop of Alexandria from 385–412. When the bishop asks to speak to Pambo, he refuses: "If he is not profited by my silence, neither will he be profited by my speech." Abba Shenoute, whose death Cyrus reveals to Pambo, died early in July 451. Therefore, the events of our story can be "dated" to that year (although the mention of the emperor Zeno, who ruled from 474–91, confuses matters). Is our monk Pambo the one who would not speak to Bishop Theophilus? It is very unlikely. Our Pambo seems to be a relatively young man, and the events of his story take place forty to fifty years after the visit of Theophilus. The Pambo who would not speak to Theophilus was already an old man in about 400 and could not still be alive half a century later. Also, our Pambo is a priest. Like the unidentified geography Pambo traverses, it is best to leave the Pambo of this story anonymous. See Derwas J. Chitty, *The Desert A City* (Crestwood, N.Y.: St. Vladimir's, n.d.), 56 and 190.

deeper understanding of God. It is an extended parable, set in its own archetypal landscape.

It is the story of a journey. The hero setting out on a journey is a very ancient and universal motif in storytelling. From classical mythology, the stories of Odysseus and Aeneas come immediately to mind. The classic American example is Huck Finn sailing down the Mississippi. The hero who journeys to find a knowledge of God is also universal. Jewish tradition offers the story of Abraham, who is called by God to journey from Ur to the land that God has promised him and his descendants; this is the story that calls Saint Theognius to the monastic life (see below, p. 147). The exodus of the Hebrew people from Egypt is the story of a journey, a story in which desert and mountain figure prominently.[3]

Pambo, unlike Abraham or Moses, is not told *why* he must journey, only that he must, and that he must go into the desert. From the beginning we are faced with expectation and mystery. Whose voice is it that commands Pambo? God's, we presume. And where is Pambo going? The desert and the mountain where he sojourns are never identified or named. From the beginning we are in a symbolic universe. Pambo's journey is more than a cross-country trek, however. He has set out to seek a deeper knowledge of God. To do that, Christian tradition tells us, a person must travel inward as well as outward.

But if this journey is as much inward as outward, it is nevertheless concretely situated squarely within the biblical landscape, a territory dominated by deserts and mountains. The Israelite people crossed through the desert of Sinai during their exodus from Egypt, en route to the promised land. In the desert they ate manna as the gift from heaven; they also built idols profaning God (Ex 32). Jesus often went out into the desert to pray. After his baptism, the Spirit drove Jesus into the desert (Mt 1:12), and it was there that Satan tempted him (Lk 4:3–13). John the Baptist came from that same desert, preaching the good news of repentance and salvation.

In the monastic story here, Pambo receives his vision on a mountain. In ancient Greek and Israelite religion, God dwelled on sacred mountaintops. For example, Moses went to the mountain to stand

3. For an excellent meditation on the desert and desert spirituality, see Kenneth Leech, *Experiencing God: Theology as Spirituality* (San Francisco: Harper and Row, 1985), chapter 5, "God of the Desert," 127–61.

before God (Ex 19). There he had a vision of God in the burning bush, and there he received the tablets of the Torah (Ex 24). On the mountain, in the company of Elijah and Moses, Jesus was transfigured (Lk 9:28–36). And it is on a mount that Jesus gives the great "sermon" collected in Mt 5.

By drawing on the deepest and richest symbols of the Christian tradition, those places where we confront God most directly, this story is laying before us a geography of the spirit, a map of the soul's quest for God. In one sense this land has been traversed before. It has a familiar biblical topography, like a three-dimensional relief map you run your hand over, getting the feel of mountain tops and the valleys below. But the desert and the mountain are also places of mystery, where each person must make his or her own journey. They are the places where bushes burn with the radiance of God, and the clothes of Jesus shine with a brightness no earthly fuller can give. Pambo's story, also, is a story of mystery. Mystery opens into mystery, opening inward into the heart of God.

It was mentioned above that Pambo is not told why he must journey, only that he must. Pambo visits three monks, and at the door of each monk's cell he knocks three times. Three is a holy number. Its holiness is the holiness of mystery, the mystery of the Trinity. Pambo is not really sure what or whom he is seeking, but the mystery is that those who await him know who he is (without ever having met him), and they have been waiting for him for a long time. His coming is the answer to their prayers.

Pambo, each of the monks declares, is a great ship that sails over the waterless desert. This, too, is something of a mystery, and an ironic one at that! Although he is a presbyter or priest, Pambo does not seem to have any great claim to knowledge or marvelous spiritual insight. When he meets these monks and has the opportunity to ask each one the most profound questions, he can only stammer incredulously about food, clothing, and health care. It's as if one of us had gone to meet Abba Hierax (the first of the monks) out in the desert, looked around, and to our amazement discovered there was no restaurant. How will we eat?

Pambo *is* like us. He still needs to grow in the faith. Although he is a priest, and although he is on a spiritual quest, when confronted with the mystery of God, he can only ask very human questions. Like us, he must sometimes ask the wrong question in order to get pointed toward the right answer. The irony is that his questions to each of the monks, though naive, turn out to be the right ones: each answer moves him ever deeper into God.

This is so because the replies the monks make go right to the heart of faith. The reason these men are holy is very simple: they trust in God. Hierax gets his food from a tree outside his cell; Pamoun finds one cloak to be sufficient winter and summer; and Cyrus finds Christ to be a sufficient visitor. "Consider the lilies, how they grow," Jesus said. "They neither toil nor spin; yet I tell you, even Solomon in all his glory was not arrayed like one of these" (Lk 12:27). These monks are they.

Pambo, however, does not see this; their answers do not satisfy him. The form of each interview is the same: (1) Pambo wonders aloud how the monk manages to survive in such a desolate place; (2) the monk tells him, essentially, that he lives by faith; (3) Pambo doesn't think this answer is worth much, so he asks for the name of the monk further down the line.

Pambo's second question, his request for the name of another monk, ironically is far more profound than he suspects. Disappointed with the answer to his first question the reader might ask (Does Pambo expect miracles?), he asks each monk, "Is there anyone beyond you?" The Coptic for this question is: *Oun son m̄pekhoun?* The word translated "beyond," *houn*, also means "interior, inside." And so Pambo's question can also be understood: Is there anyone further inside? Is there a deeper reality? Is there more to God? Does the interior journey need to go further?

It does. When Pambo meets the third monk, Abba Cyrus (after whom the story is titled in Coptic), he asks the same questions. But this time Pambo is shown death. (Earlier, Pamoun spoke about his own death and foreshadowed this.) When Cyrus commands Pambo to sit down, is there a suggestion, an implicit stage direction, that Pambo, hearing about death and judgment, is about to head unceremoniously for the door? Pambo needs to look no further. Face to face with mortality, with the limits of human knowledge and understanding, he is shown faith and trust, judgment and mercy—and this despite himself. Pambo assumes that a monk like Cyrus, because of the holiness of his life and ascetic labors, need not worry about God's judgment. (His spiritual naivete is dramatically pointed out later when Christ does not give him the kiss of greeting.) But Cyrus quickly sets him straight. Because of Cyrus' faith before death, Pambo is shown death and resurrection. He is, finally, given a vision.

It is, I believe, a vision of the incarnation. At the end of his vision, the heavenly Christ descends with all the choir of angels, with prophets, apostles, and martyrs. This is what we (and Pambo) would expect from a vision. But this takes place *only* after a very human Christ has walked through the door of a very simple monastic cell and wept over the death of one of his beloved children. This is the Christ who wept over Lazarus (Jn 11), the Christ through whom all things were made (Jn 1:3). This is Christ weeping out of love.

This, then, is the vision God offers Pambo, the mystery of the incarnation. That it is a mystery—the human, weeping Jesus and the heavenly, cosmic Christ are one—is clear because the vision is explained by the apostle Peter, who himself is part of the vision's deep mystery. Peter steps forth from the "multitude of angels and archangels and apostles and all the righteous"—but he is lame. Pambo does not recognize him. How could he? The incarnation and resurrection are intimately related in this vision: without the incarnation, there is no resurrection. How could we expect this mystery to be made clear by a crippled angel?

Pambo, almost unwittingly, has journeyed into the heart of God. But his real journey has now just begun. Now he must journey back. Not *back* to the world, because that might suggest that the spiritual journey and our life in the world are two separate things. They are not. Pambo has never really left the world. Although he has seen the transcendent, he has done so amid the very earthly terrain of mountain and desert, amid the very basic human concerns of food and shelter and, finally, death.

Because of his journey into the heart of God, Abba Pambo has been transformed, made a new person in Christ. He is now worthy to be kissed. Yet if that were how the story ended—with Christ kissing Pambo—it would be untrue to the Christian understanding of life; it would make theophanies prizes to be won on television game shows. Pambo has indeed been to the heart of God. Now he must continue, into the heart of the world. Pambo's vision, though granted to one person, is not self-centered. He still has work to do among his fellows, the daily round of manual labor and prayer that was the life of the Egyptian monk. Pambo's world is the monastery, and so he returns there and writes down for others the story of his vision. He is now an evangelist, a proclaimer of good news.

Pambo's story is now fully our own. It has moved from the most universal of archetypes to the most intimate of gospel messages. Like Peter, each of us, though lame, has been chosen by God to be an apostle of Christ. Like Pambo, each of us is called to journey into the heart of God. And then, transformed by our vision of God, we are called to continue that journey, to proclaim the good news, to transform the world.

## THE STORY OF ABBA PAMBO [1]

*The life and ascetic practice*
*of our holy father who was glorious in every way,*
*Saint Abba Cyrus, the perfect governor,*
*which Abba Pambo, priest of The Church of Scetis, set down.*
*the Holy Abba Cyrus went to his rest*
*on the fifteenth of July in the peace of God.*
*May his holy blessing come upon us and save us. Amen.*

### Pambo Receives a Vision to Make a Journey

It came to pass in the time of Abba Pambo, the priest of the church of Scetis, after he had protected the body of the blessed Hillaria, the daughter of the Emperor Zeno,[2] that a vision was revealed to him: "Rise and journey to the coast, and you will find a great anchorite whose sandal straps no one on earth is worthy to untie."[3] So the blessed Abba Pambo journeyed into the desert, sustained by the strength of God that was with him, as it was with the blessed Antony when he journeyed and went a second time to see the blessed Abba Paul.[4]

### Pambo Meets Abba Hierax

Now the blessed priest Abba Pambo rose and journeyed into the desert and came to a monastic cell. He stood and knocked at the door for a considerable length of time and cried out three times according to the

---

1. The translation is based on the Coptic text published by E. A. Wallis Budge, "The Life of Apa Cyrus," *Coptic Texts*, vol. 4, *Coptic Martyrdoms Etc.* (Oxford: 1914, reprinted N.Y.: AMS Press, 1977), 128–36. Paragraphing and section titles are the translator's.

2. *Emperor of the East*, 474–91.

3. See Lk 3:16.

4. This detail is not found in the *Life of Antony.* See Jerome's *Life of Saint Paul.*

custom of the monastic brethren, saying, "Bless me!" While I, Pambo, was standing at the door, the monk inside answered me, saying, "Greetings, Pambo, priest of the church of Scetis, and mighty ship that sails over the waterless desert. For a long time I have desired to see you. Now God has fulfilled for me my wish this day! Come in, blessed Pambo!" Abba Pambo answered and said, "Greetings, Abba Hierax. Because of your purity you have become a friend to the angels of God."

So Abba Hierax opened the door and welcomed him inside. They sat down together, and Pambo said, "My beloved brother Hierax, how many years has it been since you came to this place?" Abba Hierax said, "I have been here eighteen years, and I have never eaten any of the foods usually eaten in this world but have lived entirely upon the fruits of trees." (Now there was a date palm growing outside of his dwelling, and it produced twelve bunches of dates each year, and he lived on the fruit.) I, Pambo, then said to him, "My beloved father, are there any brothers beyond you in the desert?" He said to me, "There are some. Bless me, and go on to them, and receive a blessing at their hands."

## Pambo Meets Abba Pamoun

After I had left him and journeyed on into the desert, I came upon a small monastic cell. I called inside according to the custom of the monastic brethren. While I was standing outside, the brother answered from inside saying, "Greetings, Abba Pambo, priest of the church of Scetis, and mighty ship that sails over the waterless desert. For many days I have longed to see you. At last the Lord has fulfilled for me my wish this day. Come in; do not stand outside." I answered him, "I am Pambo, my beloved father Abba Pamoun, Lord Pa-m-porek.[5] Greetings, my beloved brother of the many-colored coat which is like the coat of the righteous man Joseph. Before God it is more glorious than all the purple of the kings of this world." (Believe me, my brothers and my fathers, I, Pambo, the most unworthy, smelled the sweet fragrance of that brother a mile before I got to his home.)

Now after we had greeted each other, we prayed together and sat

5. Coptic: *pamporkkuri. Pork* refers to an outer mantle or tunic worn by clerics or monks, a pallium. The exact meaning here and immediately below is not certain. Pamoun apparently wore, either literally or figuratively, a cloak like that of Joseph; see Gen 37:3.

down. I said to him, "My father, I know you must be cold in winter. And wearing such a tunic, you certainly won't get hot in the summer!" Abba Pamoun said to me, "'Pa-m-porek' it is, because this most certainly is its name, my beloved brother Abba Pambo. Believe me, my beloved father, I came to this place twenty years ago, and with this single garment I have been able to keep myself warm during the winter and to moderate the heat in the summer. And I confess to you that this tunic will be sufficient for me until the day of my death. When I die, it will be large enough for them to roll me up in it until the day of judgment."

I said to him, "My beloved father, are there any brothers beyond you in the desert?" He said to me, "There is one whose sandal straps no one on earth is worthy to untie. I myself went to see him many times, wishing to visit him, but he would answer me from the inside of his cell, 'Go away! In coming here you've unnecessarily troubled yourself. No human will see my face except Pambo, the priest of the church of Scetis.' And now, my father, perhaps it has been ordained and it is not for this purpose that I have come here. But I will remember you if the Lord makes straight my path to meet that brother. My father, do remember me until I enjoy the blessing of that brother."

## Pambo Meets Abba Cyrus

When I had journeyed more than a mile further up into the mountain (I, Pambo, the most unworthy, swear to you by the terrible judgment seat of God that I am not lying about what I am about to tell you) someone took hold of me through the power of the Spirit and brought me to that brother's cell. It was he who long ago seized the prophet Habakkuk and led him, carrying the food he had prepared, and brought him to the lions' den where he gave the food to Daniel in the lions' den.[6] I knocked on the door according to the custom of the monastic brethren and called out three times, "Bless me!" I stood at the door a long time. After awhile, the brother answered me from inside, saying, "Greetings, Abba Pambo, priest of the church of Scetis and mighty ship that sails over the waterless desert. Many days have I desired to see you. This day has God fulfilled for me my desire. Come in; do not stand outside."

When I was going through the door of the cell, I looked and I saw

6. Bel and the Dragon, 33–39.

a huge stone that twelve men would scarcely be able to move. That brother moved forward and rolled the stone along and planted it at the door of the cell. When I saw this I was greatly amazed. But then I remembered the patriarch Jacob, how he, when he fled from the face of Esau his brother, went to Mesopotamia of Syria. When he came to where Laban had his sheep, he went up to the well and rolled away the stone that had covered it without anyone helping him. He gave water to Laban's sheep and then sent them away to graze.[7] Then I finally understood: God helps the saints in everything that they do.

I said to him, "My holy father, tell me your holy name, for God has hidden this from me." He said to me, "Cyrus is my name. I am the brother of the Emperor Theodosius,[8] and I was fed at the same table with Arcadius and Honorius. And, indeed, Honorius said to me many times, 'Take me into the desert with you so I can be a monk.' But I refused to take him because he was the son of the emperor. Now when I[9] saw that oppression was increasing, that the emperors were breaking the law[10] and the rulers were violently robbing the poor, and that everyone was turning away from God and corrupting their path before him, I rose and set out and came to this wilderness, where I have dwelled because of the multitude of my sins. May God forgive me these!"

I, Pambo, said to him, "My beloved father, where will you find any one in this deserted place to comfort you in your sufferings?" Abba Cyrus said to me, "Believe me, my beloved brother, Abba Pambo, my God and Lord Jesus Christ is the one who visits me in this deserted place where I live. Indeed, I have never seen anyone who came to see me except a certain fellow-monk, who came here wishing to see my face. Besides him, I have never seen anyone. On the contrary, when anyone did come, while he remained outside I commanded him from inside, saying, 'Go away! You've troubled yourself for nothing in coming to see me. Truly, no human shall see my face except Abba Pambo, the priest of the church of Scetis.' These events have taken place through the dispensation of God, and now God has fulfilled for me my wish this day."

I then said to him, "My brother, are there any brothers beyond you in the desert? He said to me, "There is nothing beyond me except

7. Gen 29:3.
8. Emperor from 408–450.
9. Text "we."
10. Or: "sinning." Greek *paranomeā*

darkness and the punishments that sinners are enduring. Sit down here, my brother, and this hour you shall see mighty wonders." For a fact, when the evening of the Lord's day had become morning and the light of the Lord's day began to dawn, I heard voices crying out, "Christ, your love has been received. You have shown mercy to us." Now I said to him, "My beloved father, what are we to do concerning these things? The mountain is going to crumble beneath us!" He said to me, "Do not be afraid, my son, that God is coming to inflict punishment. He has commanded the angels who punish souls to give them a respite, because today is the Lord's day and the day of his resurrection." He also said to me, "The Lord will come here today according to his custom, and I will kiss him on the lips."

While he was saying these things, to my amazement Christ opened the door of the cell and came in. Now the door opened suddenly of its own accord, and when he came in—believe me, my fathers and brothers—I, Pambo, the least of all men, saw Christ go up to that brother and kiss him on the lips, as a brother does when he has come from a distance and greets his friend. Now I, Pambo, the most unworthy, was not worthy at that time to be greeted with a kiss by him.

Then he left us, and we did not know where he had gone. Now I thought he was a fellow-monk. I said to Cyrus, "My beloved father, didn't you tell me that you'd seen no human come to your door except me? Tell me, then, who this fellow-monk was who came in and kissed you while I was not worthy to be kissed by him." He said to me, "This was the lord of earthly and heavenly things. This was the son of the holy virgin Mary. This was the one who fills the desert and is with everyone who calls upon him."

He also said to me, "A great prophet and monastic leader[11] has gone to his rest today, Abba Shenoute the priest. Truly, the whole world has lost a great teacher today" (for that day was the fourteenth of July). He added, "This is the one who did not lie down on his bed, drowse off, or sleep until he found the Lord's house, the habitation of the God of Jacob, his helper. Truly, he fought the good fight and defeated the devil in this world. He has gone to his lord and now is perfected in the kingdom of heaven. May his blessing and prayers be with us. Amen."

He also said to me, "My beloved brother Pambo, I am sick. Do me the favor today of praying for me until I journey over the road of fear

---

11. Archimandrite.

and terror." I said to him, "My beloved father, are you afraid, even you, in spite of the many ascetic labors you have performed in the world?" He said to me, "I have done a few ascetic labors that God has appointed for me, but how can we not be afraid of what many witnesses have shown us—the fact that there is a river of fire and that we are to appear before the Judge? And as for the river, everyone is bound to pass over it, whether righteous or sinner, and it is right that you should pray for me until I journey over that terrible road." He also said to me, "Even if a person's life on this earth lasted only a single day, he would not be free from sin."[12]

Now it came to pass that at nine in the morning on the fifteenth of July, Abba Cyrus became very ill, and he said to me, "I greet you in the Lord, my beloved brother." And he prayed in this way, reciting the Lord's prayer,[13] and he opened his mouth and yielded up his spirit, like one who lies asleep. I sat down and began to weep over him, and as I was weeping over him, Christ opened the door of the cell! He came in and stood over the body of the blessed Abba Cyrus and wept over him.

I saw the tears of Christ that fell upon the body of the blessed Abba Cyrus. At last Christ turned slowly and departed through the door of the cell. When [he][14] had gone out, I saw a multitude of angels and archangels and apostles and all the righteous standing there. One of them walked toward me. He was lame. He said to me, "Do you know who I am?" And I said to him, "No, sir, I do not." He said to me, "Listen, and I will tell you. I am Cephas, the one who was given the name of Peter. I am the one whom Christ called 'Bar Jona' in the Gospel, that is to say, 'Son of the dove.'[15] The blessed Abba Shenoute went to his rest yesterday. Christ has now taken the souls of the blessed Abba Cyrus and Abba Shenoute the archimandrite to the place of rest. As it is written: 'There are many rooms in my Father's house.'[16] May their holy blessing be with us! Amen."

After all this, I was confused and trying to think what I should do with the body of the blessed man, whether I should bury it, and where I should lay it. The Savior came through the door of the cell and closed the door behind him. The Savior had his hand upon the door of the

12. See 1 Cor 3:13.
13. Literally "the prayer in the Gospel."
14. Text "I."
15. Mt 16:17.
16. Jn 14:2.

cell, and he was carrying the body of the blessed man. He became a bulwark and protection for him until the day of righteous judgment. The Savior went up into heaven with his angels.

Now I journeyed and came to the brethren Abba Pamoun and Abba Hierax, and I told them what I had seen, and they glorified God. I remained with them a few days. Afterwards I departed to my monastery in Scetis. I wrote the life of the blessed Abba Cyrus and placed it in the church of Scetis for the profit and consolation of those who should hear it read. To the glory of the Holy Trinity, the Father, and the Son, and the Holy Spirit, now and forever. Amen.

# 3

# A WOMAN IN THE DESERT: SYNCLETICA OF PALESTINE

## Introduction

"WOMEN IN THE DESERT?" LUCIEN REGNAULT POSES THIS QUESTION in his recent study of fourth-century monasticism.[1] In a chapter entitled "Women and Children," Regnault unintentionally suggests that women were peripheral to the early monastic movement—and that they remain on the margins in modern studies of early monasticism. Referring to Palladius's *Lausiac History*, he comments:

> Of all the female saints whom he presents to us in his work, none lived in the "great desert." When one thinks about the lack of security that reigned there, one realizes that a woman, even if herself courageous, could not have lived there by herself without running great risks as much to her honor as to her life.[2]

Regnault sometimes seems to define monasticism as that which can be lived only in deepest desert—and women could not live as monks in this wilderness because they were "a permanent temptation."[3] The earliest *ammas* ("mothers," the female counterparts of the *abbas*, or "fathers"), therefore, did not live in the full desert and were by implication not "real" monks: they remained close by the Nile or in the suburbs of cities like Alexandria.[4]

---

1. Lucien Regnault, *La vie quotidienne des pères du désert en Égypte au IVe siècle* (Paris: Hachette, 1990), 37.
2. Ibid.
3. Ibid.
4. Ibid. The equating of the "real" monk with those who leave home to live in the desert goes back to the image of the monk presented by Jerome and by Athanasius in the *Life of Antony*.

It is true that many, perhaps most, male ascetics regarded women as temptations and therefore as obstacles to holiness (see, for example, paragraph 11 of Syncletica's narrative below). But is that why few female ascetics ventured (or seem to have ventured) farther into the desert? Our sources suggest otherwise. Most monks, whether male or female, lived along the Nile. Even many monasteries considered to be in "the desert" were within sight or walking distance of "civilization," the fertile, inhabited areas watered by the Nile.[5]

The origins of monasticism lay not in the desert but in the towns, suburbs, and cities. The first "monks" were, apparently, "village monks," ascetics who lived lives of poverty and celibacy, but who remained in their villages and towns.[6] Antony's originality was that he left his village for the desert. In the villages, towns, and suburbs, many (most?) of those living a monastic, or proto-monastic, life would have been women, the widows and virgins of the early church.[7] This form of "monasticism" goes back to the earliest days of the church.[8]

It is true, however, that we know very little about early female ascetics or monastics, whether in village or desert. But our lack of knowledge does not mean they were not there. For example, Shenoute's White Monastery, according to one source, had 2,200 men and 1,800 women.[9] A paucity of sources awaits anyone who wishes to learn from the lives and writings of early Christian female monks. The *Pachomian Koinonia* gathers into three sizable volumes writings con-

5. H. Caddell and R. Rémondon, "Sens et emplois de *to oros* dans les documents papyrologiques," *Revue des études grecques* 80 (1967): 343–49.

6. See E. A. Judge, "The Earliest Use of Monachos for 'Monk' (P. Coll. Youtie 77) and the Origins of Monasticism," *Jahrbuch für Antike und Christentum* 20 (1977): 72–89.

7. See JoAnn McNamara, "Muffled Voices: The Lives of Consecrated Women in the Fourth Century," in John A. Nichols and Lillian Thomas Shanks, eds., *Medieval Religious Women*, vol. 1, *Distant Echoes* (Kalamazoo, Mich.: Cistercian Publications, 1984), 11–29.

8. See J. C. O'Neill, "The Origins of Monasticism," in Rowan Williams, ed., *The Making of Orthodoxy: Essays in Honour of Henry Chadwick* (Cambridge: Cambridge University Press, 1989), 270–87. O'Neill argues that Christianity, or at least part of it, is inherently monastic or ascetic, and that monasticism is not of fourth-century origins but has deep Jewish roots. He adduces the widows and virgins as an "order" going back to the primitive church.

9. J. Leipoldt, *Schenute von Atripe, Texte und Untersuchungen* 25.1, N.F. 10.1 (Leipzig: J. C. Hinrichs, 1903), 93–94. For some of what we *do* know, see Alanna M. Emmett, "An Early Fourth-Century Female Monastic Community in Egypt?" in Ann Moffatt, ed., *Maistor: Classical, Byzantine and Renaissance Studies for Robert Browning,* Byzantiana Australiensia 5 (Canberra: The Australian Association for Byzantine Studies, 1984), 77–83; and Susanna K. Elm, *"Virgins of God" The Making of Asceticism in Late Antiquity* (Oxford: Clarendon Press, 1994).

cerning the male Pachomian monks, but virtually nothing survives about the female monks who lived in separate communities along the Nile beside their more famous brothers.[10] The voluminous correspondence of Jerome, Paulinus of Nola, Augustine, and Basil of Caesarea stands in painful contrast to the exceedingly few surviving letters by female ascetics.[11] Gregory of Nyssa wrote the *Life* of his sister Macrina, and yet their brother Basil, the "father of Eastern monasticism," whom Macrina profoundly influenced, does not once mention her in his writings (four volumes in the *Patrologia Graeca*). Thus the mother of Eastern monasticism remains essentially unknown.

Syncletica's story, therefore, is valuable simply because it exists. As Elizabeth Castelli has poignantly asked:

> How many women lost their places in the written record of the church because no one chose to write their biographies and because the men whose lives they influenced omitted any mention of them? How many exceptional women may have been only mentioned and been otherwise lost without a trace? How many "ordinary" virgins are absent from the record altogether?[12]

Syncletica's story is, really, a simple one. Daughter of a Constantinopolitan aristocrat (whence her name; "Syncletica" means "the nobleman's daughter"), at eighteen she is betrothed to the son of another aristocrat. She, however, wishes to devote her life to Christ and does not want to marry. She talks her father into allowing her to make a pilgrimage to the Holy Land before her marriage, but she has no intention of returning. While in Jerusalem she flees her retinue, and thus her family, and becomes a hermit in the desert. For twenty-eight years she sees no one until she is accidentally discovered by another monk, Silas, who narrates her story.

The narrative is inherently plausible and appears to be historical.

10. Armand Veilleux, ed. and trans., *Pachomian Koinonia,* 3 vols. (Kalamazoo, Mich.: Cistercian Publications, 1980–82).

11. A point made by both McNamara, 11–12, and Elizabeth Castelli, "Virginity and Its Meaning for Women's Sexuality in Early Christianity," *Journal of Feminist Studies in Religion* 2, no. 1 (1986): 62–63. The one exception Castelli notes, 62 n. 4, is Melania the Elder, some of whose letters to Evagrius Ponticus survive, along with his, in Armenian.

12. Castelli, "Virginity," 63. For a good discussion of the Syrian ascetic women portrayed by John of Ephesus (who died about 589), see Susan Ashbrook Harvey, *Asceticism and Society in Crisis: John of Ephesus and The Lives of the Eastern Saints* (Berkeley: Univ. of California Press, 1990), esp. 108–33.

Syncletica follows the example of many aristocratic women, and men, of the late Roman empire (fourth through sixth centuries). Dissatisfied with the life she is leading in the city ("my inner concern was to put an end to the deceit of a frivolous life"), she flees to the desert so she can fully dedicate her life to God. The beginning of *The Life of Melania the Younger*, written more than a century earlier, describes Syncletica, as well as Melania:

> Wounded by the divine love, she had from her earliest youth yearned for Christ, had longed for bodily chastity. Her parents, because they were illustrious members of the Roman Senate and expected that through her they would have a succession of the family line, very forcibly united her in marriage. . . .[13]

Syncletica, therefore, fits a type, but it seems to be a historical, as well as a hagiographical, type. The theme of a woman fleeing an unwanted marriage to lead the (greater) ascetical life is a common one in the monastic literary tradition.[14] What immediately impresses the reader of Syncletica's story, though, is how thoroughly this hagiographic theme is grounded in the specifics of local geography and lifestyle. There is no doubt that the author knows the desert east of Jerusalem and especially the Jordan region. The "concrete details," the editors believe, are sufficient to indicate "the palestinian authenticity" of the text.[15]

The author, moreover, seems also to know something of the aristocracy of Constantinople.[16] Either he (or she) knew both the milieus of Constantinople and the Palestinian desert, which is possible (the author, like Syncletica, may have been from upper-class circles in the capital); or the author really is the monk Silas (or someone who listened to his story and wrote it down) who visits Syncletica in her cave (he knew the desert, and got his "aristocratic details" from Syncletica herself). This second possibility seems more likely, even probable. A text thus "sufficiently well localized," according to its editors, gives the story "real historical value."[17] Although it is difficult to date precisely the nar-

---

13. Chapter 1; trans. Elizabeth A. Clark, *The Life of Melania the Younger*, Studies in Women and Religion 14 (New York and Toronto: The Edwin Mellen Press, 1984), 27.

14. Bernard Flusin and Joseph Paramelle, "De Syncletica in Deserto Jordanis (BHG 1318w)," *Analecta Bollandiana* 100 (1982): 291–317. For examples, see 300–301.

15. Ibid., 302.

16. Ibid., 303 n. 24.

17. Ibid., 303.

rative, its editors situate the action in the sixth century and suggest that it was undoubtedly written shortly after the action took place.[18]

Why did Syncletica choose to spend her life as an anchorite? For someone contemplating the monastic vocation, then as now, the answer is complex, involving familial, societal, and personal (including spiritual) reasons. The most common answer in early monastic literature is twofold: the monk leaves the cares and concerns of "the world" and does so in order to devote himself or herself fully to God. This is in fact what Syncletica says: "For I desired especially to be free from marriage and to pray, and I called upon God's assistance in bringing this about" (paragraph 5).[19] What would such a decision mean for a woman of Syncletica's station? The most striking thing about Syncletica's reason is that her desire to pray is explicitly linked to her desire to be free from marriage; in fact, the former is dependent on the latter (her father's reply in paragraph 6 confirms this: he replaces her prayer with a husband!). While this was true for male ascetics in late antiquity,[20] it was undoubtedly more important for women: in order for a woman to devote herself completely to God in the ascetic life, she had first to escape her obligation to marry.

In late antiquity a woman's person, literally, was not her own. Syncletica states the case quite clearly (paragraph 5): "I am a woman. I was born the daughter of a certain eparch in Constantinople." She then immediately adds: "A certain illustrious friend of my father sued for my hand and asked that I be his son's wife." The legal rank of an aristocratic woman depended on the rank of her husband or father.[21] Such women were often betrothed by their fathers at a young age, as early as twelve or younger: "in the Roman world a girl's body was the token which sealed agreements between families, her virginity being the measure of her value."[22]

---

18. Ibid., 303.

19. Recension **b** is less explicit ("For I was happy to be unmarried [*emonazon*]"), but with the use of *emonazon* it implicitly says the same thing.

20. Amoun of Nitria on his wedding night persuaded his bride not to consummate their marriage. Many years later he left, with her approval, to found the famous monasteries of Nitria. See *Palladius: The Lausiac History* 8, trans. Robert T. Meyer, *Ancient Christian Writers* 34 (New York and Ramsey, N.J.: Newman Press, 1964), 41–43.

21. A. H. M. Jones, *The Later Roman Empire 284–602: A Social, Economic, and Administrative Survey* (Norman, Okla.: University of Oklahoma Press, 1964), 1: 528–29.

22. Castelli, "Virginity," 86; see 81 n. 97 for bibliography. Macrina was already betrothed at age twelve. *The Life of Saint Macrina by Gregory, Bishop of Nyssa*, trans. Kevin Corrigan (Saskatoon, Saskatchawan: Peregrina Publishing Co., 1987), 4 (PG 46: 961–62).

Syncletica's family appears to have been Christian, and so her virginity (clearly referred to in the text, paragraph 6) takes on added meaning. Socially, it (and she) had two functions: in late antiquity children (1) passed on the family's fortune and (2) assured the continuity of the family itself. Thus families, especially aristocratic ones, often opposed their children's desires to embrace the ascetic life and so *remain* virgins. In Syncletica's story this opposition is in the open, although the reasons for it are not explicitly stated. There is the assumption on her father's part that marriage is the proper norm for a young woman (paragraph 6), and the story reflects implicitly "the larger social problems of money diverted from family inheritances, and of eligible women refusing to serve as the social cement binding noble families in marriage."[23] By taking up the eremitical life, Syncletica goes against both norms: (1) By becoming a hermit, and thus remaining a virgin, she threatens the continuation of the family line. (2) Instead of passing on the family wealth, when she gives her traveling money to the monks (paragraphs 7 & 11) she symbolically gives away the family fortune, and thus she is like Saint Antony, who gives up his inheritance for the monastic vocation. Such action as Syncletica takes understandably aroused opposition because it could have profound effects, not only on the woman's family, but on her entire class.[24]

The most common form of aristocratic female monasticism was probably "home asceticism," where the women stayed with their families, often, though not always, under the control and authority of men.[25] Next in popularity was "familial monasticism," where aristocratic women, accompanied by their household slaves, relatives, and dependents, would establish monasteries, still very much under the influence, if not the control, of men.[26] Syncletica, however, becomes an anchorite, and so really does become free, like any man, to seek her own salvation in the presence of God alone.

Elizabeth Clark has observed that "in many respects, the patristic

23. Elizabeth A. Clark, "Ascetic Renunciation and Feminine Advancement: A Paradox of Late Ancient Christianity," *Anglican Theological Review* 63, no. 3 (1981): 241.

24. See Anne Yarbrough, "Christianization in the Fourth Century: The Example of Roman Women," *Church History* 45 (1976): 156, where Melania is the subject.

25. "In 393, a church council at Hippo recommended 'home asceticism' for virgins *if* they were under the careful eyes of their parents." Clark, "Ascetic Renunciation," 248.

26. One thinks of Jerome and Paula in Bethlehem. On "familial monasticism," see Clark, "Ascetic Renunciation," 246–47.

assertion that ascetic women were 'virile' is based on an accurate repre-
sentation of the concrete conditions of their lives, conditions that
resembled the men's."[27] Concrete conditions, and the accurate repre-
sentation of those conditions, were often in strong and striking opposition to the assumptions and stereotypes of both secular and
ecclesiastical thought. Gregory of Nazianzus praises his sister, in her
funeral oration, for remaining silent "within the established boundaries of women's faith"[28] (see 1 Cor 14:34), while Gregory of Nyssa
begins the *Life* of his sister Macrina by saying that she was a woman
but had managed to overcome that disability.[29] So disabled, women in
the desert often turned into men. Amma Sarah, one of only three
women whose sayings survive in the *Sayings* of the desert fathers and
mothers, reportedly said, "According to nature I am a woman, but not
according to my thoughts." Apparently her strongest words of rebuke
to her brothers were, "It is I who am a man, you who are women."[30]
"Transvestitism," women dressing as men, was not uncommon in the
desert.[31]

Syncletica is not required to become a man. She becomes, simply, a
monk, and is clothed, apparently, in the same monastic habit as the
men (paragraph 11).[32] Abba Silas, the narrator of Syncletica's story, certainly reveres her sanctity, as he would that of any holy man. Silas does
indeed mistake Syncletica for a eunuch (paragraph 3), but when he
asks, "Is this a woman? Could it be a eunuch?" she rebukes him:
"Why, my father, do you have so many questions concerning me?" She
quickly disabuses him of his suspicions by beginning her self-narrative
with "I am a woman" (paragraph 5). Syncletica has essentially told
Silas that his question is irrelevant; her narrative will teach him about
the equality of the sexes before God. Silas and Syncletica together act
out this equality: he left on his journey anticipating a blessing from his

27. Clark, "Ascetic Renunciation," 245.

28. Quoted in Ruth Albrecht, "Women in the Time of the Church Fathers," *Theology Digest* 36, no. 1 (Spring 1989): 5.

29. *The Life of Saint Macrina* 1.

30. *Apophthegmata* Amma Sarah 4 and 9; *The Sayings of the Desert Fathers: The Alphabetical Collection*, trans. Benedicta Ward (Kalamazoo, Mich.: Cistercian Publications, 1975), 230. The three are Sarah, Syncletica, and Theodora. See Ward, "Apophthegmata Matrum," *Studia Patristica* 16, no. 2 (1985): 63–66.

31. See *Apophthegmata* Bessarion 4; Ward, *Sayings,* 41.

32. Though not without first being regarded as a temptation for the monks. Palladius, *Lausiac History* 33 (Meyer, trans., 95), says that the women "had the same sort of manage-ment and the same way of life, except for the cloak."

male friend in the caves of Calamon (paragraph 1); at the end of the narrative he asks for, and receives, a blessing from Syncletica, "having possession of her blessing as spiritual food" (paragraph 14).

Syncletica stands firmly within the tradition of the widows and virgins in the first four centuries of the church. As an aspiring female ascetic, she continues the tradition begun by aristocratic Roman women in the fourth century: detaching herself from the world and its values, she strengthens her attachment to God through the study of scripture and by her "passion for the historical concrete elements of the Christian tradition."[33] She forsakes father, family, and marriage and moves to the Holy Land. Once there she becomes a monk; purchases, apparently, a Bible; and secludes herself in order to contemplate God. In her veneration of the sacred places of the Holy Land, Syncletica is like Paula in the fourth century, who came to Palestine and settled in Bethlehem, and Melania the younger, who founded a monastery on the Mt. of Olives.[34] The sites of the Holy Land, though, mark the *beginning* of Syncletica's pilgrimage. Unlike Melania and Paula, she leaves her retinue, and the Holy Land sites, and journeys into the wilderness. Her ultimate desire is to disappear into the holiness of the land—and the Lord.

Syncletica transformed herself from being just one more Constantinopolitan matron into an ascetic *par excellence,* from being one more traveling aristocrat with a retinue into being a solitary contemplative fed by the hand of God (paragraph 12). According to Elizabeth Castelli, this theme of renunciation (*an*nunciation, really)

> paradoxically offered women the possibility of moving outside the constraints of socially and sexually conventional roles, of exercising power, and of experiencing a sense of worth which was often unavailable to them within the traditional setting of marriage.[35]

This is indeed true, but those of us who read Syncletica's story today need to be wary of seeing her choices as primarily social or sociological. If we take her at her own word (paragraph 5), her choices were

33. Yarbrough, 159.

34. On Paula, see Jerome, Epistle 108.9, *Nicene and Post-Nicene Fathers*, 2nd ser. (N.Y.: The Christian Literature Co.; reprint, Grand Rapids, Mich.: Wm. B. Eerdmans, 1976), 6:198–99. On Melania, see *The Life*, chapter 41 (Clark, trans., 55). On the subject of Holy Land pilgrimage, see E. D. Hunt, *Holy Land Pilgrimage in the Later Roman Empire A.D. 312–460* (Oxford: Clarendon Press, 1984).

35. Castelli, "Virginity," 61. For a bibliography on this theme, see 61 n. 1.

spiritual and theological, as well as social. The one does not exclude the other; in fact, they are intertwined. The social, as for many men, was often an impediment to the spiritual, as it is today. So Syncletica threw it off. As a woman, however, Syncletica could not just walk away from her social contract, as Antony apparently did. (But here again we must beware of idealizations in our sources, or ourselves, that obscure the social costs of becoming a monk. Pachomius honored his social obligations by becoming a monk after his military tour of duty was over; Melania, hers by taking on ascetical practices after the deaths of her children. Antony honored the social contract by becoming a holy man.) The fact that Syncletica used subterfuge shows the boundaries she was breaking.[36]

Within the desert silence of God, Syncletica had moved beyond the social boundaries of her time. As a result, she no doubt struggled all the more with the personal boundaries that separated her from her God. Discovered by Silas, she broke her silence of twenty-eight years and so moved into history, with its own shifting boundaries and territories of deep silence. Silence and proximity to God brought her peace. Recognizing the holy, Silas speaks of her with the reverence more commonly due a Saint Antony or Daniel. Looking upon men and women like her, modern commentators have felt something of this same appreciation. Elizabeth Clark, a sensitive student of early monasticism, has spoken of the "courage, intelligence, and ardor of these social iconoclasts."[37] However we view their motives, whatever we make of their faith, or their God, we can agree on that.

---

36. Armand Veilleux, trans., *The Life of Saint Pachomius* 7–8 (Kalamazoo, Mich.: Cistercian Publications, 1980), 26–28; *The Life of Melania the Younger* 2–6 (Clark, trans., 28–30). As Yarbrough notes, 159–60: "This ascetic life offered mortification of the flesh indeed, but it also offered something more. It must have seemed an adventure of the highest kind, to throw over everything that was tedious and boring in Rome and to strike out for a life of freedom and the company of saints and wild monks in the desert."

37. Clark, "Ascetic Renunciation," 257.

# A NARRATIVE ABOUT SYNCLETICA WHO LIVED IN THE JORDANIAN DESERT[1]

1. A certain one of the holy and spiritual fathers, Silas was his name, an Arab by birth, who lived in one of the caves of Pharan[2] in the vicinity of Hierama,[3] told this story to the brothers, saying: Some years ago[4] a certain anchorite, a close friend of mine, lived in one of the caves of Calamon[5] that were occupied by anchorites. It was my custom during the annual feast days to visit him and take him some of the things he needed and be blessed by him.[6]

So when the holy festival of Easter had arrived, I took in my sheepskin cloak[7] a little soaked pulse[8] and small gifts of bread,[9] and I left

1. The translation is based on recension **a** of the Greek text, published by Bernard Flusin and Joseph Paramelle, "De Syncletica in Deserto Jordanis (BHG 1318w)," *Analecta Bollandiana* 100 (1982): 291–317. The title of recension **b** is simpler: "Life of a Certain Holy Virgin."

2. The "caves of Pharan" essentially means the "community" or "monastery" of Pharan, and is an accurate description of the monastic communities of the laura type, where the monks lived alone in caves or cells but joined together for meals and worship. For this type of monasticism, see chapter 4 on George of Choziba. On the lauras, see Yizhar Hirschfeld, *The Judean Desert Monasteries in the Byzantine Period* (New Haven: Yale University Press, 1992), 18–33. Pharan, about six miles northeast of Jerusalem, is the modern 'Ein Fara. Founded by the famous monk Chariton around 330, Pharan was the first monastery in the Judean desert. See Hirschfeld, 10–11, 21–23.

3. Flusin and Paramelle, "De Syncletica," 298–99, are unable to identify this place, but they prefer the reading of "Hierama" given by recension **a** to the "banal" reading of "Jerusalem" supplied by **b**. See also 302 n. 17.

4. Recension **b** is more specific: "thirty years ago."

5. Founded in the fifth century, modern 'Ein Hajla is about three and a half miles southeast of Jericho. For Pharan and Calamon, see the map in Hirschfeld, *Desert Monasteries,* xviii–xix.

6. There were a number of monasteries between Pharan and Calamon, a distance of twelve to fifteen miles. Silas would have followed the footpaths between monasteries until he joined the main road from Jerusalem to Jericho.

7. The *mēlōtarios,* which the monk wore in addition to the simple tunic. Antony of Egypt wore one, and willed one of two that he owned to Athanasius. See the *Life of Antony* 91. The sheepskin cloak or cape could be used as a bag. Sabas "empties his sheepskin bag in front of them, which contained nothing but roots of *melagria* and hearts of reeds." See Cyril of Scythopolis, *Life of Sabas* 13; trans. R. M. Price, *Cyril of Scythopolis: The Lives of the Monks of Palestine* (Kalamazoo, Mich.: Cistercian Publications, 1991), 105.

8. Pulse is the edible seed of leguminous plants such as peas, beans, and lentils. See Palladius, *Lausiac History* 18.1. Hirschfeld, *Desert Monasteries,* notes, 86: "Pulses were a staple food of the peasants, and they were usually found in the monks' diet as well. The relative ease of growing and storing them made them suitable for a monastic diet, especially in the desert."

9. It is not clear whether this bread has been blessed; since, as we discover, Silas was a priest, this seems possible. The practice of sending blessed bread was common in monastic circles; see Paulinus of Nola, Epistles 3.6 and 5.21, and Augustine, Epistle 34.

according to my custom and went to the servant of God. Now it happened—not by chance, I think—that I forgot my directions as to where the cave lay, and after looking for a long time and not finding it, I grew dejected. While I was wandering around there in the hills and gullies, the burning heat overtook me and I became very thirsty.

2. Suffering from fatigue and thirst and the blazing heat of the sun, I was calling out to God not to deprive me of the precious sight of the holy man.[10] While in such a state, I saw footsteps between the hills and, filled with joy, I studied them and realized that they did not belong to a grown man but rather were those of a child or a woman. I closely followed the footsteps then, searching them out, but I did not find their destination. Greatly distressed, I saw a large pile of kindling heaped together.[11] Dragging this burden with me and continuing on my way, with God's help I saw a cave and a small entrance leading up to it. Thinking it improper to go right in, I called out, "Bless me, father." When no one answered, I called out again with the same greeting. When once again no one answered, I again called out the same greeting, and for a third time, and no one answered. I then decided to be bold and went inside, and I found a monk sitting quietly.[12]

3. After we bowed to each other and embraced,[13] I suspected him to be a eunuch. He urged me to offer a prayer. I begged him, rather, to offer it, and after I insisted for a long time, he said to me, "*You* should pray, for you are a priest." When I denied this and attempted to hide it, he encouraged me, saying, "You are a priest. Do not lie, reverend father, but rather pray." Amazed, therefore, and afraid, I offered the prayer and the two of us sat down. Very much at a loss what to think, I said, "Is this a woman? Could it be a eunuch?" But he was silent. Then he said to me, "Why, my father, do you have so many questions

---

10. Greek *andros*, from *anēr*, "man." I have translated *anthrōpos* in this book as "human" or "person."

11. Recension **b** adds: "which are (from the plant) called Malōas or Halmuris." *Malōas* "is a desert plant which was often eaten by monks. It is mentioned in Job 30:14 and is to be identified with the shrubby Orache which grows on river-banks and by the roadside. Its leaves are still eaten when other food is in short supply." See *Cyril*, Price, trans., 17; 86 n. 37 (*Life of Euthymius* 11); and 75 (*Euthymius* 56). Flusin and Paramelle regard the mention of this plant as an authentic detail. The name would be dropped, as in recension **a**, when the manuscript moved out of its local Palestinian environment.

12. Greek *hēsychōs*, an adverb related to *hēsychia*, the monastic term for "quiet, stillness, peacefulness, quiet contemplation."

13. Syncletica was sitting when Silas entered the cave. Silas, appropriately, entered and sat quietly while Syncletica finished her prayers.

concerning me?" When I denied this and said I didn't, he replied, "Yes, he thinks to himself, 'Is this a woman? Could it be a eunuch?'" Amazed even more at this, I bowed my face to the earth.

4. Then he said to me, "Give me your word that you will tell no one about me while I am still alive, and I'll tell you about myself, who I am and how I got here." I said, "You know very well through the Holy Spirit that is in you that I will be pleased to learn about this." And after I promised not to make known to anyone what I learned about him,[14] he then began to speak thus:

5. "I am a woman. I was born the daughter of a certain eparch in Constantinople. A certain illustrious friend of my father sued for my hand and asked that I be his son's wife. I, however, did not wish to enter into marriage, but I did not openly express my intentions to my parents. I desired especially to be free from marriage[15] and to pray, and I called upon God's assistance in bringing this about. One day, therefore, my father said to me, 'Make yourself ready, child, for the time for the wedding has arrived, and your betrothed is importuning me to go ahead with the wedding.' But I said to him, 'It isn't possible, my lord, for me to be given to a man before my own personal vow is fulfilled.'

6. "When he asked what the vow was, I answered, saying, 'I have promised[16] to God first to worship at the holy places.' He said, 'First be joined in marriage, child, and after the wedding has been completed, take your "own personal"[17] husband with you, and the two of you can go in peace and worship God as you wish.' I said, 'I have promised to worship my Master there while I am still a virgin. Therefore, if you desire my well-being, do not cut me off from what I aim to do, my

---

14. Recension **b** omits "about him" and, with a feminine participle, indicates that "she" is speaking.

15. Greek *scholazein*, "to be free," of a woman, to be free from marriage, unbetrothed. See Basil, Epistle 199, canon 22; Roy J. Deferrari, *Saint Basil: The Letters,* Loeb Classical Library, vol. 3 (Cambridge, Mass.: Harvard University Press, 1953), 112–13: "But if anyone takes a girl who is not betrothed [*scholazousan*], it is necessary to take her away and restore her to her relatives, and commit her to their discretion, whether they are parents or brothers, or whoever have authority over the maiden." Recension **b** has "For I was happy to be unmarried (*emonazon*)." *Monazein* can mean "be single, unmarried," but in patristic Greek came to mean "live in solitude," and then "become a monk."

16. Greek *epangellesthai* can also mean "to profess" and could be used of monastic vows (see Basil, Epistle 217, canon 60; Deferrari, *Saint Basil,* 250–51), a sense that also seems present here and later in the paragraph.

17. This passage is written with some literary skill and a fine sense of irony. Syncletica's father repeats, ironically or derisively, a number of his daughter's words: "first," "complete," "worship," and here, where he replaces her prayer with a husband.

father, or something evil might happen to me on account of this.'

"Hearing this,[18] he was persuaded to send me, in the meantime postponing the wedding, not without sorrow. Thus my father gave me male and female slaves and eunuchs as a retinue and guard and three thousand coins[19] by means of a stamped document, so that I might distribute them as I wished wherever it was necessary.

7. "Thus I entered the Holy City, and after worshiping at the holy[20] places, I went around to the desert sites, distributing the money to the holy fathers. We went, therefore, toward those places where the caves of Coprotha are, to the so-called laura of the Egyptians.[21] For there lived there at that time three old men, of whom one was a holy wearer of sackcloth who also had a two-volume Bible. Now, my inner concern was to put an end to the deceit of a frivolous life, and I was seeking to find some monk who was capable of comprehending this[22] mystery with no possibility of scandal[23] and of providing me with the holy habit. When I saw the old man who wore sackcloth I said to myself, 'This man can fulfill my intentions, if it is pleasing to God.'

8. "Now when we had finished the distribution, we returned to the Holy City. After spending some days in the city, those who were with me were eager to bring an end to our business there. I, too, thought it would be good to do this expeditiously; therefore, I secretly wrote two letters, one to my parents, and one the chamberlain who was with me, explaining myself thus: 'I have offered myself to the God of the universe. Do not, therefore, search for me any longer, for you will not find me. I am leaving here to go where God will lead me.' When we were ready to leave the city, they prepared the litter for me, and our remaining animals walked ahead of us to the gate.

---

18. Recension **b** adds "and becoming afraid."

19. Greek *nomismata* (whence "numismatics"). *Nomisma* often indicates the gold aureus or solidus, the latter of which weighed about four and a half grams. More generally, nomismata can mean "coins."

20. Recension **b** adds "and venerated."

21. On this monastery, see Flusin and Paramelle, "De Synclectica," 302, esp. n. 20. They suggest that the name comes from its founders. John Moschus mentions this monastery in the *Pratum spirituale* 51, John Wortley, trans., *The Spiritual Meadow of John Moschus* (Kalamazoo, Mich.: Cistercian Publications, 1992), 42. Apparently little is known about it.

22. Recension **b**: "my."

23. Greek *askandalistōs*, the adverbial form of *skandalon*, "offense," "scandal." Syncletica is eager not to trigger any sexual desire in him; she is fully aware that she is young and attractive. For an interesting story with a "scandalous" exchange between a male and female monk, see Palladius, *Lausiac History* 37.12–16 (Meyer, trans., 108–10).

9. "At that point I said to the chamberlain, 'I desire once more, before we set out on our journey, to have the benefit of worshiping at holy Golgotha and the Holy Sepulchre.' He said to me, 'All of our things have gone ahead and none of your clothes are here. And how will you be able to depart in this fashion, when none of those who ought to accompany you are with you? So, are you going to travel like a commoner?'[24] I said to him, 'Yes, I *will* travel like a commoner, so no one will learn who I am.' He said, 'Then take the one female servant who has remained with us and go—and go quickly, so we can catch up with our animals.'

[9b.[25] "I said to the chamberlain, 'I wish to go away and say my farewells to the church of the Holy Resurrection.'[26] He said to me, 'Then take your female slaves and the eunuchs with you.' I said to him, 'I wish to go away secretly now, and I'm taking only one slave girl with me.' He said to me, 'Do as you wish; only make haste, my lady, in leaving.']

10. "I took the two letters I had written, rolled them up, and put them in my traveling clothes, and so I left with the girl.[27] We came to holy Golgotha, and standing there I said, 'Wait for me here a while until I can go and pay my respects to the Holy Sepulchre and come back.'[28] And so I left the city and went to Jericho on foot.[29]

11. "With God as my protector,[30] I went to Coprotha to the old man wearing sackcloth who, when he set eyes on me, was very surprised. He said, 'What can this be about?' I said to him, 'I am seeking God, and so I have come. Therefore I ask that you stand and clothe me with the holy habit, for I have desired this[31] for a long time.'

---

24. Greek *paganē* ("pagan"). Syncletica, as her name clearly shows (see p. 39), is an aristocrat, a *synkletikē*; without proper clothing she is "out of uniform," "unofficial," a commoner. In essence, she will be in disguise, shedding, with her clothes, her old identity.

25. Recension **b** differs significantly in paragraph 9, so I have supplied its reading.

26. The church built by Constantine in Jerusalem, situated on Golgotha. See Eusebius, *Life of Constantine* 3.25 and 3.28, *Nicene and Post-Nicene Fathers*, 2nd ser., vol. 1 (reprint, Grand Rapids, Mich.: Eerdmans, 1979), 526–28.

27. Recension **b**: "Carrying three hundred coins secretly [literally, "within"], I placed the letters with the clothes in the carrying case, and I covered my robe because without a doubt I was bound to worship in secret." (See Mt 6: 5–6 and parallels.)

28. On the holiness to Christians of the sacred places in Palestine, see Robert L. Wilken, *The Land Called Holy* (New Haven and London: Yale University Press, 1992), esp. 149–92.

29. A distance of about fifteen miles. The actions of Asella, a fourth-century Roman woman, parallel those of Syncletica. See Jerome, Epistle 24.3, *Nicene and Post-Nicene Fathers*, 2nd ser., vol. 6 (Grand Rapids, Mich.: Wm. B. Eerdmans, 1976), 43.

30. Recension **b**: "Guided by God."

31. "This" refers either to the whole action or to the monastic habit, or both.

"The old man said to me, 'See that you have not been sent as a temptation for the monks!' (for I was in the prime of life then, brought up in great luxury). But I prostrated myself to him and, throwing down three hundred coins, I said, 'Know, holy father, that you will honor me with the habit and clothe me in sackcloth and provide me with your books.' And so it happened, for when he saw my desire and my weeping, he stood and gave me the holy habit, clothing made out of rough fabric,[32] while I with joy gave him the money and my worldly clothes and the world that had ruled over me.[33]

12. "Finishing that day with him, I entreated him, saying, 'Stand and offer a prayer for my sake and I will go.' When the old man heard this, he was moved with sympathy and began to cry out, saying, 'Where will you go, my child?' I said, 'Wherever with the aid of your holy prayers God will lead me.'

13. "Thus after the old man prayed for me and supplied me with the books, I cast all my concern upon the Lord[34] and prayed that I be veiled from human sight, having given myself to that desert. Through the prayers, therefore, of that holy old man, God led me to this place, and when I saw this cave, I entered it with joy. At that time I was eighteen years old, and I've been here now for twenty-eight years. Up to now I've seen no person here except you alone."[35]

14. It was possible to look at her face and see it give off flashing sparks of light. When, therefore, she stopped talking, I begged her to share with me in the necessities I was carrying.[36] But she did not agree, saying, "*You* eat, for you are worn out." For a long time I requested that she share with me, but she steadfastly refused, saying, "If I share in these material foods that you have brought, he who has fed me all the years I've been here will no longer send me my customary food."[37]

32. Literally "clothes made of hair," as opposed to the worldly clothes Syncletica will give up. Clothes made of hair are reminiscent of the hairshirt Antony wore (*Life of Antony* 91) and the camel's hair coat of John the Baptist (Mark 1:6 and parallels).

33. Recension **b**: "With joy I gave him what I had in exchange for my habit."

34. See Ps 54:22; 1 Peter 5:7.

35. Recension **b** adds, "Then I realized that that woman, Godlike and angelic in form and intelligence, had removed her own footsteps with the Maloas (branches) and hidden in the grotto of the cave." See John Moschus, *Pratum spirituale* 179 (PG 87.3: 3049): "And know this, father, that his [God's] goodness has so sheltered me that no one has seen me these seventeen years except you alone today." See also *Spiritual Meadow*, Wortley, trans., 149. See Flusin and Paramelle, *"De Syncletica,"* 300.

36. The pulse and bread, mentioned in paragraph 1, that Silas was taking to his friend.

37. The theme of God supplying food to monks in the wilderness is a common one in early monastic literature, see "The Life of Onnophrius" below, pp. 170–71, 184–85.

When I heard this I sighed for myself and begged her to bless my food, but she would scarcely do even this, and so I ate, having possession of her blessing as spiritual food. Turning my attention to her face, I was astounded at her beauty: it was a wonder how, having spent so many years in such spiritual discipline[38] and solitude,[39] she remained at the peak of her youthful beauty.

15. Now at the same time I went in to see her in the cave, all of my burning thirst went away. After eating, I was concerned that when I returned I would again encounter thirst, but her piety said to me, "Be confident that you will not be thirsty until you arrive at the door of your cell." As I was leaving, then, I begged her, saying, "Have mercy on me and do not leave this place, so that over the years I may come and be blessed by you." She promised, and after we offered our prayers, I left. On my journey I was not thirsty until I entered my cell, just as the holy daughter of Christ had predicted.

16. After some days, I went in search of her in that place but did not find her, whether because she had fled into the inner desert or because she had hidden herself some way or another, I do not know.

Glory to Him who ordains these things, for ever and ever. Amen.[40]

38. Greek *askesei*, "ascesis."
39. Greek *hēsychia*.
40. Recension **b** has a much longer doxology.

# 4

# WHAT IS SPIRITUAL IS LOCAL: SAINT GEORGE OF CHOZIBA

## Introduction

WHAT IS SPIRITUAL IS LOCAL. ALL TOO OFTEN WE THINK OF SPIRI-
tuality as all soul and no body. Thus disembodied, what is spiritual drifts without hometown or date of birth, homogenous and
homogenized, as though a twentieth-century American (or the church
he or she attends) should be exactly the same as a sixth- (or first-!) century Palestinian. The spiritual, though, is more complex, and more
interesting, more connected to local terrain, literally and metaphori-
cally.[1] The *Life of Saint George of Choziba*, written by George's disciple
Antony in 631, offers us spirituality localized: we are in the Judean
desert; the weather is hot and the cliffs precipitous; there are snakes;
the Persians are invading; miracles occur; the monastic regimen is austere and spare, if not downright severe. Most of this will probably not
be to our liking. But we need to pay attention anyway, because what is
local—life here in Byzantine Choziba—gives flesh to the universal
calling to live out the gospel. Stripped to essentials, naked, these lives
can seem as uncompromising as the desert landscape: the monks of
Choziba carved their lives, like their cells, church, and monastery, out
of the rocks themselves; they oriented their monastery church in order
to fit the cliff's embrace.[2] It's as though they had inscribed in their

---

1. As The *Celtic Vision* by Esther de Waal (Petersham, Mass.: St. Bede's, 1990) and *The Syriac Fathers on Prayer and the Spiritual Life* by Sebastian Brock (Kalamazoo, Mich.: Cistercian Publications, 1987) show, to name just two books.

2. C. R. Conder and H. H. Kitchener, et al., *The Survey of Western Palestine*, vol. 3, *Judea* (London: The Committee of the Palestine Exploration Fund, 1883), 198.

dwelling places and in their hearts the injunction of Saint Jerome: *Nudum Christum sequere nudus* ("Follow, naked, the naked Christ").

We need to remember, though, that these monks had ovens and bread and gardens. They lived just a few miles outside of Jericho, and their monastery was close to the highway that ran from Jerusalem down to the Jordan, the road so busily traveled by pilgrims to the Holy Land.[3] The numerous footpaths connecting the monasteries seemed indeed to make the desert a city.[4] These monks are foreign, but not completely strange. The gospel they followed, in its essentials, is ours: hospitality, prayer, charity, love of God and neighbor, worship, community. If we sympathetically visit them in their spiritual as well as physical landscape, temporarily dislocated from our own, we can better see ourselves in their faces, and by searching out our kinship with them better discern both the gifts and the deficiencies of our own time and place.

## History of the Monastery of Choziba

The monastery of Choziba lies at the eastern end of the Wadi Qilt, three miles west of Jericho. Alfons Maria Schneider has given a vivid description of the area:

> When one, coming from Jerusalem, leaves the old Jericho road. . . approximately three miles outside of New Jericho and, following the riverbed, climbs up the Wadi el Qilt, one arrives after several hundred yards at a deeply furrowed valley of especially wild beauty. The walls of the gorge drop almost vertically and are so pressed against one another that there is little room on either side of the rocky streambed. The sides of the cliffs are composed of rock masses of varying hardness in horizontal layers that have taken on fantastic shapes through erosion. Along the valley bed runs a narrow green strip of vegetation that owes its existence to the water channeled to Jericho from sources above. The deep melancholy quiet of the gorge

3. One of the few major roads in the Judean desert in late antiquity, the Jerusalem-Jericho road utilized "the drainage basin of Wadi Qilt." See Yizhar Hirschfeld, *The Judean Desert Monasteries in the Byzantine Period* (New Haven: Yale University Press, 1992), 10. On pilgrims to the Holy Land, see E. D. Hunt, *Holy Land Pilgrimage in the Later Roman Empire A.D. 312–460* (Oxford: Oxford University Press, 1982), and Robert L. Wilken, *The Land Called Holy: Palestine in Christian History and Thought* (New Haven and London: Yale University Press, 1992), esp. 101–22.

4. Hirschfeld, 205–12; see 206 for a map of the footpaths between monasteries, and below for a discussion of the cells and footpaths.

is disturbed now and then only by the loud call of a bird of prey circling overhead. The oppressive heat between the cliffs, which one encounters during the day, is dissipated late in the afternoon by a cool breeze coming from Jerusalem. A well-kept trail, which first follows the rivulet and then flows into the Wadi, meanders down the south side of the valley to a bridge spanning the brook and then runs up to the monastery which is boldly fastened to the precipitous north wall of the rocky valley.[5]

Monks had been living in such places in the Judean desert since early in the fourth century, when Chariton, "the father of Judean monasticism," founded his first monastery at Pharan, five miles northeast of Jerusalem.[6] About a hundred years later, monks were living at Choziba; they chose this location in the Wadi Qilt for the same reasons Chariton founded his monasteries there. The common characteristics

reflect a clear understanding of the necessities of monastic life. [These monasteries] were built on cliffs near perennial water sources, not far from the settlements of the desert fringe. The steep and broken terrain offered a number of advantages to the monks: natural shelter from the harsh climate and desert predators in caves and recesses in the rock, solitude (on account of the difficulty of access), and minimal friction with locals, since the cliffs were—and are—of little interest to the residents of the desert fringe (by contrast with the grazing and arable lands in the temperate zones of the desert).[7]

Written evidence for the origins of the monastery of Choziba, as with most of the monastic settlements in the Judean desert during the Byzantine period, is meager. According to the *Life of Saint George of Choziba* and the *Miracles of the Most Holy Mother of God at Choziba*, five Syriac monks lived consecutively in a cell at Choziba from around 430 to 480.[8] While this may seem improbable, there is little doubt that

5. Alfons Maria Schneider, "Das Kloster der Theotokos zu Choziba im Wadi el Kelt," *Römische Quartalschrift* 39 (1931): 297.

6. For an excellent, accessible, study of Judean desert monasticism, especially of its archeology and daily life (though not its spirituality), see Hirschfeld. See also Derwas J. Chitty, *The Desert a City* (New York: St. Vladimir's Seminary Press, n.d.). On Palestinian monasticism, see also John Binns, *Ascetics and Ambassadors of Christ* (Oxford: Clarendon Press, 1994) and Joseph Patrich, *Sabas, Leader of Palestinian Monasticism* (Washington D.C.: Dumbarton Oaks, 1995), both of which appeared too late to use in this book.

7. Hirschfeld, *Desert Monasteries,* 11.

8. For a discussion of the sources and a history of Choziba, see Schneider, "Das Kloster," 299–305.

monks from Syria were the first ascetics at Choziba; the Judean wilderness attracted pilgrims and monks from all parts of the Roman Empire.[9] At this time the "monastery"—actually monks living scattered in caves—was probably not independent but was connected with a monastery in Jericho.

Sometime later a monk named John came to Choziba. We know very little about John's early life other than that he came from Egypt.[10] After arriving at Choziba, John undoubtedly lived at first in a small cave, or cave cell, then later built a *monē*, a simple monastery, around the oratory of Saint Stephen. John was a contemporary of the great Sabas, founder of numerous monasteries in the Judean desert (d. 532), and must have been a person of some renown. Cyril of Scythopolis, in his *Life of Sabas*, refers to "the sainted John the Egyptian, who was then refulgent with virtues at Choziba."[11] John must have been influential in church circles in Jerusalem because he later became bishop of Caesarea, next to Jerusalem the most important city in Palestine.[12] As bishop of Caesarea, he was a signatory at a synod in Jerusalem in 518.[13] He later retired to Choziba, where he died.

Unfortunately, 518 is the only firm date we have for John. He probably lived from 440–450 to 520–530.[14] We possess even less chronological information after John's time.[15] George came to the monastery sometime in the second half of the sixth century, and Antony, his disciple and biographer, became a monk at Choziba before the Persian invasion in 614, when the monastery was probably looted. Peace was restored between the Persians and the Romans in 629, but in 638 Jerusalem—and with it, all of Judea—fell to the Muslims.[16] We today

9. At Choziba, George was from Cyprus; Epiphanius, a Cilician, from Byzantium. A noble woman also comes to the monastery from Byzantium. Vitalius is "a Roman." Jerome's list in Epistle 107.2 includes "crowds" of monks from India, Persia, and Ethiopia.

10. See S. Vailhé, "Répertoire alphabétique des monastères de Palestine," *Revue de l'Orient chrétien* 4 (1899), 526, and Schneider, "Das Kloster," 300.

11. *Sabas* 44; Price, trans., 144. John tells a miscreant who has fled to him for judgment, "If you want to be saved, go to our Abba Sabas and do what he tells you." John is also mentioned in John Moschus, *Pratum Spirituale* 25 (PG 87.3: 2872). For an English translation, see John Moschos, *The Spiritual Meadow (Pratum Spirituale)*, trans. John Wortley (Kalamazoo, Mich.: Cistercian Publications, 1992), 17.

12. Schneider, "Das Kloster," 301.

13. Schneider, "Das Kloster," 301.

14. Schneider, "Das Kloster," 301. Vailhé, "Répertoire alphabétique," 526, places his birthdate "around 450."

15. Conder and Kitchener, 3:193; Schneider, 310.

16. Incursions of Saracens had begun in the sixth century, and monastic life for the next century and more was often precarious. See Cyril, *Life of John the Hesychast* 13 (Price, trans.,

can hardly imagine the loss felt by Byzantine Christians: not only had their sacred city fallen; its capture was also a profound breach in the walls of the Byzantine Empire. The Jerusalem above wept over the Jerusalem below.[17] Since sacred space is rarer now, analogies are imperfect, but perhaps it was like what an American Roman Catholic would have felt if, at the height of the Cold War, both Washington, D.C., and Rome had fallen into the hands of the Communists. Just as in modern times, however, Christianity outlasted communist Russia, so many early monasteries survived the Muslim era. Unfortunately, we have very little information about Choziba. The monastery was still standing at the end of the twelfth century. Sometime after that it fell into ruins.[18] In 1878 the monk Kallinikos began construction of a new monastery on the site of the old one, and the monastery is known today as the Monastery of Saint George.[19]

## The Monastery of Choziba

We can only stand in awe of the present-day monastery of Saint George at Choziba, the Deir Mar Jariys, carved out of and into the massive cliff face of the Wadi Qilt.[20] The ancient monastery was much smaller and simpler, about 300 feet long and 35 to 100 feet wide, encompassing 5,900 square feet, about three times as much space as the four-bedroom suburban home where I live.[21]

Choziba is "a classic example" of a monastery built next to a

230), and *Life of Sabas* 72 (Price, trans., 184), where Sabas petitions Emperor Justinian: "and on account of the inroads of the Saracens we beg Your Serenity to order the most glorious Summus to build at public expense a fort in the desert at the foot of the monasteries founded by your humble servant."

17. Antiochus Strategos, *The Capture of Jerusalem;* quoted by Wilken, 221. See Wilken, *The Land,* 216–32.

18. John Phocas visited the monastery in 1177 (PG 133.19: 949), as did an anonymous Greek in 1253 (PG 133.13: 988). See Vailhé, "Répertoire alphabétique," 527. Apparently some wall paintings in the chapel dedicated to Saints John and George were painted in the thirteenth century. See Asher Ovadiah and Carla Gomez de Silva, "Supplementum to the Corpus of the Byzantine Churches in the Holy Land. Part I: Newly Discovered Churches," *Levant* 13 (1981), 214.

19. George is buried in a niche in the south wall of the chapel behind the church, and his skull rests over the niche. See Ovadiah and de Silva, *Levant,* 213–14. There is no doubt that the monastery of Saint George is the site of the ancient Choziba; see Schneider, "Das Kloster," 298. For the later history of the monastery, see Schneider, 304–5.

20. See Hirschfeld, *Desert Monasteries,* 37, for a marvelous photograph.

21. Hirschfeld, *Desert Monasteries,* 38; based on the plan of Conder and Kitchener. See "Plan 1" in Schneider, "Das Kloster," 311.

cliff.[22] It combined a cenobium, an enclosed monastic settlement where monks lived together, with a laura, "a community of recluses," who lived in individual cells but who came to the cenobium for worship and, at Choziba, meals and work.[23] Choziba, as we have seen (above, pp. 55–56), began as a hermitage around 430 when the five Syrian anchorites lived there. It later became a laura-like community called the "Cells of Choziba" (see *Life* 12).[24] In the middle of the fifth century, Gerasimus, who along with Sabas and Euthymius was one of the great founders of monastic settlements in the desert of Judea, "founded a new kind of laura, which consisted of . . . a central cenobium, surrounded by hermits' cells."[25] The cenobium included "a church, a storeroom, a refectory, a kitchen, and living quarters for the staff, including cells for the abbot, the steward, and the priest."[26] Novices lived in the cenobium. (John the Hesychast was a cenobite at the monastery of Castellium for a year, after which time he received his own cell.)[27] As the *Life* also shows, though, cell-dwellers (*kelliotai*) like George were often present at the cenobium. Gerasimus's foundations became the model for other monasteries around Jericho, including Choziba.

Choziba became a "laura annexed to a cenobium" late in the fifth century under the leadership of John of Thebes, later called John the Chozibite (see above, p. 56), probably in order to accommodate the steady flow of pilgrims who traveled the road from Jerusalem to Jericho;[28] the *Life* and *Miracles* are rich in stories about pilgrims, and Choziba may have been the only monastery in the Judean desert to receive female guests (*Miracles* 1).[29] A story told by John Moschus

22. Hirschfeld, *Desert Monasteries,* 36.

23. Hirschfeld classifies Choziba as a "laura annexed to a cenobium." See Hirschfeld, 10–11, for a discussion of lauras and cenobia; 18–47, for different types of monasteries in the Judean desert; and 38, for the reconstruction drawing of the monastery of Ein es-Sakhari, which the monastery of Choziba probably resembled. J. Patrich points out, though, that Choziba, with its cells a mile removed from the cenobium, was unlike a regular laura where at least some of the cells were clustered around the central nucleus. See J. Patrich, "The Cells (*ta kellia*) of Choziba, Wadi el-Qilt," *Christian Archaeology in the Holy Land: New Discoveries,* ed. G. C. Bottini, et al. (Jerusalem: Franciscan Printing Press, 1990), 206.

24. Hirschfeld, *Desert Monasteries,* 37.

25. Ibid., 13.

26. Ibid.

27. Cyril, *Life of John the Hesychast* 6–7; Price, trans., 224–25.

28. Hirschfeld, *Desert Monasteries,* 16.

29. On women not being permitted in the monasteries, see Cyril, *Life of Euthymius* 54 (Price, trans., 74), and *Life of John the Hesychast* 24 (Price, trans., 238).

about an unnamed elder at Choziba vividly demonstrates the importance of hospitality (and self-denial) to the monks and may character-
ize a good portion of the monastery's ministry:

> He would travel the road from the holy Jordan to the Holy City [of
> Jerusalem] carrying bread and water. And if he saw a person over-
> come by fatigue, he would shoulder that person's pack and carry it
> all the way to the holy Mount of Olives. He would do the same on
> the return journey if he found others, carrying their packs as far as
> Jericho. You would see this elder, sometimes sweating under a great
> load, sometimes carrying a youngster on his shoulders. . . . To some
> he gave a drink of the water he carried with him and to others he
> offered bread. If he found anyone naked, he gave him the very gar-
> ment that he wore. You saw him working all day long. If ever he
> found a corpse on the road, he said the appointed prayers over it and
> gave it burial.[30]

The monastery where this elder lived, in antiquity variously called a
"laura," a "monastery," or a "cenobium,"[31] was built of limestone,
which was plentiful, and was supported with wood. Archeologists have
found framework that supported a structure at least two stories high.[32]
Walls were coated with plaster made of loam, lime, and water, and the
*Life* describes the monks of Choziba carrying lime from the kiln to the
monastery (paragraph 26).[33] Monks like these built the monastery

> on a long, narrow shelf at the foot of an immense cliff on the north-
> ern bank of the wadi. The entrance gate was in the eastern part of
> the rock shelf. . . . Entry was through two gates and a passageway
> leading to an inner courtyard. The courtyard gave access to the
> church, behind which, on a higher level, stood the refectory and the
> kitchen. The monastery of Choziba provides a good example of a
> departure from the classical square cenobium, resulting from the
> need to adapt the shape of the monastery to the rocky terrain of the
> wadi.[34]

30. John Moschus, *Pratum Spirituale* 24 (Wortley, *Meadow*, 16 [altered slightly]).

31. Evagrius Scholasticus, *Ecclesiastical History* 4.7, calls the settlement the "laura of
Choziba," while the *Life* (3) terms it "the monastery of our Lady the Mother of God." John
Moschus, *Pratum Spirituale* 24–25 (PG 87.3: 2869B and D), speaks of "the cells of Choziba"
and "the cenobium of Choziba" (Wortley, *Meadow*, trans., 16–17).

32. Hirschfeld, *Desert Monasteries*, 37–38.

33. See ibid. 64–65.

34. Ibid., 37–38 and 33. Schneider gives a walking tour of the ancient monastery, "Das
Kloster," 305–9. See also Conder and Kitchener, *Survey*, vol. 3, who gave the first systematic
description of Choziba, the only one that predates the building of the modern monastery.

Because Antony situates virtually all of his story in the extended area of the monastery (that is, the cenobium, the cells, and the near-by gardens and footpaths), he provides us with a more intimate view of the monastery and the activities of the monks than is often the case.

## Footpaths and Cells[35]

About one to one and a half miles east of the monastery, linked by two footpaths that follow the contours of the Wadi Qilt, lay the cells of Choziba, "a well defined and integrative monastic colony."[36] These cells formed a small laura, connected with the cenobium, of fourteen cells about thirty-five yards apart, spread over 50,000 square feet.[37] The two paths that lead to the monastery figure prominently in the *Life* and the *Miracles* and are often the scene of precipitous falls and miraculous escapes from harm. One path "linked the monastery with the main road descending from Jerusalem to Jericho and served the many pilgrims who came to the monastery."[38] One such pilgrim, a noblewoman from Constantinople, ordered her servants to carry her on her litter "down to the river and to the monastery on the right side," but her servants said that it was impossible "to go down there with a litter"—besides, women were not allowed in the monastery. She persisted, and with the help of the Virgin, made her way safely down, apparently on a horse (*Miracles* 1). This trail, certainly more accessible by foot than in a litter, "is used to this day, plunging to the streambed, crossing it via a bridge, and ascending northward to the cliff on which the monastery stands."[39]

A second path, less precipitous, "leads to the monastery from the direction of the Jericho oasis, without crossing the stream. Many sections of retaining walls from the Byzantine period have been found along its length."[40] This may be the path the monk Zenon took when

---

35. For a discussion of monastic cells in the Judean desert see Hirschfeld, *Desert Monasteries*, 176–90, and for a discussion of footpaths, 205–12. For a detailed discussion, see J. Patrich, "The Cells," 205–25.

36. Patrich, 209. See Hirschfeld, *Desert Monasteries*, 207, for a map of the cells, and Patrich, 207, for a more complete map.

37. Hirschfeld, *Desert Monasteries*, 31.

38. Ibid., 207–8.

39. Ibid., 208. He notes that the modern path has been paved by laborers employed by the monastery. See the picture of the remains of the ancient bridge on 208.

40. Hirschfeld, *Desert Monasteries*, 209.

he went to Jericho to bring eucharistic bread back to the monastery (*Miracles* 4). The cells of Choziba "are situated on the cliff below the trail. The path forks, and one section descends directly to the cells."[41]This is the path that George took to and from the cenobium (*Life* 21) and the trail the brothers walked when going out to gather capers (*Life* 42). Such travels could, however, become adventurous: "A certain brother was walking along the single-lane path between the cells and he came to a certain precipitous place where the rock was also high above him. And there the brother ran into a leopard" (*Life* 21).

Monks in the Judean desert lived simply, and their cells were spare.[42] But the word *cell*, with its connotations of prisoners and bars, may conjure up too austere an image. One monastic cell excavated at Choziba—cells were almost always occupied by a single monk—was a complex that included a small cave, a room in front of the cave built of masonry and wood, a courtyard with a bench and cistern, and a small garden of about a hundred square feet.[43] Such a living arrangement, in addition to offering quiet and seclusion, water, and vegetables, provided more: the courtyard offered light and warmth when desired, and the cave provided shade from the blistering heat. It was small, though. One of the best-preserved cells in front of a cave, similar to the one at Choziba, includes a cave 10.5 feet long and 7.4 feet wide and high. The room in front of the cave is small, 8.2 feet by 9.0 feet.[44] The ceiling is low, about 6 feet high (though we should remember that the ancient monks were considerably shorter than we are, averaging perhaps five feet in height), and is constructed of wood beams. The courtyard is also small, 18 feet by 7.2 feet, but it includes a bench and a cistern. Many of the cells at Choziba had small ovens.[45]

Life in such a cell was simple and secluded—but that was the purpose of such a life: to keep distractions to a minimum so the monk could devote himself to God. While alone, though, the hermit always knew that the footpath was not far from his door and that the monastery was

41. Ibid., 210.
42. For a good discussion of the meaning of the cell to the monks of the *Apophthegmata*, see Graham Gould, *The Desert Fathers on Monastic Community* (Oxford: Clarendon Press, 1993), 150–7. The monks depicted in the *Apophthegmata* are mostly semi-anchoritic, therefore much like George.
43. Hirschfeld, *Desert Monasteries*, 184, see 185 for a plan and cross-section of this cell. See Patrich, *Survey*, vol. 3, 208–20, for detailed archeological descriptions and numerous illustrations.
44. My children's bedrooms are ten by thirteen feet.
45. See Patrich, *Survey*, vol. 3, 214 and 218.

about half a mile to a mile away. Such an awareness could be both a comfort and a distraction. Interestingly, the *Life* does not often describe monks alone in their cells at prayer. As Antony reveals, George kept his spiritual way of life very private: "No one, the whole time he lived in the cell, was able to know his way of life" (*Life* 12). The monks were often speaking, working, journeying, and undergoing various small adventures; such activity made the monastery feel domestic and busy. The monastery indeed was a community of prayer, but it *was* a community, one whose everyday activities included both prayer and "business." Thus, we see George more often at the cenobium than alone in his cell. Undoubtedly, though, the hermit did spend most of his time at his cell. As Abba Poemen pointed out several centuries earlier—in words that will strike our era of self-gratification as harsh:

> Living in your cell clearly means manual work, eating only once a day, silence, meditation; but really making progress in the cell means to experience contempt for yourself wherever you go, not to neglect the hours of prayer and to pray secretly.[46]

## Daily Life and Spirituality

The monks' lives consisted mostly of work and prayer, often done together. The *Life* and the *Miracles* do not, unfortunately, offer us an intimate view of the monks' prayer life. We are like the modern visitor to Choziba unable to climb up to the hermit's cell—in this case, the cell of the interior life.[47] We can nevertheless learn a great deal about the spirituality of these ancient monks from their daily life, from both what Antony considered important, and from what he took for granted and mentions only in passing.

An early scene in the *Life* shows what the monks valued: piety and work. After leaving the monastery of Calamon, George entered the monastery of Choziba. When "the superior saw the great stability and monastic piety in him, not long afterwards he tonsured him and clothed him with the monastic habit" (*Life* 4). The superior then apprentices George—in work and in spirit—to tend garden with an

---

46. *Apophthegmata* Poemen 168, *The Sayings of the Desert Fathers*, trans. Benedicta Ward, rev. ed. (Kalamazoo, Mich.: Cistercian Publications, 1984), 190.

47. This reticence was also true of the earliest desert monks, as Douglas Burton-Christie has observed: "The monks we meet in the Sayings are generally reticent to speak of their spiritual experience. . . ." See his *The Word in the Desert: Scripture and the Quest for Holiness in Early Christian Monasticism* (New York and Oxford: Oxford University Press, 1993), 299.

elder "who was advanced in the ascetical life." This old man, however, turns out to be rather hard-hearted, but George performs his first miracle and in doing so heals the elder in body and soul (*Life* 5). We might call this story typically hagiographical because it holds up the narrative's hero as a saintly wonderworker. But if we do we should not overlook its realism: the story acknowledges that monks have real human weaknesses, something that George's harsh words on slander and backbiting in the community (*Life* 48–50) make abundantly clear!

The real emphasis, however, is on the monastic virtues: the old man, by mistreating the novice, represents arrogance or spiritual pride, a passion the monks sought to eliminate or bring under control. (The struggle against pride and arrogance is a central theme of the *Life*, so much so that a later writer attributed a long speech against it to George.) George, by contrast, shows great humility, patience, and forgiveness to an extent that surprises the community for one so young. But George is not the only example. When George's brother, Heracleides, dies, he is praised as "a good man, if ever there was one, full of faith and adorned with every virtue, his praises sung by everyone in the Jordan plain, a virgin and quiet solitary, detached from possessions, merciful, continent" (*Life* 9). Leontius, a superior of Choziba, was "a good man, merciful in every way and a friend to the poor" (*Life* 11).

We can see from Leontius and Heracleides that the monks valued someone whose interior and exterior life were one: quiet allowed for prayer, and prayer made one peaceful; detachment gave the monk inner peace, which made him merciful and "a friend to the poor." Virtues, of course, can be lost through inattention or worn away through indifferent habit. The Virgin appears at the monastery as a woman "poor in appearance" and, in a story with fairy-tale qualities, sets right the monks' work and reminds them that "this holy place is a shelter for the poor and for visitors, and not a shelter only for the rich" (*Life* 25). Situated as they were along the Jerusalem-Jericho road traveled by wealthy pilgrims, the monks probably had to learn and relearn this lesson.

The Mother of God reminds the monks that poverty, and giving to others out of that poverty, are outward manifestations of spiritual humility. The spirituality of the monastery of Choziba, as represented to us by the *Life* and the *Miracles*, centers around humility, the honest assessment of one's self before the presence of the Almighty.[48]

48. For a good discussion of humility in the *Sayings* of the early desert fathers and mothers, see Burton-Christie, 236–60.

Heracleides "possessed the mother of virtues, I mean humility of spirit" (*Life* 9). An exemplar of humility, Heracleides would not stand in choir with the monks, "but always stood in a corner of the church wearing ragged clothes and having a hood over his head until, with many tears, and without conversation or distraction, he finished the holy psalmody of the liturgy. . ." (*Life* 9).

Such humility, placing themselves below all others, led George and Heracleides to severe—and presumably atypical but admired—ascetical practices, especially with regard to food. George and Heracleides were examples to be admired—and partially imitated. The *Life* gives no indication that their asceticism was the norm.[49] Such extreme practices as theirs may be kept—barely—palatable for us by an ambiguous image: George, emaciated by asceticism, still feels the pleasure of light and warmth as he suns himself, a spiritual lizard, "among the rocks, warming himself in the heat of the sun (for he was very thin on account of his great abstinence), boiling over with the desire of spiritual love to do the work that God wills. . ." (*Life* 30). What motivated George and others like him, "circumspect in all things," keeping their eyes to themselves "like the Cherubim" (*Life* 14), to such asceticism and self-denial? I believe it was both love and fear: an abiding, almost overwhelming horror of pride and arrogance—hubris. Most of the teaching offered by George in the *Life* (14, 38–39, 43–56) is on the subject of arrogance and its opposite and antidote, humility. George's words evince a clear-headed and sensible understanding of arrogance. It

> anchors itself in the wind and our self-conceit drifts in the air like fleeting smoke. What, really, is arrogance except the counterfeit image of puffed-up thought, the momentary crashing of a wave? It's a bubble, ready to burst, floating for a little while on the surface of the water; suddenly it breaks, and comes to nothing (*Life* 14).

Much of this wisdom, of course, was gathered from the Psalms, Proverbs, and Ecclesiastes—and from life itself. In a world controlled by often brutal imperial—and ecclesiastical—power, George looked to

---

49. The monk Aphrodisius had a strikingly similar ascetical practice: "Taking the leftovers of the cooked food, whether greens or pulses or roughage, he would put them in a single bowl and take a little from the bowl each day, and was satisfied with this. If the food in the bowl began to smell or produced worms, he did not throw it away but simply added more cooked left-overs" (Cyril, *Life of Sabas* 44; [Price, trans., 144]). But Aphrodisius' practice is penitential: "His wailing throughout the night left his neighbors no peace."

Christ, and Christ's love and compassion for humanity, as the model of humility. Humility and honoring one's neighbor, Antony believed, were "the full profession of our monastic habit and the kingdom of God" (*Life* 60). For George, in a seeming paradox, humility "has a height: the only Son of God 'who humbled himself even unto death, death on the cross'" (Phil 2:8) (*Life* 14).[50] The incarnation, then, and the incarnation's cross, are at the center of George's asceticism: all the monastic virtues—humility, charity, compassion, hospitality, peacefulness—radiate like rays of light from the nimbus adorning the head of the resurrected Christ on one of the frescoes at Choziba. And, always together because resurrection and cross coinhere, they penetrate like the thorns spiking his earthly crown.

## Work and Daily Life

Immediately after George is clothed in the habit of a monk, he is set to work. The monks at Choziba probably spent much of their daylight hours in manual labor. Absent from Antony's accounts is the basket-making of the Egyptian solitaries. Instead, we observe the monks of Choziba at a wide variety of tasks befitting a busy monastery: as gardeners, cellarers, doorkeepers, bakers, provisioners, wood gatherers, quarriers, mule drivers.[51]

The monks would have tried as much as possible to be self-sufficient, but most Judean desert monasteries were not, if only because they could not grow the grain needed to make bread. The monastery had an agent, a *proagorastēs*, in charge of "buying provisions for the monastery." He "came from Arabia and asked the superior for a sum of money to purchase grain. At the moment the superior did not have what was necessary, so he proposed that he send someone the next day either to Jericho or to the Holy City to obtain it" (*Life* 25).[52] The monks were apparently able to supply their need for firewood by harvesting

---

50. The image—and spirituality—of humility's height was an old one in monasticism. Isidore of Pelusia had said: "The heights of humility are great and so are the depths of boasting; I advise you to attend to the first and not to fall into the second," a merciful one-sentence summary of the long address attributed to George in *Life* 43–56. See *Apophthegmata* Isidore of Pelusia 5 (Ward, trans., 98).

51. Each of these was a "ministry" or "office"; see *Life* 35 and 37; and *Life of Sabas* 44 (Price, trans., 143).

52. In 1977, Yiannis Meimaris met the father superior of Choziba, Amphilochios, outside the Damascus gate in Jerusalem, "loaded with supplies for his Monastery." See Meimaris, "The Hermitage," 171.

*manouthion*, a woody shrub. They would go out on an organized harvest once a year, taking monks from both the cenobium and the cells, and even recruiting non-monks as workers (*Life* 14). Monks would also go out individually to gather *manouthion*, and capers for food (*Life* 42). We should not underestimate how difficult—even dangerous—some of the work at Choziba was. The desert heat and precipitous cliffs were constant work-companions. One scene vividly shows both the extreme heat at Choziba and George's reputation as a fearless worker:

> In the bakery, in addition to his other duties he would also heat up the oven. You all know what sort of difficulties and afflictions the place caused in the summer. For we often found the candles in the choir stalls melting and dripping because of the extreme heat. But the old man would persevere in this same heat, lighting the oven two or three times a day—frequently on the day the slave was expected to work in the bakery. Many of the brothers tried to do the same thing but were unable to do it by themselves without someone relieving them. So the brothers would also say, "This old man is made of iron" (*Life* 23).

George's lighting of the oven several times a day shows that the monastery baked far more bread than the monks could eat. In fact, the *Life* tells us "most of the bread was consumed by visitors" (23). Life at the cenobium, then, was strongly influenced by the care of visitors, and even cell-dwellers like George were affected. (We saw above how one unnamed monk cared for travelers, p. 59.) There must have been a steady stream of guests: Epiphanius, the wrestler from Byzantium, stops by on his way to the Jordan—and stays (*Life* 16); the uncle of one of the brothers "would come down to the monastery of Choziba in order to pray and at the same time see his nephew" (*Miracles* 2); a rich noblewoman from Byzantium comes to Choziba carried on a litter (*Miracles* 1). The visitors, like the monks, would eat vegetables (grown in the monks' gardens) and beans, in addition to bread (*Life* 12).[53] Wine seems to have been available, in quantity (*Life* 14 and 28 and *Miracles* 2)!

---

53. The edible seeds of various legumes (peas, beans, lentils), often called "pulse," "were a staple food of the peasants, and they were usually found in the monks' diet as well. The relative ease of growing and storing them made them suitable for a monastic diet, especially in the desert." See M. Dembińska, "Diet: A Comparison of Food Consumption between Some Eastern and Western Monasteries in the 4th–12th Centuries," *Byzantion* 55 (1985): 431–62, cited in Hirschfeld, *Desert Monasteries*, 86. Recent research, interestingly, has suggested that "an enriched diet of restricted calories" can help extend the human life span to 140 years or more. See Betty Friedan, *The Fountain of Age* (New York: Simon and Schuster, 1994), 127. The spare diets of the early monks may in fact have contributed to longevity.

Besides work, the *Life* and the *Miracles* provide other details about the monks' day. We see the monks in church, reciting the psalms together (*Life* 9); the noblewoman arrives when "the fathers were finishing the evening office" (*Miracles* 1). During the winter George recites the divine office and psalms in his cell, a small shed (*Life* 13). The *Life* suggests at times that George was at the cenobium almost every day, but this is probably due to the compressed "action" of the narrative. The narrative also states that each Lord's day (Sunday), George would come to the cenobium with the other cell-dwellers (*Life* 16 and 20), and that "late on the Sabbath day [that is, Saturday], the monks who lived in cells were accustomed to going up to the cenobium to participate together in the divine office and the liturgy of the undefiled mysteries and in a meal with the fathers in the monastery" (12). When Epiphanius comes to George for counsel George tells him to go to the monastery and wait for him until the Lord's day (*Life* 16).

The monks usually worked and slept in the same short-sleeved tunic, the regular monastic clothing. George kept one tunic, a *synaktikos*, as his "Sunday best," which he wore to the *synaxis*, or weekly liturgy. For his workaday clothing "he would go around to the garbage heaps and gather together rags and, sewing these together, would make himself clothing. From these rags he would also make his bed" (*Life* 12). He would sleep on his "patchwork mat on the pavement" (*Life* 36). Antony tried sleeping on the floor, but it affected his health, so George told him to gather straw or leaves for a sleeping mat (*Life* 40). These glimpses of the everyday life of the monks suggest that some monks like George, rigorously ascetic, lived very austerely; others, like Antony, emulated them—or tried to. For most of the monks at the cenobium, life was probably not austere (at least by their standards), but was, rather, simple, devoted to prayer and hard work.

## Holy Man and Holy Wonders

The *Life of Saint George* is subdued hagiography. George's asceticism is exemplary—and probably unusual—but Antony only occasionally seems awestruck in its presence, as he is when describing George's dehydrated balls of food (*Life* 12). The *Life*, for the most part, simply notes and accepts the old man's way of life. In the monastery, George seems to have been held in some awe for his ascetical strength, but probably more important was his role as a spiritual counselor.

Epiphanius comes to the monastery seeking someone "advanced enough from whom he could seek counsel" and is told, "We have someone who is wonderful in every way." Antony also records several of George's addresses to the monks on spiritual topics (*Life* 14; 18–19; 38–39; 43–56, an interpolation). Whether or not these are verbatim reports, it is clear that George was a spiritual leader and teacher in the monastery during his life, deeply respected for his hard work and spiritual counseling, and revered for his wonderworking.

George was revered indirectly, though. The *Life* and the *Miracles* describe a number of his miracles, and Antony clearly believes they are due to the patronage and protection of our Lady, the Mother of God:

> like an unfathomable sea are the many mighty works and wonders of our holy Lady in this holy place concerning spirits and thieves and wild beasts and snakes, and also concerning rocks that have fallen from cliffs and come down upon the monastery, and how the glorious and grace-giving Mother of God has brought security and great protection from all harm (*Life* 29).

As a narrator, Antony really has two stories to tell—that of George and that of the Mother of God. He wants to tell the story of the wonderful old man George, whom he knew personally, but at times he gets so excited about telling the wonders of our Lady that he gets sidetracked. At the end of paragraph 24 Antony promises to stick to his narrative about George, and then proceeds to report—for five paragraphs—marvelous wonders of "our Lady! After the quotation above—which interrupts his narrative of the Persian invasion—Antony realizes (once again) that he has wandered away from the old man's story: "But we need to return to our account, from which we have digressed, concerning the narrative about the old man."

Antony's world is one of wonder and miracle, so different from our own, or at least from the way we allow ourselves to perceive it. "Like a huge eagle tall as a man," the devil appears on top of George's cell, standing "on the edge of the roof of the dwelling; spreading his wings, he blocked out the sky." But the devil is impotent: George leaps at him and "the eagle crashed down from the precipice; making a very great noise and crying out with a pitiful screech, with a wail it vanished like smoke" (*Life* 13). Another time an evil spirit attacks George on the footpath at a "precipitous place." The old man rebukes the demon—and forces it to carry him to his cell (*Life* 20)!

When George defeats the devil in the bakery, Antony attributes it to "our blessed Lady" (*Life* 24). The *Life* and the *Miracles* differ, therefore, from most other descriptions of the holy man in late antiquity: in the *Life of Sabas* by Cyril of Scythopolis, when a camel falls from the cliffs, its master importunes Sabas and then sees "an elder of sacred appearance sitting on the camel as it rolled" who rescues the beast (*Sabas* 81; Price, 195). Nothing like this occurs in the *Life* and the *Miracles*; there is no "cult" of the holy man as mediator between God and humanity. When a similar accident happens in the *Miracles* (3), it is the Virgin who is responsible for rescuing the muledriver. The Virgin guides the rich noblewoman to the monastery (*Miracles* 1), appears as a poor woman to teach the monks about hospitality (*Life* 25), protects the monastery from bandits (*Life* 28), and rescues monks from dangerous falls (*Miracles* 3). Abba Leontius, who served at the church of the Mother of God in Jerusalem, summed up this marian spirituality: when asked about his almsgiving, he replied, "Forgive me, father, but it is not I who gives. It is my lady the Mother of God who provides for both me and for them."[54]

The Holy Mother of God is the protector and guardian of the monastery, but holiness resides in her servants, too. For Antony the relationship between holiness and wonder (miracle) is clear: the five Syrian monks at the beginning of Choziba's history

> were perfected in their godly behavior and virtuous life; eagerly embracing the eremitic struggle and enduring the ascetic life, they exchanged them for the heavenly kingdom. Therefore they also had great authority before God, both on behalf of those at the monastery and those outside; they bestowed numerous gifts of healing while lying in the same tomb which unceasingly poured forth oil for healing so that it covered the slab on top of the tomb (*Miracles* 6).[55]

Holiness, the monks of Antony's world believed, resides in the saints on earth if in faith they "call upon God, who is very compassionate and merciful." In a deeply moving story, a farmer from Jericho,

54. John Moschus, *Pratum Spirituale* 61 (Wortley, trans., 47).

55. Both healings at tombs and anointing with holy oil from the tombs of the saints are common in Judean monasticism. See Cyril, *Life of Euthymius* 47 (Price, trans., 65); 50 (69); 51 (73); 52–53 (73–74); 54 (74); and 58–59 (79–80). See *Euthymius* 42 (58) for an example of a crucible placed on a tomb that "pours forth every kind of benefit for those who approach with faith," and 21 (30) for the "abundant charisms of healing and against impure spirits" that "we see even today welling up from his tomb."

"a dear friend" beloved by George and Heracleides, loses his only son. The farmer "then placed him in a basket, along with some of the first fruits from his farm, covered him with grape leaves and, carrying him, hastened to the laura. . . . And the all-merciful Lord, the lover of humankind, who creates the will of those who fear him, heard their prayers and raised the child" (*Life* 8).

The *Life of Saint George* is, finally, a story of deep faith. That faith may not be ours in some of its particulars, but its deep-running waters can, if we acknowledge our thirst, help sustain us in our modern, myriad wastelands. Holiness, the *Life* suggests, can finally become not a matter of body and spirit but a movement of spirit into spirit:

> When he set his eyes on me, [George] embraced and kissed and blessed me and turned to the east and said, "Depart now, my soul, in the Lord depart." After saying this sentence three times, he offered up his spirit to the Lord who was within him and along with whom he had fought the fight for this good and holy way of life. And so he exchanged his life as someone might change his pace as he walks, with complete peace and tranquility (*Life* 57).

# THE LIFE OF SAINT GEORGE OF CHOZIBA[1]

Translated with Apostolos N. Athanassakis

*The life and ascetic practice of our father among the saints, George of Cyprus who lived in Choziba*

## Chapter I[2]
## George's Origins and the Beginnings of His Monastic Life

1. George was by nationality a Cypriot, and his parents were devout and moderately wealthy, as is the case with those who are from Ktēma.[3] He had an older brother called Heracleides who, while his parents were still living, went to the Holy City of Christ our God to pray. After going down to the Jordan and worshiping God there, he withdrew to the laura[4] called Calamon and became a monk. Left as his parents' only child, George was raised with all piety and was conspicuous for his holiness.

2. When his parents passed away and their child was left orphaned, George's uncle took charge of him and the family property. Having an only daughter, the uncle wished to marry her to him. But the young man disliked worldly things; moreover, he refused to live with a wife. Since he had another uncle who was the superior of a monastery, he

---

1. For our translation we have used the text edited by C. House, "Vita sancti Georgii Chozibitae auctore Antonio Chozibita," *Analecta Bollandiana* 7 (1888): 95–144, with House's corrections, "Nota in Vitam Sancti Georgii Chozibitae," *Analecta Bollandiana* 8 (1889): 209–10.

2. Chapter and paragraph divisions are those of the published text. Descriptive headings are the translators'.

3. *Ktēma* may stand for ancient Paphos, as it does today, or the phrase may be translated "as is the case of those who live on an estate [*ktēma*]."

4. Lauras at this time were communities of hermits where many or most of the monks lived in individual cells, often at some distance from the monastery; they would gather on Saturday and Sunday (the Sabbath and the Lord's day) for community meetings, including the Eucharist. Some monks, especially novices, would live in community in the cenobium; such was the case at Choziba. For a good introduction to monasteries like Choziba and Calamon, see Yizhar Hirschfeld, *The Judean Desert Monasteries in the Byzantine Period* (New Haven and London: Yale University Press, 1992).

fled to him, wishing to follow the monastic way of life, as his brother Heracleides had also done. But his uncle, the one who held his family's property, learning that he was there, went and fought with his brother[5] over the return of the boy. But the latter answered and said to him, "It was not I who brought him here, and I will not send him away. He is old enough. It's right that he choose for himself."

3. The young man, knowing of the conflict between his uncles concerning him, left everything and secretly fled the island.[6] He went away to the Holy City and venerated the holy places of Christ our God, and after going down to the Jordan and praying there, he withdrew to join his brother at the laura of Calamon.[7] But when his brother saw that he was still a young man and beardless—which is against the rules of the holy fathers—he refused to receive him into the laura because he was beardless.[8] But taking him to the monastery of our holy mistress the Mother of God,[9] which is called Choziba, he entrusted him to the superior and returned to his own cell.

## George's Novitiate; His First Miracle

4. When the superior saw the great stability and monastic piety in him, not long afterwards he tonsured him and clothed him with the monastic habit. He then summoned one of the monks who was advanced in the ascetical life and who had the ministry of the "new little garden" (as it was called), and he assigned the novice to him as a fellow minister. The old man was tough, a Mesopotamian by birth. One day, then, he sent the young man down to the stream to fetch water, but the young man went and returned without any, for he was unable to get to the water because his clothes got in the way and the water had been dammed by sticks and reeds tangled together. Then the old man made him take off his cloak and, with the boy's cowl serving as a loincloth, he sent him to go and fetch the water.

5. That is, George's uncle, the superior of the monastery, not George's brother.

6. For a similar story, see Cyril of Scythopolis, *Life of Sabas* 1–2 (Price, trans., 95–96).

7. Calamon is five miles southeast of Jericho, at Deir Hajla. See Price, 214 n. 58. See also the index in Hirschfeld, *Desert Monasteries*, 299.

8. Monasteries at this time routinely refused to accept aspirants who were too young, that is, who had not yet reached puberty. In 1893 on Mt. Athos, Athanasius, a young monk, "having no beard, had to live outside the Monastery." See Archimandrite Cherubim, *Contemporary Ascetics of Mount Athos*, vol. 1 (Platina, Calif.: St. Herman of Alaska Brotherhood, 1992), 106.

9. Greek *theotokos*.

When the boy delayed in leaving the water, the old man hid his cloak and left when it was time for Holy Communion.[10] When the boy returned and found neither his supervisor nor the cloak, he went to the monastery naked except for a loincloth. When he knocked, the guestmaster opened the door. Seeing that he was naked, he inquired of him, "How did this happen?" and he explained to him what had happened. The guestmaster brought out a cloak, gave it to him to put on, and conducted him into the monastery. When his supervisor came from the morning meal,[11] he met him in front of the place where five of the holy fathers were resting.[12] When the old man saw him, with angry threats he struck him, saying, "What took you so long?" And immediately his whole arm became stiff and paralyzed.

5. Falling before the boy, the old man pleaded, saying, "Child, please do not make me a public spectacle nor make an example out of me. I have sinned. Forgive me, and entreat the Lord on my behalf so I can be healed." The young man spoke to him with humility and respect: "Go, father, and kneel in repentance at the tomb of the saints, and they will heal you." But the old man stopped him, saying, "I have sinned against *you*. Please intercede on my behalf." Then the boy took the old man by the hand, and they went together to the tomb of the saints. There they knelt in repentance and offered prayers, and immediately he was healed. From that time on the man was gentle and mild and completely respectful.

Now when a rumor about all this spread through the brotherhood, and they all marveled and praised God for the unexpected miracle that had occurred—especially from a youth and a novice—the boy, fearful of this fish hook of vanity, secretly left the monastery and went away to his brother at the laura.

10. Greek *metalēpsis*.

11. Greek *ariston*, which sometimes means "Eucharist," here signifies the late morning meal after the liturgy, of which *metalēpsis*, Communion, was part.

12. See paragraphs 5–6 of the "Miracles of the Most Holy Mother of God at Choziba" in Tim Vivian and Apostolos N. Athanassakis, trans., *Antony of Choziba: The Life of Saint George of Choziba and the Miracles of the Most Holy Mother of God at Choziba* (San Francisco and London: International Scholars Publications, 1994), for the story of these five saints and the healing power of their tomb.

## Chapter II
## George's Life with His Brother
## at the Monastery of Calamon

6. George lived, then, with his own brother, the two of them occupying what was called "the old church." Holding fast to this way of life and ascetic practice, not once did they cook anything for themselves, unless someone came to visit them. Instead, they asked the doorkeeper of the fort[13] to watch over the leftover food for them from one Lord's day to the next,[14] both that from the fort and what was brought to the doorkeeper by the fathers. And taking this food, they lived off it. The pot in which the food was kept was never washed or emptied out but was full of maggots and gave off a very foul-smelling stench for quite a distance. They abstained from wine, and with these arrangements they were content.

7. One day Abba Heracleides[15] said to his brother, "Take an ax and let's go cut some wood," for they had a barren date palm, and he ordered him to cut down this tree. But George knelt before him and entreated him, saying, "No, father, let's not cut it down. We might get a palm-branch from it." His brother threateningly said, "Cut it down! Look how long it's been since it bore any fruit. Why should it take up wasted space?" But George once again with humility knelt before him and said, "I myself swear that from now on it will bear fruit." And so his brother acquiesced, and from then on it bore dates both good and plentiful, more than the other palm trees.[16]

---

13. Greek *kastron* (Latin *castrum*). See Cyril of Scythopolis, *Life of Sabas* 72 (Price, trans., 184): "to build at public expense a fort in the desert at the foot of the monasteries. . . ." John Climacus, in *The Ladder of Divine Ascent* 6, refers to a sixth-century monastery in the Sinai (the present-day monastery of Saint Catherine) as a fort. See Colm Luibheid and Norman Russell, trans., *John Climacus: The Ladder of Divine Ascent* (New York: Paulist, 1982), 134.

14. "Leftover food": *erēmōmena*. A saying from the *Apophthegmata* (PG 65:301A; Megethius 3) shows that the asceticism of George and his brother may be atypical: "Some of the Fathers questioned Abba Megethius, saying, 'If some cooked food remains over for the next day, do you recommend the brethren to eat it?' The old man said to them, 'If this food is bad [*ērēmōtai*], it is not right to compel the brethren to eat it, in case it makes them ill, but it should be thrown away'" (Ward, trans., 149).

15. "Abba": "Father," a title of respect accorded to monks, especially to older or prominent ones. Possibly "abbot," but the narrative has not identified Heracleides as the superior of the monastery.

16. See Lk 13:6–9. George assumes the role of the gardener in Jesus' parable.

## The Raising of a Dead Child

8. There was a certain farmer from Jericho, a dear friend who was beloved by them. He had an only son, still a child, and this child died. His father then placed him in a basket, along with some of the first fruits from his farm, covered him with grape leaves, and carrying him, hastened to the laura. When he knocked at the cell, Abba George came out, opened the door, and showed him in. The beloved man went inside to see the old man. Begging his pardon, he set the basket in front of them, entreated him to bless the fruits of his farm, and left.

When the brothers lifted the fruits out of the basket, they found the dead child. When the old man, Abba Heracleides, saw this, he was shaken and said to his brother, "Call this fellow, for temptation has come to us here today. From what I can see, he has come to tempt us sinners." His brother, by then forty years old or older, knelt before him and said, "Don't be dispirited, and don't be angry, father. Come, let us in faith call upon God, who is very compassionate and merciful. And if God overlooks our sins, and when we call upon him, raises the child, our friend will depart, according to his faith, with his child alive again. If, however, God's goodness does not wish to do this, we will cry out to God and say that, because we are sinners, we have not attained such authority, nor do we have the liberty to do so."

And so the old man was persuaded and they stood for prayer with tears and a heart shattered with contrition. And the all-merciful Lord, the lover of humankind, who creates the will of those who fear him, heard their prayers and raised the child. Then they called the child's father back and said to him, "You see, you have your son, restored to life through the compassion of God. See that you say nothing about this to anyone or you will cause us troubles and afflictions."[17] So he took his child and left, praising and glorifying the beneficent, merciful, and life-giving God.

## Abba Heracleides' Way of Life and His Death

9. They lived, then, in this way with complete devotion and peace. For no one heard them argue or be inconsiderate to one another, nor to anyone else. For the old man had great piety and forbearance, and

17. See Mk 5:43 and 7:36.

Abba George great obedience and humility. But the old man came to the end of his life, having reached about seventy years of age or even more. He was a good man, if ever there was one, full of faith and adorned with every virtue, his praises sung by everyone in the Jordan plain, a virgin and quiet solitary, detached from possessions, merciful, continent.

For the diet that we have written about above he followed all the days of his life, and he would follow this diet by fasting two or three days or even each day of the week. Through this diet he attained so great a virtue that if at any time there was an *agapē* for the fathers and he was compelled by them to eat, he would leave the tastier dishes, and if he did not mix his own food with what was offered to him, he was not able to eat. In any case, he would become ill. Indeed, this happened to him many times when he was forced to eat their way.

Now he also possessed the mother of virtues, I mean humility of spirit. For he never allowed himself to stand in the choir of holy fathers during the singing of the psalms, judging himself unworthy of such a position, but always stood in a corner of the church wearing ragged clothes and having a hood over his head until, with many tears, and without conversation or distraction, he finished the holy psalmody of the liturgy—wherefore, indeed, the many wondrous deeds of his life in Christ are sung. But this man, Abba Heracleides, so conspicuous for his holy and God-pleasing way of life, finished his life in a good old age, and was buried there in the tombs of the holy fathers, and he confidently intercedes without ceasing along with the choirs of saints to God on behalf of us and the whole world.

## Abba George Continues the Way of Life of Abba Heracleides

10. Abba George, although left alone in the cell, saddened, and mourning his brother's death,[18] held securely to his way of life and ascetical practice, loved by all. He often ministered to the fathers, being among them peacefully and faithfully and strengthening[19] every-

---

18. Greek *koimēsis*, "dormition."
19. Greek *oikodomein*, "edifying," "building up."

one in every way (for he accepted the office of minister[20] with fear and compunction), always serving and ministering to others.

One day he had to go out on some business and, opening the door, he saw a lion lying in front of the doorway. Calmly, he nudged the lion with his foot, commanding him to move away from the door so he could leave to take care of his urgent business. But the lion quietly roared in a friendly way and wagged his tail that he didn't want to get up. Abba George nudged the lion two or three times with his foot so he would move, but when the lion did not get up, he spoke to him quietly, "Since you do not obey what scripture says—'The Lord has shattered the lions' teeth; blessed be the Lord!'[21]—open your mouth so I can look." The lion opened his large mouth and allowed him to feel around as much as he wanted. Then, after he placed his hand in the beast's mouth and felt around, he said firmly, "Just as a stake in a wall, a loose one, feels, so too are a lion's incisors!"[22] Then the lion stood up and went on his way and George, going out, finished the business he was supposed to do.[23]

## Chapter III
## George's Way of Life at Choziba

11. When the superior of the monastery at that time died, a great uproar took place in the laura, and there were two sides fighting over who was going to rule the monastery. They began to destroy the rules of the monastery and the customs of their fathers. On account of this, the old man was distressed and deeply troubled, and he fervently called upon God to make known to him where he wanted him to move. And he saw in a vision two great mountains shining like light, one much higher and more resplendent than the other. And the one who showed him the

20. Greek *diakonia*. The meaning may well be "servant," less probably "deacon"; it does not appear that George's ministry here is an ordained one. The *Pratum spirituale* of John Moschus shows that there were servants in the monasteries who, in fact, may not have been monks. See *Pratum spirituale* 16 (PG 87.3: 2864A), and 138–39 (PG 87.3: 2977C); (Wortley, trans., 12 and 113).

21. See Ps 57:7 (58:6).

22. There is a play on words here: "incisors" are *passaliskoi*, while a stake is *passalos*.

23. Stories of meetings between lions and monks are very common in monastic literature. For examples, see Cyril of Scythopolis, *Lives of the Monks of Palestine*, and John Moschus, *The Spiritual Meadow*. The latter has the famous story of Gerasimus' lion (c. 107, PG 87.3: 2965–69; Wortley, trans., 86–88), which ends with this theological moral: "how the beasts were in subjection to Adam before he disobeyed the commandment and fell from the comfort of paradise" (Wortley, trans., 88).

vision told him to go and settle wherever he wanted, and the old man asked for the higher mountain. And that one said to him, "Go, then, to the monastery where you were tonsured and dwell in the cells there."[24]

So he immediately left and asked the superior at Choziba to give him a dwelling among the cells. Leontius was in charge of this monastery, a good man, merciful in every way and a friend to the poor. For he was so advanced in the virtue of being merciful that when he died, one of the old men saw him standing in front of the altar, turned completely into fire. (I have a number of things to say about the mercifulness of this father—these I shall leave aside because this is not the time for me to give them. But I will say that blessing flowed from him as from a fountain which the [blessed][25] Mother of God abundantly furnished according to his wish. He was always ready to give freely, serving and ministering to the blessed Virgin in mercy, according to his ability, and even beyond.)

12. The old man, overjoyed at having such a suitable disciple, gave him a cell right away. As a result, he moved immediately from Calamon and went and lived at the cells of Choziba. No one, the whole time he lived in the cell, was able to know his way of life, except that he acquired neither wine, nor olive oil, nor bread, nor clothing except for one short-sleeved tunic[26] that he wore to church.[27] But he would go around to the garbage heaps and gather together rags and, sewing these together, would make himself clothing. From these rags he would also make his bed. He would ask the cellarers at the appropriate time to keep for him from one Lord's day to the next what was sponged off the tables of the fathers and the guests,[28] whether it was vegetables or beans or bones.[29] And taking these things and grinding

---

24. For similar heavenly guidance, see *Life of Antony* 49 (Gregg, trans., 67–68).

25. Reading *eulogē menēs*, instead of the unattested *eulegomenēs*.

26. Greek *kolobion*. Jerome, in his Preface to the *Rule of Saint Pachomius*, comments: "They have nothing in their cells except . . . two *lebitonaria* (or *colobia*), which is a type of clothing without sleeves that the Egyptians wear, and one worn for sleeping or working" (House, "Vita Sancti Georgii," 108 n. 1).

27. Greek *sunaktikos*, of a garment reserved for the *synaxis*, or community liturgy. For another example, see *Apopthegmata Patrum* Theodore of Pherme 29 (PG 65:196B and note 72 there; Ward, trans., 78).

28. Greek *xenos*, literally "stranger," that is, those who are not monks but who are received in hospitality at the monastery. See Palladius, *Lausiac History* 14.3 (PG 34: 1036A): A monk "built a monastery for himself and took in a few brethren. Then he took in every stranger, every invalid, every old man, and every poor one as well, setting up three or four tables every Saturday and Sunday" (Meyer, trans., 50).

29. Hirschfeld suggests that since the monks rarely ate meat (sometimes the sick were allowed it), these "bones" must be fruit or olive pits (Hirschfeld, *Desert Monasteries*, 86). But guests dining at the monastery (mentioned above) may have been allowed meat.

them in a stone mortar, he made balls and dried them in the sun for two or three days, and—if he made use of them at all—he would eat them in his cell, moistening them with water. For late on the Sabbath day, the monks who lived in cells[30] were accustomed to going up to the cenobium to participate together in the divine office and the liturgy of the undefiled mysteries and in a meal with the fathers in the monastery. Believe me, honorable fathers and brothers, that I myself, after the incursion of the Persians,[31] when we returned to the monastery, went with some of the brothers to the cells, and we found some of these very balls left there, and we all marveled at how he made use of them.

13. He lived in a kind of shed,[32] a small cell four to five feet in length, or even much smaller, in which he recited the divine office in the summer. One night, then, when it was scorching hot, the enemy of our life wanted to make him negligent so he would skip the divine office. Like a huge eagle tall as a man, he stood on the edge of the roof of the dwelling; spreading his wings, he blocked out the sky. When the old man saw this, he at first marveled at the size of the bird, but then realizing that it was a stratagem of the one who hates what is good, he rushed forward to strike it. But the eagle crashed down the precipice; making a very great noise and crying out with a pitiful screech, with a wail it vanished like smoke.

On the porch of his cell lay an old clay jar left by those who had lived there before him. A swarm of bees had come and hidden in it and were busy at work inside. One day a thought greatly troubled him: "Gather the honey and do what you need to with the pot." But he took the pot and, heaving it off the edge of the roof, cast down the thought along with it. And what was troubling him immediately ceased.

---

30. Greek *kelliōtai*, literally "cell-dwellers," those monks who lived in cells away from the monastery (the "cenobium") itself.

31. In 614.

32. Greek *exōstēs*. In rural Greece today, a *xōsti* is a structure attached to a dwelling, usually reserved for animals.

## Abba George Speaks to the Monks
## about Arrogance and Humility

14. It was the custom at the cenobium from time to time to cut *manouthion*.[33] For they would cut at one time what they needed for the whole year, and would call together to help both the monks from their cells and, if they could also help out, some others who were not monks.[34] One day, then, after they were done cutting wood, they sat down to eat at about the fourth hour,[35] and the old man also sat down at one of the tables.

Now one of the brothers, acting in a disorderly way, began to tell frivolous and indecent stories and make faces at the brothers who were sitting there, snatching at the food on the table. When the old man, having endured these things once and twice, saw the brother being so strongly tempted, he leaned forward and with his eyes fixed on the face of the brother, said to him in a severe voice, "We are monks, father. You are behaving shamefully, child, and boasting arrogantly, not considering that the monk is completely circumspect in all things and ought to be like the cherubim, keeping his eyes to himself[36] and not allowing himself to get completely carried away. I say to you, child, the ant will come up and eat you and humble your arrogance." (For this was the expression he used instead of an oath, for he never swore but instead used this expression: "I say to you.") But the brother laughed at the old man and mocked him, saying, "Sure, old man, the ant's going to come up and eat me."

Now when they got up from the meal, each one rested a little wher-

---

33. *Manouthion* occurs three times in the *Life* (here, 19, and 24) and once in the *Miracles* (3). It occurs three times (with a different spelling: *mannouthion*) in Cyril of Scythopolis (see the index in Price, trans., 302, where, however, the last three entries should be deleted). Price translates the word as "faggots," but Festugière suggests "thistles" (see Price, 91 n. 106). *Manouthion* may have been the tumble thistle (*Gundelia tournefortii*; Arabic *aqub* ), "found widely on the desert fringe in Palestine. When it first sprouts in February or March, all its parts—stems, leaves, roots, flowers, and seeds—are edible. Toward the summer, the leaves turn yellow and become prickly. Indeed, if manouthion is tumble thistle, it may have been eaten shortly after being harvested, with whatever was left over or gathered out of season being used for fuel" (Hirschfeld, *Desert Monasteries,* 89). As firewood, the "bushes were gathered and stored in the monastery storerooms"; at Choziba, the monks kept a supply near the oven (*Life* 24).

34. "Others who were not monks": *xenous.* See above.

35. Roughly 10:00 A.M.

36. A reference to Is 6:2? But there it is *seraphim* who cover their faces with their wings. See paragraph 49 below.

ever he found a place until the sun passed its height. This brother rested under some sheltering rock, sound asleep, for he was drunk from consuming a great deal of wine—or, rather, it was so that what the old man had said might be fulfilled. And, sure enough, as sometimes happens to those cutting wood, he got a little nick near his ankle from the *manouthion* and bled a bit. Now a nest of ants lay beside the rock, and when they caught scent of the blood, they began to eat at him in such a way that before long they had stripped the flesh and made the wound almost as wide as his hand. The brother woke up from his sleep and felt the piercing pain in his foot. Rubbing it with his hand, he saw calamity strike as a couple of handfuls of ants around his foot threatened the wound, and he began to cry out, "Lord, have mercy on me!" When the brothers gathered around him to learn the reason for his shout, he showed them his foot and said, "What the old man said has now happened!" While all of them stood there astonished, he got up and ran and threw himself at the old man's feet, asking him to forgive his sin and to pray for his healing.

Then the old man admonished the brothers and said, "You see, sirs, fathers and brothers, that human arrogance is nothing, nor is the self-conceit of our hearts. For arrogance anchors itself in the wind and our self-conceit drifts in the air like fleeting smoke. What, really, is arrogance except the counterfeit image of puffed-up thought, the momentary crashing of a wave? It is a bubble, ready to burst, floating for a little while on the surface of the water; suddenly it breaks, and comes to nothing. Tell me, what profit, really, do we gain from it? It cannot add an inch to our height,[37] and yet it makes us fly above the heavens. It cannot add a penny to our possessions, and yet it makes us conceited like rulers and kings. It doesn't provide us with extravagant foods or luxurious clothing, and yet it inflates our thoughts the way luxury bloats the bodies of the self-indulgent. It doesn't add one day to our lives, and yet like the immortals we keep our brows raised skyhigh! Earth and dust, we forget the stench of the tomb and fly away on the air. Arrogance is like the swelling of the sea which sometimes is calm and smooth, while at other times its every drop rises and crests; yet one wave after another crashes onto the shore and vanishes. In the same way arrogance also brings down the mind that it holds captive through self-important thoughts and then dashes it against the gates of Hell.

37. Mt 6:27 and Lk 12:25

"And let us reflect on this in our hearts, honored fathers: Neither the virtuous and holy person—even if he is like Peter and Paul, even if he is more highly esteemed[38] than any person—neither saints nor those who are impious can fly in the air a single inch above the earth, but all of us, whether righteous or sinners, measure off the same steps, equally, in the flesh, upon the selfsame earth. But who can judge whether the righteous person lives soaring in his principles and deeds? 'For our citizenship,' he says, 'is in heaven.'[39] But he says to the arrogant person, 'You will now be dragged down to Hades, for everyone who exalts himself will be humbled.'[40] Wherefore, humility has a height: the only Son of God, 'who humbled himself even unto death, death on the cross.'[41]

"Know then, beloved, how great is the indescribable humility by which God descended even unto death. Piety is the foundation for the whole society of the saints. Indeed, I say to you, brothers, that it is neither the Greek nor the Jew nor the Samaritan who has true piety and gentleness, and who is beloved and cherished before both God and humanity. For among every race, the person who fears and honors God is acceptable to him. In order that we might demonstrate for ourselves how beneficial piety is, let us learn from the four-footed animals and wild beasts and birds: we associate with those that are the most holy and most gentle, while we go after those that are wild and savage.

"Let us, then, acquire these virtues, beloved, I mean humility and piety, through which we will be beloved by both God and humankind. Let us take the yoke of Christ upon ourselves, and let us learn from it[42] that he is gentle and humble in heart, and we will find rest and peace for our souls,[43] and he will receive us as joint partakers in his eternal kingdom." Having said these things, the old man prayed on behalf of the brother, made the sign of the cross over his foot, and healed him.

---

38. Greek *hyperēphanos*. Throughout this section, "arrogance" translates the Greek *hyperēphania*.

39. Phil 3:20.

40. A conflation of Mt 11:23 and 23:12; parallel Lk 10:15 and 14:11.

41. Phil 2:8.

42. Or "him."

43. See Mt 11:29.

## Chapter IV
## The Story of Epiphanius the Wrestler

15. There was in Byzantium a certain wrestler, a Cilician by nationality, at the top of his profession. His opponents, who were causing problems for him among the wrestlers, poisoned him, and he was suffering. In desperation the friends of this fellow took him around from oratory to oratory and monastery to monastery, grieving for him. Finally, out of great despair—or rather, lack of faith—these so-called Christians took him to sorcerers, rejecting the saints in favor of the farces of magicians. The sorcerers bound an evil spirit on him for two years, and as a result he was invincible as a wrestler on account of the great strength of his body and the workings of the demon.

Now when the two years were over, he was once again suffering terribly, just as before, and the threat of God's punishment was bringing him to repentance because God, in his ineffable mercy, wishes no one to perish but receives everyone into repentance, overlooking our iniquities as one who loves humankind. This fellow's friends, dishonored and reproached by his enemies on account of him, furnished him with provisions for a journey and sent him to the Holy City.

16. Having then arrived and worshiped at the holy places, he came down also to the holy Jordan in order to pray and passed through Choziba. By chance he came upon Abba Dorotheus, who later became the Guardian of the Cross[44] at the time of our holy father Modestus,[45] patriarch of the Holy City of Christ our God, and he asked him whether they had an old man advanced enough, one from whom he could seek counsel. He said to him, "We have someone who is wonderful in every way. He lives in the cells and each Lord's day comes to the cenobium." He said, "I'm in a hurry to go down to the Jordan, but I beg you to take me to him." Abba Dorotheus took him to the old man, and kneeling before the old man, said to him, "This brother here has come to the cenobium and asked me whether there were an old man from whom he could seek counsel, and I have brought him to

---

44. For the names of earlier Guardians of the Cross, see Cyril of Scythopolis, *Life of Euthymius* 20 (Price, trans., 29), 22 (31), 37 (52), 40 (57), 48 (66), and *Life of Sabas* 19 (Price, trans., 113). See also John Moschus, *Pratum spirituale* 49 (PG 87.3: 2904–5; Wortley, trans., 39–40).

45. Modestus in 632 succeeded Zachariah as patriarch of Jerusalem; he died in 633 or 634.

you." The old man said to the brother, "Go, child; wait for me at the monastery until the Lord's day, and I will come and offer you counsel." The old man did this because he wanted to learn about Epiphanius through God's providence. For such was the way of life and practice of the old man: he would not quickly offer counsel to anyone, waiting until he was informed by God. And so thus persuaded, the brother went away and stayed in the cenobium.

17. The old man came on the Lord's day and said to Epiphanius (for this was his name in the world), "Child, if you listen to me, I will offer you counsel, and your soul will be saved." Epiphanius kneeled before him and begged him, saying, "This indeed is what I seek, reverend father." The old man said to him, "Stay here with the fathers for, as you can see, the work of this place of hospitality is good. And your soul will be saved." He said, "I want, father, to ask your advice privately." But the old man said to him, "What do you want to ask, child? What you are seeking is not possible." He said, "Why, reverend father?" The old man said to him, "Because you have abandoned the saints and gone off to sorcerers, and from them you have received false help; you have dishonored your faith, and God has become angry on account of this wrongdoing and impiety."

## Saint George Speaks to the Monks about True Faith

18. And he said to the brothers, "Look, beloved, at what Christians do! Woe to this world because of its scandalous acts! How have we become Christians? Haven't we sworn allegiance to Christ, rejecting the enemy and all service to him and all his pomp and all his works?[46] We have been baptized in the name of the Father and the Son and the Holy Spirit. How then can we turn back again, like a dog to its own vomit?[47] We call ourselves Christians, and yet we submit to the yoke of the enemy of Christ: some become sorcerers, while others seek out help from them! What fellowship[48] does light have with darkness, what agreement does the temple of God have with an idol, or what agreement is there between Christ and Belial?[49] For these are the pomps and

---

46. Those "swearing allegiance" to Christ and those "rejecting" the enemy are *suntaxamenoi* and *apotaxamenoi*, respectively.

47. See 2 Peter 2:22 (Prov 26:11).

48. Greek *koinōnia*.

49. 2 Cor 6:15.

the rituals of the enemy of our life that indeed we have rejected because we swear allegiance to Christ. How, then, can such as these share in the Lord's food and the food of demons, or the Lord's drink and the drink of demons?

"Do you see, beloved, that such a transgression is no small matter? Do you see that the shame brought to our faith by these fellows[50] is no small thing? Do you see that Saint Peter spoke well when he said, 'It would have been better for them if they had not known the way of truth since they have shamelessly turned away from the holy commandment passed on to them'?[51] How, therefore, can God not be angry at our people? How can he not turn his face away from the evil generation that does such things? Who will persuade him not to bring cataclysm upon the earth or once again rain down fire and brimstone or consume the earth with fire like Sodom and Gomorrha?[52] I myself, children, am filled with fear and trembling because of the evils that are coming upon the earth on account of our wicked practices.

"You, beloved, I know, ought to be moved to repentance on account of what you have heard—and, even more so, be strengthened in your rejection of this world and the love of it, and persevere in the patient endurance of the monastic way of life and its form, and with tears and great humility earnestly entreat God night and day so his ineffable goodness will spare his people, and he will have mercy on his inheritance. Perhaps the world will be spared the terrible things expected of it.

"But you, Epiphanius my child, if you heed the words of your humble servant and remain in this place and turn away from the world, you will be rid of the demon for the rest of your life. You abandoned the saints and ran to sorcerers and received help from them and made a spectacle of your faith, yet because of the match you have wrestled against your opponent and the chastisement and training you have received for the sin you committed, your soul will be saved."

## Epiphanius Becomes a Monk; His Way of Life

19. The young man fell at the feet of the old man and beseeched him with tears, saying, "Yes, reverend father, whatever you command me, I

50. Or "actions," "deeds."
51. See 2 Peter 2:21.
52. Gen 19.

will gladly do, only let my soul be saved." And he became a monk, reliable in everything, having undertaken great ascetical discipline. For frequently he would go several days eating only carobs and dates, and he did these things while living in the cenobium, undertaking ministries and completely humbling himself with the most onerous duties, achieving unceasing vigils. Indeed, a little before the hour when the signal[53] is given for the night office, after sitting in deep meditation and prayer on a stone bench before the small sepulcher of the five holy fathers who were lying there, he would sleep a little. He never slept after the divine office, but would go out for *manouthion*, often returning to the monastery at sunrise.

He did not use bedding of any sort from the time when he left the world. He acquired very great simplicity of heart[54] and never swore an oath, using in place of an oath the phrase "Thy will, Lord." We do not have the leisure now to narrate his virtues and his entire way of life. But he also received divine grace[55] and would see the evil spirit, and often he would scare it away so it would not come near him. For according to what the old man said, it was never far from him, up to the day of his death.

## Chapter V
## Wondrous Happenings at Choziba

20. It was the custom for those monks who lived in the cells to come each Lord's day to the cenobium. Now when the old man also had come, the ministers[56] took him around in the afternoon on the Lord's

---

53. Greek *krou(s)ma*: a striking on wood or metal as a signal for the divine office. See Cyril of Scythopolis, *Life of Sabas* 43 (Price, trans., 143): "The saint arose one night before the hour of striking. . . "; and *Life of Euthymius* 44 (Price, 62). Abba Cyriacus told Cyril that when it was his duty, "I would not stop beating the summoning-block for the night psalmody until I had recited the whole of the 'Blameless' Psalm [Ps 119 (118)]" (*Life of Cyriacus* 8; Price, 250). See also John Moschus, *Pratum spirituale* 11 (PG 87.3: 2859C), 50 (2905A), 104 (2961B), 105 (2964A) (Wortley, trans., 10, 41, 82, 83).

54. Greek *akakia*. See John Climachus, *The Ladder of Divine Descent* 24 (Luibheid and Russell, trans., 215): "Simplicity is an enduring habit within a soul that has grown impervious to evil thoughts."

55. Greek *charisma*.

56. Greek *diakonētai*, servants, attendants or ministers in a monastery. See n. 20 above. See *Apophthegmata* Macarius the Great 1 (PG 65:260A; Ward, trans., 125), and Arsenius 37 (PG 65:104A; Ward, trans., 17): "A Father went to see Abba Arsenius. When he knocked at the door the old man opened it, thinking that it was his servant." These servants may have been slaves.

day to their own ministries so he could bless them and offer prayers for them.[57] Some also communicated to him their own thoughts. Now it happened one Lord's day that he was offering counsel to one of the brothers until the second or third hour of the night. It was the old man's custom not to sleep at night in the monastery after the second hour. Going outside, therefore, to the doorkeeper's cell, he called on the doorkeeper to open the door and let him leave, but the doorkeeper stopped him, saying, "But it's time for bed, reverend father—and where are you off to just now? Better lie down and rest, and you can leave early in the morning." But the old man said, "No, child, let me leave now." The doorkeeper said, "I'm afraid, reverend father, that I'll be to blame if something happens to you on the road." He said to him, "It is God, child, who comes to our aid." The doorkeeper importuned him at length but, not being able to persuade him, at last let him leave.

Going out, the old man took the single-lane path to his cell. Then an evil spirit came at a precipitous place and tried to hurl him down.[58] But he knew the spirit and rebuked it, saying, "Get away from me!"[59] Now this occurred many times. At last, when the demon would not give in, the old man said, "Since you behave shamelessly and refuse to go away—the Lord be praised!—you will carry me and bear me to my cell." And immediately the spirit submitted, and carrying him, took him to his cell. And the old man said, "Now go, and do not behave shamelessly and contend with us humble sinners."

21. After this had happened and become known, one of the brothers said to the old man one time, "If you were hurt, father, by a leopard or a snake or by some other wild creature, what would you do?" The old man said, "Child, spirits I do not fear, so how shall I be afraid of wild beasts? Besides, beloved, no one has ever heard of anyone being harmed here by a leopard, except for one fellow, and it happened like this: A certain brother was walking along the single-lane path between the cells, and he came to a certain precipitous place where the rock was also high above him. And there the brother ran into a leopard. When he saw it, he was afraid to turn around, but the beast also refused to back down. So they stood there, looking at one another. Now when the brother saw that the beast was not going to give way, he said to it, 'In the name of our Lord Jesus Christ, move so I can go by!' When the

---

57. In Greek these last two pronouns refer to the ministers.
58. "Precipitous" is *krumnōdeis*, while "to hurl down" is *krumnizein*.
59. Similar to what Jesus says to Satan; see Mt 4:10.

leopard heard the name of the Lord, it shot down onto a ledge about ten feet below. But the brother did not fear God, before whom the beast trembled, so he picked up some large rocks and stoned the beast. Enraged, the leopard went away by another route and, overtaking the brother, cuffed him two or three times and went away, leaving him wounded. But it did not touch him with its mouth at all. We found him and brought him to the infirmary, and after a few days the brother got well.

22. "Now concerning snakes that are poisonous and dangerous in this region, I know a certain gardener who killed a snake in his garden and hung it up in the shed. And he left it hanging there for two weeks, and neither bird nor beast dared to touch it, but the ants went in through its eyes and mouth and devoured its flesh. And another time while we were cutting *manouthion*, one of the brothers picked up a rock to place upon the load, and there was a snake beneath the rock. It stretched out its neck in order to seize the brother but did not succeed, striking and biting instead the root of a large piece of wood lying there, as though that were the brother (for they were deaf and blind because of the great amount of poison in them). And in truth the wood withered as though from a fire. Such, then, are the really dangerous snakes, but no one has ever heard of anyone being bitten by a snake in the holy precinct of our holy Lady, the blessed Mother of God, who protects her servants everywhere."

## Abba George and the Miracle in the Bakery

23. The old man used to ask those who were cellarers at the time not to do the baking without him. For he said that it was an especially great reward to do such work in this holy place, for most of the bread was consumed by visitors. He also took on the ministry of the cisterns that were along the road to Jericho. He would help and work along with the gardeners, too, and willingly perform each ministry. He was eager to show great cooperation concerning the monastery's work on behalf of visitors, not only on account of the reward but also because he was eager and wished to be an example for the brothers.

In the bakery, in addition to his other duties, he would also heat up the oven. You all know what sort of difficulties and afflictions the place caused in the summer. For we often found the candles of the choir stalls in the sanctuary melting and dripping because of the extreme heat. But the old man would persevere in this same heat, lighting the oven two or three times a day—frequently on the day the slave was expected to work. Many of the brothers tried to do the same thing but were unable to do it by themselves without someone relieving them. So the brothers would also say, "This old man is made of iron."

24. One day, then, after the morning meal, each monk lay down to rest wherever he wished. But the old man for a long time would only lie down for a little while, not sleeping but reciting verses from scripture. Suddenly fire came out of the oven—which had been opened by the work of the enemy—and it spread to a bunch of *manouthion* lying nearby (there was a lot of it), and the fire reached to the chimney roof. And he saw the holy blessed Mother of God standing between the ground and the roof, which she touched, acting to put the flames out. When the old man saw this he was astounded. When the brothers got up, he told them what had happened, and they were amazed and gave praise to her. For the burning of the *manouthion* was a true and wonderful witness.

There were many other wonders that the blessed Lady did in this holy place which, if they were written down, would be too many for us to relate even in a large book.[60] Recalling a few things for the joy of those who read about them and for her glory, I shall keep my account to a narration of the way of life of our holy father George.

## Chapter VI
## Miracles of Our Blessed Lady
## the Mother of God at Choziba

25. The monk in charge of buying provisions for the monastery came from Arabia and asked the superior for a sum of money to purchase grain. At the moment the latter did not have what was necessary, so he proposed that he send someone the next day either to Jericho or to the Holy City to obtain it. After vespers, quite late in the evening, a certain woman, poor in appearance, came and said to the doorkeeper, "Please show charity and call the superior for me; I need to meet with him." The doorkeeper went and summoned the superior. He said to

---

60. See the collection of stories about Mary in *The Miracles of the Most Holy Mother of God at Choziba* (p.73 n. 12 above).

him, "Go. If she wants counsel, give it to her; if she needs something to eat, prepare it for her. Because of our visitor, I don't have time to go out now." The doorkeeper communicated this to the woman, and she said, "I need to speak with him so I can resume my journey before dawn." The doorkeeper again went and spoke to the superior, and he angrily replied to him, "I told you, brother, that I am unable to leave our visitor and go right now to speak to the woman."

These words the doorkeeper told to the woman, and she said to him, "Why do you care for the wealthy and disregard the poor? For this reason you justly lack money. But take this gift of alms and give it to him." And she handed to him a money-pouch with sixty pieces of gold in it. The doorkeeper ran and gave it to the superior and also told him what the woman had said. The superior took the pouch and said to him, "Go, see to her needs and apologize, and I will make arrangements for these people and come out to see her." The doorkeeper left, and he went around the whole outside of the doorkeeper's lodge but he did not find her. And he ran around to all the roads, but he did not see her. It was our blessed Lady setting right their work, for this holy place is a shelter for the poor and for visitors,[61] and not a shelter only for the rich.

26. Now some of the brothers used to transport unslaked lime from the furnace to the mixing troughs. One of the brothers reached the gong-shed where the mule drivers waited on a certain rock until the fathers could meet them and take their load. One basket tipped over and the brother wanted to set it right. The mule got spooked, and the basket was overturned because of the work of the enemy, and both were thrown down the precipice, a height of about sixty feet. The basket was thrown off and dragged away by the stream that was still running. The brother, however, went unharmed with the mule through the garden up to the monastery, giving thanks with everyone to God.

27. A certain brother was hauling with the mule drivers outside the side entrance to the monastery, and he knelt down in order to tighten the reins; these reins were made of rope plaited with strips of hide. When this broke, it hurled the brother onto an overhanging ledge as far as the garden, which had a height here of about 120 feet. But this fellow, too, got out safely, a little shaken up from fright, and he went on up to the monastery, going around praising God with the brothers.

28. One evening the doorkeeper, feeling sleepy and blissfully drunk

---

61. Greek *xenous,* see n.28 above. On the importance of hospitality, see Cyril, *Life of Euthymius* 17 (Price, trans., 22–23).

from a large quantity of wine, laid himself down on the pallet inside the door and went to sleep there before he had closed the door. Then, with the door open, some thieves secretly came in who wanted to plunder the place. And when they had reached the second door inside, suddenly they heard what sounded like a large company of foot soldiers and men on horseback coming towards them. The thieves, thinking it was the emperor's soldiers, fearfully turned around with such a great uproar that the doorkeeper was wakened by the commotion and flight of these fellows and closed the doorkeeper's lodge.

When dawn came, the thieves returned like ordinary people, wishing to find out exactly what had happened. So they inquired of the doorkeeper whether the emperor's soldiers had slept there that night, and he said, "No." Then they of their own accord confessed what had happened that night. And everyone knew that it was the grace of our Lady the Mother of God and the saints, and they praised God. But three days later when the thieves sat camped across from the monastery, learning in detail how to get in to plunder it, they saw a fire encircling the monastery the whole night, and they were amazed among themselves how the fire surrounded the monastery by night but by day they saw nothing such as this. And, once again, they revealed this of their own accord for the glory of God and our holy and immaculate Lady, the Mother of God.

29. Now when the Persians seized the Holy City of Christ our God and marched down to Jericho, departing for Damascus with their prisoners, one of the elders saw our Lady exhorting the saints and saying, "Hurry! Let us go! Let us join with the holy cross and escort it, forming a procession with it."[62] And as we have already said, like an unfathomable sea are the many mighty works and wonders of our holy Lady in this holy place concerning spirits and thieves and wild beasts and snakes, and also concerning rocks that have fallen from the cliffs and come down upon the monastery, and how the glorious and grace-giving Mother of God has brought security and great protection from all harm.[63] But we need to return to our account, from which we have digressed, concerning the narrative about the old man.

62. In 615 the Persians conquered Jerusalem, massacred a large number of its citizens, and hauled away the True Cross, to which the Virgin refers. In 629 a peace treaty restored the Cross, but in 638 "Patriarch Sophronius surrendered the city to Sultan Omar," which marked "the end of Byzantine Jerusalem" (Price, trans., lii).

63. For similar modern-day miracles aided by Saints Nicholas and Anastasia, the Roman at the monastery of Gregoriou on Mt. Athos, see Archimandrite Cherubim, *Contemporary Ascetics,* 126–30.

## Chapter VII
## Abba George and the Persians

30. After the attack of the Persians resulted in the capture of territory up to Damascus, there was no little confusion in the land. One day, then, our holy father George was sitting among the rocks, warming himself in the heat of the sun (for he was very thin on account of his great abstinence). Boiling over with the desire of spiritual love to do the work that God wills, with fervent tears he was calling upon God, the lover of humankind, asking him to be merciful to his people. And he heard a voice: "Go down to Jericho, and you will see the works of humankind." So he stood up, and finding some brothers from the cenobium who were going down to Jericho, he went down with them.

Now when they came to the small gardens outside the city, suddenly he heard in the sky a great noise of a crowd of people thrown together against each other, and they were clanging their weapons and crying aloud as though lined up for battle. Raising his eyes to the sky, he saw it filled with Indians, and they were attacking one another as though armed and crashing together as in battle. And the earth shook and trembled beneath him. The brothers said to him, "Come, father, let's go into the city. Why are you standing so long looking at such a sight in the sky?" But with tears and sorrow he said to them, "We must flee, brothers, and go back! Haven't you seen and felt the earth shaking?" And as soon as he had said these things, suddenly from the city some armed horsemen came out, and some other young men as foot soldiers, wearing daggers and carrying spears in their hands and running here and there. And the brothers realized that this was the shaking of the earth that the old man was talking about, so they returned to the monastery with great fear because he told them also about the vision in the sky.

Now the old man returned to his own cell, and he bewailed and mourned the people's confusion and even more their ignorance and impiety. He then went outside and sat on the rock for the sun's warmth (for this was his practice on account of the weakness of his body), and he called upon God and implored him, saying, "Lord God of mercies and Lord of pity, you who wish everyone to be saved and to come to the knowledge of truth, take up your staff and smite this people, for they walk in ignorance." And suddenly he saw a fiery staff stretching in the sky from the Holy City to Bostra. And the holy man knew that the people would be severely disciplined. And he bewailed and mourned everything.

31. When the Persians attacked and surrounded the Holy City, at that time both the brothers from the cenobium and those living in cells left. Some fled to Arabia with the superior of the monastery, while some went to live in caves, and others hid themselves in Calamon. With them also was the holy man George, for after numerous entreaties from the brothers, he left and hid himself with them. Now the Saracens tested the river and searched the mountains for those who were living there. They found the old man and many other fathers, and they took them to another river. Among the fathers was the old man Abba Stephen the Syrian, who was about a hundred years old or more, the holy father and witness to the faith, whom they killed there.[64] The rest they led away as prisoners.

But when they saw Saint George, his voluntary poverty, ascetic emaciation, and goodness, and perceived his way of life—or rather, they were moved by God—they gave him a food basket filled with loaves of bread and a little jug of water and let him go with these words: "Save yourself by whatever means you wish." Now he went down at night to the Jordan, and there he moved about until the Persians passed by through Jericho to Damascus, taking with them the prisoners from the Holy City. And he went up from there to the Holy City until he once again returned to Choziba.

## Chapter VIII
### Antony, the Narrator, Speaks of His Life with George [65]

33. But the time has come for me now to speak also about those things concerning myself and how I attached myself to the old man. For my life had been filled with numerous, even innumerable, sins, leaving me wounded by my licentious and filthy behavior. But God, who is most compassionate and loving, who wants all persons to be saved and to come to the knowledge of truth, and who does not desire death for the sinner but wants him to reform and live, this God was good enough to extend his grace even to me, a worthless sinner, and through his ineffable goodness, offer compassion and mercy.

---

64. In the north wall of the chapel at Choziba "is a reliquary with the skulls of fourteen martyred monks from the period of the Persian conquest in 614." See A. Ovadiah and C. G. de Silva, "Supplement to the Corpus of the Byzantine Churches in the Holy Land," *Levant* 13 (1981): 213.

65. In the *Life of Euthymius* 49 (Price, trans., 68), Cyril has a similar autobiographical section.

And so forsaking my father's house, I left in secret—none of my household found me out—taking with me also one of my accomplices. We wanted to go to Raïthos,[66] but because the Saracens were robbing and terrorizing the highways, we were unable to do so. Having put ourselves in the care of some holy fathers, we came to Choziba and were received by the superior at that time and were tonsured shortly thereafter. I do not know what my companion decided to do, but he went up to the Holy City with the superior and without letting him know, he secretly entered Raïthos. Now I mourned for and lamented the loss of my companion, and I resolved to find him. Since Abba Dorotheus held great love for me, he dissuaded me from doing this.

33. Now when these admonitions and entreaties did not succeed, when the old man came to the cenobium on the Lord's day, Dorotheus related my story to him. The holy man took me aside and began to admonish me, saying, "Child, do not think that it is the place that makes you a monk; it's the way you live.[67] Neither is it father or mother or family or friends. Intention is what counts. No one will help us on that great and fearful day. All that matters is what each of us has done. See what holy scripture says: 'It is the person and his work.'[68] And again: 'You will repay each according to his works.'[69] If then, child, you have renounced the world and its works, why do you again run after its forms, seeking worldly companionship and friendship and society? For the Lord says in the Gospels: 'If someone does not deny father and mother and family and friends and even his very self, and take up his own cross and follow me, he cannot be my disciple.'[70] The cross, child, represents every temptation and affliction and persecution and suffering, even unto death for Christ's sake, and steadfast endurance.

"Therefore, child, cleave to the one to whom you fled, and do not ever in this life separate yourself from him until the day you die. For the godly apostle says: 'In whatever condition each was called, brothers, let him remain there with God.'[71] For if God wanted you to be in Raïthos, just as he brought you out of the world and such a way of life into his goodness, so can he all the more lead you there with the great-

66. Raïthos (or Raïthou), present-day Tor, was on the Gulf of Suez, not far from Sinai.
67. There is a play on words in the old man's advice: "place" is *topos*, whereas "way" is *tropos*.
68. See James 2:24.
69. See Rom 2:6.
70. A conflation of Lk 14:26 and 9:23.
71. 1 Cor 7:24.

est ease. Know this, child: that if the enemy, through whatever sort of pretext, tries to get someone to renounce the monastic life by moving him from where he is and putting him in danger, the monk needs to maintain his position all the more firmly. For he who disregards his own father and mother—I mean the place where he was spiritually begotten—how will some other place save him unless at last, advanced in years, he acquire virtue at that time and know how to harmonize his coming and going according to God? Therefore, child, pay heed to my humility and remain here meanwhile, and from now on you will also have me to look after you."

When I heard these things, and more than what I've recorded, I knelt before him and said, "See, reverend father, that I am entrusting myself to God and to our Lady and to you. As you wish, be merciful with me, my sinful and passion-filled ways, and save my poor soul."[72]

34. From that day on, then, I did hardly anything without him. I also took on the ministry of lighting the oil lamps, and when the old man came on the Lord's day and was spending time in the church, I was not separated from him night or day.[73] When, therefore, I endured numerous battles and illnesses and temptations and afflictions, the old man eased my pains and healed me, body and soul. Now when the Persians had surrounded Diospolis,[74] I offered my thoughts to him, saying, "Look, our superior is fleeing to Arabia, and he is asking me to go away with him, along with other brothers who wish to go."

He said to me, "Child, it is right for us to remain here where we have renounced everything, whether for life or for death, and it is better to die in this land. For the Lord, even if he chastises us for our sins as a merciful and affectionate father, will not forsake his Holy City. His eyes watch over everything that happens to her, and to this land as a land of promise, until the consummation of the age, according to his promises." After listening to him, I remained there, and with the brothers we left the monastery for the caves. Often I was in danger of falling into the hands of the Saracens and Jews, but I was never taken, protected as I was by the prayers of the old man, obedient to his word.

72. Or "life"; Greek *psyche*.

73. Antony, a novice at this point, would live in the cenobium, while George lived in a cell outside the monastery.

74. Diospolis (Lydda) lies between Jericho and Joppa, which is on the coast.

## Antony and George Return to Choziba

35. After the Persians' attack, while we were staying at a guest-house in Jericho, they made me the cellarer. Because of this distraction and because I had to do business with worldly folk and with women, I found myself at war. So I said to the superior, "If you wish for me to return and stay at the monastery, I will gladly remain there. Nevertheless, I can no longer remain here." He, however, was not persuaded, because he was toughening the brothers there, so I secretly left and returned to the Holy City to the old man, and I laid out my conflict to him. He prayed on my behalf and healed me by word and deed, and he kept me there by his side.

Now when I perceived that I was recovering so quickly, I said to him, "If you wish, I will go back down." He said to me, "Stay, child, and tomorrow they will come after you." And it happened just as he had said: The following day two priests and a deacon came, and they urged the old man to persuade me to go down with them, since the fathers, persuaded by the superior, had already returned. Overjoyed, I went down with them. When they had settled me in my ministry, I sent word urging the old man to come down to join us.

36. And when after a few days he came down, he had me prepare his patchwork mat on the pavement in the cenobium facing the little window to the east and to position his pillow so he would lie facing east. And he said to me, "Child, do not get upset, and do not speak with me, and do not allow anyone else to come near me." And stretching himself out on his back, he covered himself with a burial shroud and remained there three days, neither moving nor turning, and without getting up at all. And the brothers said to me, "Let us bring the old man out and bury him before he begins to stink and we face the risks of a delayed burial." But I touched his feet and found that they were warm, and I urged the brothers to go away, while at the same time I kept the promise I had made to him. Sitting down beside him, I mourned for him and wept bitterly.

Suddenly, while I was sitting there beside him, on the third day he shook himself and stripped off his covers, and sat up. Breathing in deeply and sighing, he said, "Praise be to you, our God, praise be to you." I knelt before him and said, "Why, holy father, have you afflicted me like this?" He said, "Didn't I tell you beforehand, child, not to get upset and not to speak with me?" Again I knelt before him and begged him to tell me what he saw, and he said to me, "Child, just now you cannot bear to hear it, either with your ears or with your mind. I will tell you when the appropriate time has come." He said this, his eyes asking me not to force him to tell me. And indeed the appearance he gave was truly frightening, as was the way his face looked when he was marveling at what he was seeing. Now I was foolish in my simplicity, and so I did not force him. And now I regret it.

37. One time when he was eating with me while I performed my ministry, I knelt before him and said, "Bless the ministry of your servant, reverend father, because we are in tight circumstances," and he said, "God will bless and increase your ministry, child." And he did: There was a big jar for olive oil standing there filled with oil, and its contents were not exhausted for three weeks, and the whole cenobium was inspired by this. One of the cooks, being tempted, said to me, "Do me a favor, father cellarer, and tell me: Did you put oil in the jar?" I said to him, "Yes." And he said, "When?" I said to him, "Two days ago." And he said, "For three weeks I've been drawing oil, and I haven't seen the level go up or down." I said, "God will forgive you, brother, because you have been tempted." And from then on it was used up. It was also this way with an abundance of bread and wine, when we unexpectedly had guests who stayed longer than usual, and I knew that the blessing had come from the prayers of the holy man.[75]

## Chapter IX
## Abba George Speaks to the Brothers about Arrogance and Humility and Judging Others

38. A certain fellow came to the monastery from the world in order to renounce it. Early one Lord's day, then, after the Eucharist,[76] we went down to the cenobium to see the old man (for after the arrival of the Persians, he no longer remained in the cells but lived with us). The old man said to me, "What do you say, child, concerning the brother who has come from the world?" I said to him, "He's a good man, reverend

---

75. "Two vats of oil stand in front of the church of the present-day monastery of Choziba . . . to commemorate George's miracle." See Hirschfeld, *Desert Monasteries*, 100, and the picture on the same page. For a similar occurrence regarding bread, see the *Life of Theognius*, p. 161 below.

76. Greek *kanōn* can refer either to the Eucharist or the monastic office.

father; his work equals that of the fathers, and he does whatever I assign him. But some say, 'It's like this,' while others say, 'No, it's like *that.*'" He said to me, "Child, do you want to have a donkey that neither eats nor drinks nor brays nor kicks? Clearly, you do not want to have such an animal." I understood the force of what he was saying and said, "Yes, blessed father, I have everything." And he added, "Go, child, harvest the brother; he's a good man."

39. And turning to the brothers, he began to speak to them by way of admonition: "My children, we have the fear of God and his perfect love in our hearts. Let us not despise anyone, especially since the apostle says, 'Why do you judge your brother, and why do you despise your brother? He stands or falls before his own Lord. He will be upheld, for God is able to make him stand.'[77] And the Lord says, 'Why do you see the speck in your brother's eye, but do not notice the log in your own eye?'[78] It is a great sin, brothers, for someone to condone his own wound while he rebukes his neighbor for the same wound; or for someone to weigh carefully the deeds of another while he overlooks his own, as though he himself were free from sin. This is not possible. 'Heaven itself,' it is said, 'is not pure in your presence.'[79]

"If a loathsome and rotten person has a certain passion, why is that important? And if one of you boasts that he has a new heart, although he has lived the monastic life so many years, this fellow most certainly deceives himself with his impious behavior. But no, this fellow accuses the one who has left the world! Look, we have spent all these years cutting ourselves to pieces in the monastic life in the desert, and we haven't even grasped the first rung on the cord: that is, to hold ourselves as sinners and to worry about our own evils, and not to get puffed up with self-righteousness and rebuke our neighbor.

"Tell me, brothers, why have we completely left the world, with its wealth and glory and luxury, and come to this desert where these things don't exist? Is it on account of our sins and passions, in order to repent of them? Or is it because we are sinless and have fled those who are sinners and subject to the passions? And if, filled with passion, we have come to repent, we are not the rulers and arbiters of ourselves so that, whenever we have the desire, we make ourselves free and glorify

---

77. See Rom 14:4.
78. Mt 7:3.
79. Job 15:15.

ourselves, already cleansed of passion. No! This happens when the righteous Judge wishes it.

"If, however, we act like righteous persons, freed from the passions, who are fleeing sinners—while we still trample upon our neighbor and boast about ourselves—we have a mighty accuser, the tax collector, who was derided by the self-important Pharisee, but who had already been preferred by God, who knows what's in the heart.[80] These two, then, humility and arrogance, stand in opposition to each other. Arrogance continually boasts, 'I shall ascend above the clouds of heaven, I shall place my throne upon the stars; I shall be equal to the Most High.'[81] The reward for such insolence is this: Now you will be thrown into hell. But humility, like a father, comforts us, saying, 'Come to me, all you who are weary and are carrying heavy burdens, and I will give you rest. Take my yoke upon you and learn from me; for I am gentle and humble in heart, and you will find rest for your souls.'[82] Believe me, children, that if a person makes a new heaven and new earth,[83] while he loudly boasts and denigrates his neighbor, his labor is for nothing and his lot will be with the hypocrites. But if we confess our sins, as John the Theologian says, God can be trusted to forgive us our transgressions.[84]

"But why, brothers, does he not free us equally from both small and great passions? What, then, do I say? There is one, and only one, passion, one sin that seems to be worthless, that is able to destroy us: He who insults his brother will be liable to the council, and he who says 'You fool' will be liable to the hell of fire for the least little thing.[85] Do you see, beloved? The one sin that does not seem to be a sin leads directly to the fire of hell. Drunkards and revilers will not inherit the kingdom of God.[86] What destroyed the sons of Eli? Wasn't it when they ate beforehand the sacrificial meats?[87] And what destroyed Ahab? Didn't the theft of some small thing cause his whole household, along with his cattle and possessions, to be stoned to death?[88] Therefore brothers, we

---

80. See Lk 18:14.
81. See Is 14:13–14.
82. Mt 11:28–29.
83. See 2 Pet 3:13.
84. See 1 Jn 1:9.
85. See Mt 5:22.
86. See 1 Cor 6:10.
87. 1 Sam 2.
88. See 1 Kings 21–22:40, although it is Naboth, not Ahab, who is stoned to death.

who are in sin, even if it seems to be a small one, let us not reproach the greater sin of our neighbor. For this would gain us nothing.

"Tell me: If someone were cut to pieces in front of us while we were pricked with a needle, which would we feel—the suffering of the person cut to pieces before us, or the pain of the needle wounding our body? And if a city surrounded by soldiers has a single enemy within its walls, which has harmed it more? Isn't it the enemy within, rather than those waging war outside? So, too, it is with us, my little children: We are not harmed so much by our neighbor—even if he is a fornicator or an adulterer or a murderer or a magician (which is the worst of all evils)—as we are by some tiny passion that we have within us. We are full of passion! Who among us will be able to boast that he is without passion or sin? And the passion of arrogance is the most vain and wretched, for the more it wanders about in the mind, the more it makes its captive what we call 'lightheaded.'

"Therefore keep up the struggle, my brothers, to help one another for the sake of humility. For each person who is righteous (without being perfect) and receives those who are sick is conspicuous because he lives his life by advancing in true knowledge. But whoever thinks he is great and perfect in righteousness, as though he were one of the saints, on top of all this, if he boasts and in trampling upon his neighbor denigrates him, this person's intentions and righteous deeds and boasting are a foolish vanity. Brothers, take hold of the beginning of virtue, which is the fear of God (as it is said: 'The beginning of wisdom is fear of the Lord')[89], grounded in humility and made secure in the bond of the love of God most perfect, who became perfect man in Christ Jesus our Lord, to whom be glory forever."

## Abba George Watches Over Antony

40. Now although I was wounded with compunction, I foolishly decided to rest myself on the ground. When the old man noticed this, he let me do this for a little while. But after a few days passed, my face changed color and my skin got cold and I completely wasted away, and the brothers said to me, "Are you sick? You've wasted away." I said, "I don't have any symptoms," but the old man took pity on me so I wouldn't be crippled and become incapacitated. He said to me, "Let's go to the

89. Prov 9:10.

cell where you minister and sleep. I wish to speak with you alone." I said to him, "Why don't you want to speak to me here?" (I did not want him—of course he knew—to see my worthless work.) He said to me, "I want to speak to you there," and he went ahead of me. Going into the cell, he said to me, "Child, where may I sit?" Now when I swept the cell, I let down the bedding that was hanging up and prepared it for him. He sat down and said to me, "If you want to do this, take a scythe; go outside and cut some grass; then make it into bundles and place these under your body and rest on them." When I did this, it was like I was resting on a mattress, and I no longer wasted away.

41. A certain brother came to the monastery from Raïthos who seemed to have knowledge and to be easy to talk to. This fellow tried to attach himself to me, but the old man would not allow it. Believe me, reverend fathers, wherever we happened to chance on one another,[90] whether it was during my ministry or in church, it was immediately found out, and the old man would come and, using some pretext that he'd make up at the time, drag me away so that finally I became distressed concerning this fellow. But this experience showed after his death what kind of guardian the old man was: Although he never in any way accused the brother of some evil, this brother badly afflicted me concerning a number of things and concerning unorthodox teachings, for he was a Galatian by birth.[91]

42. One day after breakfast I said to the old man, "I'm going to the river to gather caper seeds,"[92] and he said to me, "I'll come with you." He was showing his concern for me, for after the Persians came, the river had been completely despoiled with wild beasts and unclean spirits. As we were walking on the path between the cells, he said to me, "Go down to those caper plants there, child, and gather some, and I'll

---

90. There is a play on words here: "to chance on one another" is *estēmen eis suntuchia*, while "easy to talk to" is *eusuntuchos*.

91. Is there a suggestion of Origenism here, mediated by Evagrius Ponticus? Palladius was from Galatia, was taught by Evagrius, and was accused by Jerome of teaching "the heresy of Origen." See Jerome, Letter 51.9. In 543 Justinian issued his edict against Origenism, and in 553 the Origenists were expelled from the New Laura in Palestine. See Sozomen, *Ecclesiastical History* 8.11–22, and Socrates, *Ecclesiastical History* 6.7–13.

92. Greek *kapparis*. *Capparis spinosa* is a Mediterranean shrub whose buds or berries are picked to make a pickled relish. Written sources mention three plants gathered by monks for food: manouthion, a wild herb; the saltbush; and the caper, which "grows throughout Palestine and is known to favor stony ground, cliffs, and walls. The edible parts are the buds of the flowers and the young fruits. In the cliffs along the banks of riverbeds in the Judean desert, caper bushes are found in abundance" (Hirschfeld, *Desert Monasteries,* 89–90).

wait for you here." So I went down and gathered some. After an hour had passed, he called to me, saying, "Come on, child; I'm tired." When I came up, he said to me, "Show me what you've gathered," so I showed him the small basket which was about a third full. Groaning aloud he said, "Oh, child, the world is an evil place! I remember one time before the Persians came, we were going from our cells to the cenobium for the evening prayers on the Lord's day when one of the brothers went down to this same caper patch and gathered a full basket, and again in the afternoon the next day when we were returning to our cells, he gathered the same amount." I said to him, "Why is it like this, father?" He said to me, "At that time holy men were walking about and treading the earth, and the earth was blessed, and everything on it. But now evil-doers and murderers dwell on the earth, and thievery and bitterness and adultery and murder are poured out upon it; blood is mixed with blood and the earth is defiled and accursed. How can such things on the earth be blessed?" These were the things he said and taught. They went into my heart so I would write them down just as he said them.

## [Chapter X] [93]

## Chapter XI
## The Death of Abba George

57. After these things, our holy father George became weak with an illness and died from it the same day. On the evening in which he was perfected, in order that it be demonstrated with what great confidence in the Lord he was sojourning, according to God's dispensation there gathered a multitude of guests, and so I was very much occupied with my ministry. [94] Some of the brothers, then, who often sat with the old man, came and said to me, "The old man is asking for you and says, 'Where is Antony? Call him for me, because I am going to die soon.'" I was torn between the two: I wanted to finish my ministry, and again,

---

93. Chapter X (especially paragraphs 44–56) is an interpolation, a speech by Saint George on the theme of arrogance and humility; for a translation of this section, see Vivian and Athanassakis, trans., *The Life of Saint George of Choziba and the Miracles of the Most Holy Mother of God at Choziba*, 73–89.

94. That is, his serving the guests, as is made clear below. See n. 20 above.

I wanted to go to the old man. Now the old man knew this through the Spirit, and he made it clear to me: "Don't be sad, child, and don't be upset; finish your ministry, and I'll wait for you until you can come." Now when the guests got up from eating, and others came, the time had stretched almost to the middle of the night; still, the old man waited. And so, when I completed my ministry and dismissed all the guests I went up to him.

When he set eyes on me, he embraced and kissed and blessed me and turned to the east and said, "Depart now, my soul, in the Lord depart." After saying this sentence three times, he offered up his spirit to the Lord who was within him and along with whom he had fought the fight for this good and holy way of life.[95] And so he exchanged his life as someone might change his pace as he walks, with complete peace and tranquility. It was clear beforehand how he would give his spirit into the hands of the Lord, as it is written: "The souls of the righteous are in the hand of God, and torment shall not touch them."[96] And again: "Precious in the sight of the Lord is the death of his holy ones."[97] When I knew that he had offered up his spirit, I fell upon his breast and bewailed and mourned the loss of the holy father. We attended his body with psalms and hymns and spiritual songs[98] and buried him among the graves of the holy fathers, and now he is with the choirs of saints who intercede together for us and all the world.[99]

## Epilogue

58. But I beg your indulgence, blessed servants of Christ. Forgive my deficiencies and feebleness of expression, my ignorant and unskilled attempt at setting down a few of the things from the many that I both saw and heard concerning the old man's way of life. For he was chaste, tranquil,[100] poor, temperate,[101] humble, full of love for everyone and, most of all, very compassionate.

95. See 1 Tim 6:12.
96. The allusion is uncertain.
97. Ps 115:6 (LXX).
98. See Col 3:16.
99. George's death is celebrated on January 8 with this distich: "For George who sowed with tears/It is time now to harvest with joy." George is buried in a niche in the south wall of the chapel at Choziba and above the niche is his skull. See Ovadiah and de Silva, "Supplement," 213–14.
100. Or "solitary, eremitical": Greek *hēsuchios*.
101. Or "continent": Greek *enkratēs*.

59. This, beloved and dear servants of God, is the life and the struggles of our holy father George of Cyprus, and this is his way of life and the completion of life and dormition of this God-pleasing man who was a friend to God. What shall I do, sinner and wretch that I am, who in this brief compass seem to be unworthy of his constancy and patience? Truly, the saying of the Lord has been fulfilled in me when he said, "The wedding guests cannot fast while the bridegroom is with them, can they? The days will come when the bridegroom is taken away from them, and then they will fast."[102] Believe me, honored fathers and brothers, that in his life most of the things he spoke about were not things of this earth. But if temptation or affliction beset me, I had only to meet with him, and everything was quickly removed, as though by a sponge, and then I could go on, in great calm and peace.

But now, after his perfecting, temptations and intolerable afflictions and persecutions and unbearable anguish one after another—I thought I would die—rose up against me. But often, with the prayers of the holy old man, I stood firm and responsible like those who partake of the sacraments endure with thanksgiving what comes upon them. This above all we celebrated continually: that on account of our sins which we committed, we were not punished as we deserved. For if God wanted to prosecute us as retribution for the deeds we have done, we would not be worthy to live. Therefore we have recovered the holy way of life of the holy father, delineating fully for ourselves both the endurances he undertook while fasting and the vigils he would make all night while standing, the unending streams of tears,[103] the patient endurance of temptations. In short, as we recall to memory the steadfastness and patience of his angelic and completely virtuous life, we are filled with hope.

60. But I beg your indulgence and entreat you, honored fathers and brothers, forgive me a little for so boldly and shamelessly begging you to make entreaty for me, a sinner and the least of your servants, through the law of love and the mercy of God. For my wretched soul has been worn down, weakened, and wounded by the worthless passions that the Lord rejects. And so, pitifully and in numerous ways, I have been justly brought forward to trial, held prisoner by deadly enemies. I prostrate myself before your concordant belief, blessed servants

---

102. Mk 2:19–20.
103. See the *Life of Theognius*, pp. 159-60 below.

of Christ, so that you, like the best physicians, might teach me some of the signs of humility—in which are life and light and joy and peace—and how not to denigrate my neighbor. For in these two virtues, I believe, are the full profession of our monastic habit and the kingdom of God. Our love for God is fulfilled in humility and in not despising our neighbor and in our love for him. Especially, beloved, zealously send forth the crown of all good things—your God-pleasing, petitionary prayers—to God on behalf of me, your passion-filled and worthless servant, that through you favored servants of Christ I, too, unworthy though I am, might be free from my passions and with you be made worthy of the heavenly kingdom of our God. To him be the glory for ever. Amen.

# 5

# THE MONK AS HOLY MAN: ABBA AARON

## Introduction

AT THE END OF THE FOURTH CENTURY, THE *History of the Monks of Egypt* recorded that the monks of upper Egypt "raise the dead and walk on the water just like Peter. And all that the Saviour did through the saints, he does in our times through these monks."[1] Jesus performed miracles, and the Acts of the Apostles records how his disciples continued to heal in his name. The monks of Egypt believed they were following their Master and the apostles and saints before them when they performed miracles, healed the sick, and raised the dead.

An especially wise and saintly monk, usually (but not always) in old age, came to be regarded as a holy man. As a person known for his sanctity and healing powers, he attracted disciples who wished to sit at his feet and learn from him. In a sense, such a Christian holy man merely replaced the non-Christian priest in his area, and in later cen-

---

1. *Historia Monachorum*, Epilogue, trans. Norman Russell, *The Lives of the Desert Fathers* (Kalamazoo, Mich.: Cistercian Publications, 1981), 118.

2. The seminal discussion of the holy man in late antiquity is Peter Brown's "The Rise and Function of the Holy Man in Late Antiquity," *Journal of Roman Studies* 61 (1971) 80–101. See also Brown, "The Saint as Exemplar in Late Antiquity," in John Stratton Hawley, ed., *Saints and Virtues* (Berkeley: University of California Press, 1987). And see Robert Markus, *The End of Ancient Christianity* (Cambridge: Cambridge University Press, 1990), 23 and n. 8, and 25–26. Markus wishes "to shift the emphasis" on the holy man, a shift with which I concur: "To understand the special place and the function of holy men in the Christian community, we have to see them as representative persons acting for the community rather than as individuals with privileged access to a reality they had to mediate to their fellows, a reality not accessible to the ordinary run of Christians."

turies, came to have more and more social and political power.² Holy men—and women—were a vital part of the life of the village. One twentieth-century holy woman may give us a clearer picture of her ancient predecessors:

> In one of the provinces in Upper Egypt, close to the desert hills, lived the *sheikeh* [holy woman] Sulūh. This woman had, during her lifetime, a great reputation for holiness, and people flocked to her, in times of difficulty, from all quarters. Her skin was very dark from constant exposure to the sun, and her head, on which she wore no veil, was covered with a crop of hair, thick and long like the wool of a sheep; from beneath her brows peered dark, sharp-looking eyes. Her clothes were scanty, consisting merely of a piece of linen rag and a sort of coat. She remained out in the desert solitude all day, and at night, so I was told, slept alone "in the mountain."³

One of Sulūh's ancient counterparts, Apollo, a monk near Hermopolis in the Thebaid, destroyed a local idol that used to "ensure the flooding of the Nile."⁴ The farmers would still need the Nile to flood to irrigate their land, and in times of distress, would still need divine help and assurance. Whether they were Christians or not, if there was a powerful man of God in the area, they went to him. Such a person was Abba Aaron, whose life and deeds occupy the final third of Paphnutius' *Histories of the Monks of Upper Egypt*.⁵

One day some men come to Abba Aaron, "terrified because the proper time for the rising of the waters had passed. And they continued to weep [and beg the holy man. He had] compassion [on them and prayed to God,] saying, 'God, do not forsake the work of your hands, man and beast. For indeed you created us all from your blood and you deigned to come into the world'" (paragraph 132). Aaron preaches a short sermon on mercy and dismisses the men in peace, saying, "God will make the river fill with water, and he will bring it to its proper level. Do not be afraid, and do not be unbelieving." The holy man then goes down to the river and prays to God:

3. Winifred S. Blackman, *The Fellāhīn of Upper Egypt: Their Religious, Social, and Industrial Life To-day, with Special Reference to Survivals from Ancient Times* (London: G. G. Harrap, 1927), 246–47.

4. *Historia Monachorum* 8.24–29 (Russell, trans., 73–74).

5. See Tim Vivian, *Histories of the Monks of Upper Egypt and the Life of Onnophrius* (Kalamazoo, Mich.: Cistercian Publications, 1993), 114–41.

Lord, you are the same yesterday, and today, and forever. It was you who burst open the rock and water flowed forth and you gave it to the people to drink. And when Samson was thirsty you caused the jawbone of an ass to bring forth water which quenched his thirst. Therefore, I entreat you today to send the river's water over the entire land so the poor among your people have enough food and bless you and your holy name.

The river rises, and "there was abundance and plenty that year through the prayers of the holy man, as it is written, 'The prayer of a righteous man is powerful and effective'" (paragraphs 132–35).

Is what Aaron does a miracle, or is it "the prayer of a righteous man," "powerful and effective"?[6] The question is undoubtedly a modern one. Phrased in this "either/or" manner, it falsely separates the miracle from the life of the holy man. It divides the singular act from the ongoing activity of prayer and contemplation, which was the monk's life.

The holy man understood that contemplation and action went together. "Action" could be something as simple as mat weaving, disposing one to contemplation. Abba Aaron plaited rope and sewed burial shrouds; Gandhi in our time sat at the spinning wheel. Action could also be pastoral; then it took on greater social importance as the holy man became community healer and reconciler. Macedonius, according to the *Histories of the Monks of Upper Egypt*, the first bishop of Philae, is appealed to by Nubian camel herders to settle their dispute.[7] Abba Aaron causes the waters of the Nile to rise. Actions such as these should be seen in their proper context: Macedonius at first declines to hear the "case" of the Nubians, but when he reads in the lectionary, "Blessed are the peacemakers, for they shall be called children of God," he goes down to them. Before Aaron performs his miracle, he speaks about justice and mercy to those who have come seeking his help.

As far back as Saint Antony—in other words, at the beginning of monasticism—monastic spirituality understood contemplation and action as a seamless garment that the monk wove with his or her life. Early in the *Life of Antony*, when the holy man emerges from his

---

6. For a discussion of the role of miracles in the lives of the monks, see Benedicta Ward's introduction in *Historia Monachorum* (Russell, trans., 39–45).

7. See Vivian, *Paphnutius*, 92–94.

dwelling, "many of those there were sick. The Lord healed them through him because the Lord gave grace to Antony in his words. And he comforted the many who mourned, while he reconciled others at enmity and made them brothers. He would tell everyone to honor nothing among the things of the world more than love for Christ Jesus."[8] The monastic life aimed not at building up of the self but, through the love of Christ, at healing the world.

The life of Abba Aaron, as told by Isaac to Paphnutius, is a paradigm of this understanding. Isaac heard a "report" about Aaron: he was "living the monastic life in a place called 'the valley,' and was performing many cures for all those who were sick" (paragraph 90). In this sentence, as in Aaron's life, the monastic life and healing are joined together. In his account of Aaron's life, Isaac gives much more space to the holy man's miracles of healing and reconciliation than to his feats of asceticism and self-denial (though the latter are certainly present). It is not an exaggeration to say that Aaron's miracles and acts of healing *are* his *politeia*, his way of life: they arise naturally and simply from his life of prayer, from the way he is present to God, God's grace, and God's world.

Death and resurrection lie at the heart of Abba Aaron's ministry, and thus the old man's *politeia* is a true *imitatio Christi*. Isaac, playing Elisha to Aaron's Elijah, relates the first miracle he saw: One day while a Nubian and his son were fishing, a crocodile seized the boy and dragged him into the river. The father, in distress, cut himself badly while running wildly up a mountain. Aaron healed the father and restored the boy, dragged underwater by the crocodile, through prayer (paragraphs 98–100).

In the next miracle related by Isaac, a fisherman's son gets tangled in a fishing net and supposedly drowns. But because of Abba Aaron's prayers the child while underwater sees a vision of light and is miraculously freed from the net: "It happened that when I got tangled up in the net and was about to lose my last breath, I looked and saw a man of light. He took me by the hand and freed me from the net and brought me up into the boat. And suddenly I no longer saw him" (paragraph 102).

The images of water, of death and rebirth, of baptism, are central to these stories. In several other stories, Abba Aaron raises the dead by

8. Coptic *Life of Antony* 14; see above, p. 23.

sprinkling water that he has blessed. For example, a vineyard worker falls from a tree and seems to be dead, but is restored when sprinkled with holy water (paragraphs 103–4), and a rich man has his sight restored when he washes his face with water blessed by Abba Aaron (paragraph 115). In a variation on this theme, a stillborn child is made alive when sprinkled with earth taken from the doorstep of Abba Aaron's house (paragraph 108): The dust of burial is the sure sign of resurrection. Another story makes it clear that such baptisms (whether through immersion or the sprinkling of water or earth) give new life: A childless woman hears about a stillborn baby brought to life and tells her husband to petition Abba Aaron for a male child. Aaron prays for the couple, and she bears a son (paragraphs 124–26).

All these miracles depend on the faith of the people who petition Abba Aaron. Their stories are like those in the Gospels where people call on Jesus: It is their great faith that allows them to be healed. But the faith—and power—of the holy man can bring a person to believe even when faith is lacking. One story, with more than a touch of humor to it, demonstrates this:

> Now it happened that one day two Nubians were walking together on their way to Aswan. One of them had only one eye. His friend said to him, "Come on, let's receive a blessing at the hands of this great man." The one-eyed man said, "He isn't a great man. If he really is, let him open my eye." And while the words were still in his mouth, his eye—which had been blind—regained its sight, but his good eye became blind! When his friend saw what had happened, he was utterly amazed, and said to him, "Didn't I tell you that he is a *very* great man?" The one-eyed man said, "It's no great loss, for one eye has been shut while the other has been opened. However, let's go to him. Perhaps he'll give light to the other eye." So the two of them came to the holy man Abba Aaron. My father said to the Nubian who was not a believer, "Since you think that it's no great loss, why are you here?" Immediately he became very [fearful] and worshiped him, saying, "[Open my] eye!" and immediately he was able to see with the other eye. And the two believed, and went away joyful, and they proclaimed throughout that whole country the miracle that had taken place (paragraph 123).

This story reveals how Abba Aaron's power could work even at a distance. The miracle stories of this holy man, because of the sequence in which they are presented, show a progression in Aaron's power: The holy man first blesses water that heals; earth is then taken from in front of his house and sprinkled efficaciously on a stillborn child; a rich man is blinded because of Aaron's prayer, and his sight is then restored by water blessed by the holy one; a gouty man believes he will be healed if the hand of someone healed by Aaron touches him and, because of his faith, he is healed.

The powers of the holy man are very much like those of Jesus. Jesus healed by touching others. The woman with the hemorrhage was healed by touching Jesus' robe. The centurion's son was healed at a distance from Jesus because of his father's faith. Aaron himself affirms this similarity by quoting Jesus' words (Jn 14:12): "Do not allow anyone to disbelieve our words. For indeed our Saviour said, '[Truly, truly, I say to you, whoever believes in me, the works which I do] he shall do also, for he shall do things greater than these.'"

The story about Abba Aaron is not unique among the stories told about the early desert fathers. The monks took seriously the words of Jesus that through belief in Christ, one could heal the sick and raise the dead. What is striking, though, are the elements the stories of Abba Aaron have in common with monastic stories from other parts of the Near East. Aphrahat (Aphraates), a Syrian monk, was entreated by a "pious man" to protect his land from a plague of locusts. He

> ordered a gallon of water to be brought to him. When the petitioner had brought the gallon, he placed his hand over it and besought God to fill the water with divine power; then on finishing the prayer he told the man to sprinkle the water round the boundaries of his property. The man took it and did as instructed and it served as an invincible and inviolable defense for those fields. . . .[9]

The *Life of Pachomius* records that the holy man Theodore was so venerated that people "would run forward, observe and take the soil on which the soles of his feet had stood and rub it on the sick."[10]

John of Lycopolis "did not perform cures publicly. More often he gave oil to the afflicted and healed them in that way." A woman with cataracts begged to be taken to John, but he did not see women. She begged only that he should be told about her and offer a prayer for her. This he did, and moreover sent her some oil. She bathed her eyes in

9. Theodoret of Cyrrhus, *A History of the Monks of Syria* 8.14, trans. R. M. Price (Kalamazoo, Mich.: Cistercian Publications, 1985), 78–79.

10. *Vita Pachomii* 150, Armand Veilleux, trans., *Pachomian Koinonia*, vol. 1, *The Life of Saint Pachomius and His Disciples* (Kalamazoo, Mich.: Cistercian Publications, 1980), 214.

the oil only three times and on the third day regained her sight and publicly thanked God.[11] A woman suffering a long time with a flow of blood said to Abba Dionysius: "I know that the man of God Abba Pachomius is your friend; therefore I want you to lead me to him so I may see him; for I am confident that if only I see him the Lord will grant me healing." She went to see Pachomius, touched him and his clothing, and was healed.[12]

Holy men like Pachomius and Abba Aaron were intercessors. Because of their way of life, others believed that these holy men had immediate access to God; they were mediators with God. At times, holy men even seem to become substitutes for Christ—at least in the eyes of those who come to them for help. The writer of a letter to a certain Abba Paphnutius (not the author of the "Life of Abba Aaron") said to him, "After God you are my salvation." Popular belief often elevated holy men like Aaron to such a position. A man with a barren wife says to Aaron, "[I believe that] God will grant you [whatever you ask] from him," and the rich blind man says, "Please ask Christ on my behalf that this darkness over my eyes cease, and I will never disobey *you* in anything."[13]

Aaron resisted such exalting. He always quotes the words of Jesus when speaking with those petitioning him. When a man has a son granted to him through the power of Aaron's prayer, he returns to Aaron with his son perched on his shoulder and exclaims, "Look! The fruit which God has given to me through your holy intercessions!" Aaron takes the child in his arms and says, "Blessed are *you*, Lord, in all *your* works."[14]

11. *Historia Monachorum* I (Russell, trans., 53).
12. *Vita Pachomii* 41 (Veilleux, trans., 64–65). For a series of miracles by Pachomius, see *Vita Pachomii* 41–45 (Veilleux, 64–69).
13. Emphasis added.
14. Emphasis added.

# THE LIFE OF ABBA AARON[1]

## Abba Isaac Tells Paphnutius about Abba Aaron

86. Now then, my brother Paphnutius, since you [asked][2] me for some information, you see, I've told you about the bishops who lived in Philae. According to what my father Abba Aaron told me personally, his parents paid money and bought him a commission in the army. And he received seven loaves of bread daily but he never ate any of them. Instead, he gave them away in accordance with the commandment.[3] His parents wanted to take a wife for him, but he refused. Instead, he remained a virgin from his birth until he completed his life.

## Abba Aaron and the Lion

87. Now it happened one day that letters were sent to the imperial troops ordering their transfer to another city. And the order came to Abba Aaron to take the troops and go with them. Now when he left the city a lion met him on the road that evening and wished to seize him. And the righteous man said, "When I remembered the words that the prophet David said, 'The lion and the bear has your servant slain,'[4] I raised my eyes [to heaven] and said, 'My Lord Jesus Christ, [if you] deliver this wild beast into my hands, I will give up my house and everything in it and all my possessions, and I will become a stranger to my parents and to all my men, and I will become a stranger to the things of this world, and I will clothe myself in the monastic habit for the sake of your holy name.'"

88. And now the holy man Abba Aaron said, "When I had said these words, I made ready the spear in my hand. I drove it through the

---

1. The "Life of Abba Aaron" is translated from the Coptic text published by E. A. Wallis Budge, "[Histories of the Monks in the Upper Egyptian Desert by Paphnutius]," *Coptic Texts*, vol. 5, part 1, *Miscellaneous Coptic Texts* (London: 1915). The "Life of Abba Aaron" is part 3, beginning with paragraph 86. For a translation of the "Histories," see Tim Vivian, trans., *Paphnutius: Histories of the Monks of Upper Egypt and the Life of Onnophrius* (Kalamazoo, Mich.: Cistercian Publications, 1993), 71–141.
2. Text: "told."
3. See Mt 6:29?
4. 1 Sam 17:36.

lion and he died. And I did not return to the city right away but went to another town a three-day march to my south. When I got there I sold my horse and my tunic with all its accouterments and all the things I had with me. I bought myself some clothes like the country folk wear, and with the rest I ministered to the poor in that place. I then went to the monastic community of Scetis, and there I put on the monastic habit. But I did not remain there because of my parents, for they were searching for [me],[5] and so I traveled south, little by little, until I came to this community." Now these things that I have just told you, my brother Paphnutius, [I heard] from my father Abba Aaron.

## Abba Isaac Relates His Own Story to Paphnutius

89. When I asked him to tell me his own experiences after he renounced the world, after a while he added: If you will pray for me, I will tell you the things I have seen with my own eyes. Now it happened that when I was a child in my parents' house, my parents sent me to school so I could be taught to write. Now my teacher diligently instructed me every day until he had taught me to write the holy letters. When I had made sufficient progress in my learning, I was able to read the passage from the Gospel that says, "Whoever will not forsake father or mother," and the rest that follows, "and follow me, is not worthy of me."[6] I pondered this passage in my heart and I continued to meditate upon it with my whole heart.

## Isaac Goes to See Abba Aaron

90. Now it happened that after some days I heard a report about our holy father Abba Aaron, that he was living the monastic life in a place called "the valley" and was performing many cures for all those who were sick. I rose and went to where he was living. I sat by the door of his dwelling until the sun set, for that day was a holiday. When evening had come and he had not come out, I rose and walked about three miles into the desert.[7] After a while I looked down into the sand

---

5. Text: "him."

6. Mt 10:37.

7. Or "mountain"; Coptic *ptoou* can mean either. And throughout.

and I saw footprints headed around a corner in the rock. I followed them and found my holy father Abba Aaron, and hanging from his neck there was a rope to which was tied a large stone.

91. Now when I called out to him, "Bless me," he withdrew his neck from the rope and threw the stone to the ground, and put on his clothes. He gazed into my face and said to me, "Where are you going, my son, in this place?" And I said to him, "Forgive me, my father, for I am lost." He said to me, "Come, sit down, my son. Indeed, you are not lost; rather, you have found the good path." When I had seated myself beside him, I entreated him, "I want to ask if you will let me be a monk with you." He spoke to me with compassion, "Our Savior says in the Gospels, 'Come to me, everyone who is weary, and I will give you rest.'[8] The monastic life has become well known, but this way of life is labor and suffering up to the very end."[9] I said to him, "My holy father, it is for this very thing that I have come here! If I am to complete my life in perfection, you must show me mercy." He said to me, "That which you seek is good, my son. Since you have put your hand to something that is good, who will be able to stop you, my son?"

## Isaac Becomes a Monk

92. Now we rose and came out from the desert, and he took me to a priest to clothe me in the monastic habit. And when we called inside the priest's house, he came outside and greeted us and took us inside his place. Right away my father told him about me, and immediately the priest shaved the hair from my head and clothed me in the monastic habit. We rose and went home. Now my holy father Aaron spent a week in helping me lay the foundations for doing work in the service of God. After a week he said to me, "Stay here while I go and visit this brother, and then I will come back to see you." (Now he did not want me to know that he wanted to go keep his own monastic observances.) And I said to him, "Will you come back today?" And he said to me, "No, my dear brother. Give me until the Sabbath."

93. The first day on which he left me was the [?].[10] And he spent the

---

8. Mt 11:28.

9. The Coptic has a play on words in this passage. "To the very end" is *jokef ebol*, the same words translated "to complete in perfection" in the next line. For a similar story, see the *Life of Pachomius* (Bohairic 10, First Greek Life 6 [Veilleux, trans.], pp. 30 and 301).

10. The meaning of the Coptic *pouosh* is not clear here.

first day and the second and the third and even the fourth and fifth away from me. Now as for me, demons were severely abusing me: "Why did your father go and leave you all alone? Why didn't he take you, so you too could be blessed by that brother?" Now when they continued to trouble me, I rose and set out into the desert to where I had found him the first time. I discovered him standing out in the sand (it was very hot, since it was the season when the Nile floods). There was a huge stone sitting on his head and his eyeballs were about to burst on account of the heat. He fell to the ground and gave himself up to die. I grabbed him and raised him up, weeping into his face, saying, "Why do you punish yourself so badly like this, my holy father?" And he said to me, "Why have you come here my son?" I said to him, "The Nubians have been tormenting me, and I've come to tell you."

94. He smiled and said, "Truly, they are invisible Nubians, my son."[11] I entreated him, saying, "I beg you, your holy Paternity, why do you give yourself to such afflictions and ascetical practices?" That very old man Abba Aaron answered, "I will not hide anything from you, my son, regarding your question. Indeed," he said, "when I remember the afflictions that my good Savior endured for us until he redeemed our race from the captivity of the devil—he gave his body and blood for us—I say, 'Since God took it upon himself to suffer on our behalf, it is right that we too should have every kind of affliction until he has mercy on us on the day of reckoning.'"[12] And when he had said these things, we rose and left and came home.

## Abba Aaron's Way of Life

95. Abba Aaron lived the monastic life in this manner: On the day he ate, he would drink no water; and the day he drank water, he would not eat. Now it happened that one night when we were both sleeping at home, the demons took on fantastical shapes and were crying out in the valley below with the voices of roaring lions. When I heard them I was terrified, and so I shook my father awake and said, "Lions are attacking us!" But he said to me, "Do not be afraid, my son, for it is written: 'Through our God we shall do a great thing,'[13] and again, 'Let

---

11. The Nubians were the "uncivilized" people living south of the first cataract in upper Egypt (present-day Ethiopia), that is, outside the *oikoumene* or civilized world.

12. See 1 Pet 2:12.

13. Ps 60:12.

God arise, and let his enemies be scattered.'"[14] After he said these things, we rose and went to the upper room. The demons were crying out as before, and some of them were saying, "Bring them here so we can kill them," while others were saying, "Let's kill them where they are." The holy one knew through the Spirit that they were demons, and he said to me, "Let us give ourselves to prayer." And as soon as we had given ourselves to prayer, the demons fled through the valley.

96. Now I was amazed and said to the holy old man Abba Aaron, "Don't the demons assume a number of forms?" And he said, "You will see, my son, that what you have accomplished is a small thing indeed. For a certain brother spoke to me, saying, 'It happened to me once that I was standing under a mountain ledge one summer's day. For six days I had neither eaten nor drunk nor sat down. A demon came, carrying a golden staff in his hand, and he said to me, "Be strong, athlete of Christ, and fight the good fight. For I have seen your sufferings, and I have been sent to comfort you."' Now that brother, when he perceived the wiles of the devil, drew the sign of the cross on the ground and immediately the demon disappeared."

97. Now it happened that when the holy man Abba Aaron said these things to me, I threw myself down at his feet, and I entreated him, saying, "Who was that brother?" And he said, "Rise, and I will tell you." And when I had gotten up, he said to me, "See that you tell no one! I was this servant, and I was completely unworthy for this to have happened to me."

## Abba Aaron and the Miracle of the Nubian's Son

98. Now it happened that on another day we were sitting with one another. A certain Nubian came out from the mountain with his son to drink water from the river. And when his young son put his hand into the river to scoop up some water to drink, a huge crocodile seized him and dragged him under and fled. Immediately his father threw himself to the ground and cried out and wept bitterly, for besides that son he had no other. Now as the man ran up the mountain crying out, he cut himself against the sharp edges of the rocks and severely injured himself. When I saw how heartbroken he was, I told my father. He got up and came to the door and gestured to the Nubian with his hand to

come to him. And when he had come, Abba Aaron saw the wounds on his body, and he wiped away the blood that had run over his body and took him and brought him inside his home. He brought him in by force and made him sit down.

99. Now when he had questioned him about what had happened (he could not understand what the Nubian was saying to him), my father said to me, "Rise, see if you can find anyone on the road. Call him. Perhaps you can find someone who knows how to speak with him. When I went out, I found a man from Philae who was going to Aswan riding on a donkey. I called to him and said to him, "Do you understand the language of the Nubians?" He said, "Yes." I took him to my father Abba Aaron. Now when that man saw the Nubian and the wounds all over his body, he was astonished and said to him, "How were you wounded?" And the Nubian told him what had happened. The holy man Abba Aaron took a piece of wood and gave it to him, saying, "Take it and throw it into the river where the crocodile seized your son." And he went and did as Abba Aaron had told him.

100. Now it happened that when he threw the piece of wood into the water, a huge crocodile appeared and cast the little boy up on the shore—and he had not been injured in any way! And his father took him by the hand and brought him to the holy old man Abba Aaron. And when the Nubian saw this miracle, he shouted with joy and hugged Abba Aaron and kissed him. Now the interpreter went to Philae and did not go to Aswan that day. Instead, he went about proclaiming the miracle that had taken place. And when the Nubian saw the miracle that had taken place, he went home glorifying God and proclaiming what had happened. And all those who heard have glorified God and the holy man Abba Aaron until this very day.

## Abba Aaron and the Miracle of the Fisherman's Son

101. Now it happened that on another occasion, one day when we were sitting at home, a fisherman came to us. His clothes were torn, his head was covered with dust, and he was weeping bitterly. I went up to him and said, "What happened to you?" And he said to me, "It happened that I and my small son, who was in the boat with me, were dragging in our net when he fell into the water and got tangled in the net, and I couldn't pull up the net because of the very strong currents. When I remembered my lord, the holy father Abba Aaron, I rose and I

have come to him to seek his mercy and favor, for this is my only son." And I got up and went and told my father. He got up and came down. The man prostrated himself at his feet and worshiped him, saying, "Help me! Ask Christ to be gracious to me and give me back my son, for I have no other."

102. Now that glorious old man said to him, "Go, my son, in the name of the Lord. I believe that you will find your son sitting in the boat." And he said, "I believe, by God, that it will happen just as you have said." And he went to the boat and found his son just as Abba Aaron had told him. He asked his son, "What happened to you?" and he said, "It happened that when I got tangled up in the net and was about to lose my last breath, I looked and saw a man of light. He took me by the hand and freed me from the net, and brought me up into the boat. And suddenly I no longer saw him." And his father took him and brought him to the holy man Abba Aaron, and gave thanks to God and to the holy man Abba Aaron.

## Abba Aaron and the Miracle of the Vineyard Worker

103. There was also a certain laborer who lived a little to the south of us and worked in a vineyard. Now it happened that when he had climbed up a date palm tree to gather dates, the belt holding him broke. He fell backwards to the ground and seemed to be dead. Now his son was sitting under the palm tree, and when he saw what had happened, he wept bitterly. And when the men who were nearby [heard] him crying out, they went to see what had happened. When they saw their friend lying on the ground as though dead, they said to his son, "Go to the holy man Abba Aaron, and get a small bowl of water from him in faith, and throw it on your father. Maybe he will wake up."

104. The young boy went weeping to the holy one. Now the holy one was sitting by the door because he had a fever and was exhausted. The young man threw himself down before him and told him what had happened. Now when the righteous and compassionate one heard what had happened, his heart was heavy and he said to me, "Bring me a little water, and let the young man take it and throw it on his father in the name of Christ. So I brought the water to him. He made the sign of the cross over it and gave it to the young man to take and throw it on his father. As soon as he threw it on him, he immediately got up. He came with his son and worshiped at the feet of the holy man Abba

Aaron. The holy one raised him up, saying, "Worship God, for I am the least of God's servants." When he rose, his son told him what had happened, saying, "When I threw the water [on] you, you trembled and then stood as though you'd just woken from sleep." And so they went away from him in peace.

## Abba Aaron and the Miracle of the Stillborn Baby

105. Now there was in Philae a woman who was about to give birth, but her child withered inside her and died.[15] And when she remembered the miracles that God had worked through the holy man Abba Aaron, she cried out, saying, "God of the holy man Abba Aaron, hear me in the hour of my distress!" Immediately she gave birth to a small child, but he was dead. And her parents greatly mourned for the small child, but when the young woman saw her parents' heavy hearts, she said to them, "Why are you so heavy-hearted about the child?[16] Had I not asked the God of the holy man Abba Aaron, I too would have sunk into death."

106. Now when her parents heard this, they took money in their hands (for they were very wealthy) and went to the holy man Abba Aaron. (Now the Spirit told him, "They will be coming to you.")[17] He said to me, "Shut the door and don't allow anyone to see me today." When they arrived, they spent a long time knocking on the door and calling inside. And he looked out through a window and said to them, "Who are you looking for?" They answered, "We are looking for your Holiness." Then he said, "What do you need?" And they said, "We have come to meet your Holiness. Accept this small gift, and pray that the child might live for his mother's sake. Indeed, his mother called upon your name when she was about to give birth. Had she not done so, they both would have died."

107. Saint Abba Aaron said to them, "The apostle has well said,

---

15. The Coptic for what is translated here as "withered" is *joht*, literally "failed, ceased." There is a play on words here: "child" in Coptic is *sherē*, and "miracle" in the following line is *shperē*.

16. The wordplay continues: the Coptic for "small child" is *pshēre shēm*; "young woman" is *tsheere shēm*.

17. On the holy man being informed through God or the Spirit, of which we have several examples in this narrative, see the *Life of Pachomius* 107 (Veilleux, trans., 158). In the *Histories of the Monks of Upper Egypt* the holy archbishops of Alexandria also have such powers; see paragraphs 58 and 84 (Vivian, *Histories*, 100 and 114).

'The root of all evil is the love of money.'[18] And Peter rebuked Simon, saying, 'May your silver and your gold go with you to perdition because you think that the gift of God is acquired by money.'[19] For it was through the love of money that Gehazi was cursed with leprosy.[20] Furthermore, our Lord said to the imperial officer, 'Go, your child lives,' and the officer had offered him neither gold nor silver.[21] Now as for you, if you believe, the gift of Christ will be given to you." They answered, "We believe, our holy father, that Christ will fulfill everything you say to us."

108. And the father of the child [*sic*] [took] a little earth from beside the door of Abba Aaron's home and tied it up in his neckerchief. And when they came into the house, they found a large crowd of people gathered together and the man's wife and her child. The child's father uncovered the little bit of earth tied up in his neckerchief and sprinkled it upon the dead child. Immediately he moved his body and opened his eyes. Those who were sitting beside the mother were astounded, and they glorified the God of the holy man Abba Aaron.[22] Now the people used to bring large numbers of the sick and diseased to Abba Aaron, and he would heal them. He was like the apostles to whom God gave power over every kind of sickness.[23]

## Abba Aaron and the Rich Man and the Poor Man

109. Now on another occasion a man from the city of Aswan came to Abba Aaron one day. He continuously wept before him and said, "There is a certain rich man in my city to whom I owe ten obeli, and I can't get the money to pay him. I have begged him, 'Be patient with me and I will repay you.' But he would not agree to this and has seized me for what I owe him. He wants to take from me my vineyard, which I inherited from my parents and from which I make a small profit, enough for my poor children and me to live on. I *am* paying him the interest I owe him. I beg you, your Holiness, to send a message to him to ease up on me, for someone from his household told me, 'He's going

18. 1 Tim 6:10.
19. Acts 8:20.
20. 2 Kings 5:27.
21. Lk 7:1–10.
22. There is another wordplay here: "child" in Coptic is *pshēre*, while "astounded" is *shpēre*.
23. See Mt 10:1 and parallels.

to press you for the principal and haul you into court so he can take away your vineyard.' But I believe that if you were to send a message, he would not refuse to listen to you." As he said these things, he wept.

110. Now evening had come, and the man rose to go on home, but Abba Aaron saw his distress and said to him, "Stay here until morning, for it's late now," and he stayed in the outer court. My father Aaron said to me, "Take a loaf of bread and some water, and give them to him and say to him, 'Stay here until morning, and God will help you.'" And I did as he told me, but the man, because of his sadness, refused to taste anything. And I went and told my father, and he came out to him and said to him, "Do not be disobedient, my son. Rise and eat a little bread, and I believe [that] God will help you." And in this way he persuaded him. The man rose and ate.

111. Now the holy man Abba Aaron rose and went to the upper room. He spent the whole night petitioning God and praying on behalf of that man. When morning came, the man tried to return home, but the holy man Abba Aaron said to him, "Stay here a little longer, and you will go home with your mind at ease." And while these words were still in his mouth, the rich man came riding on a donkey, which was being led, and two other men were following him in order to guide him to the righteous one. His eyes were open but he could not see. He threw himself down at my father's feet and worshiped him. Abba Aaron took hold of him and raised him to his feet. Then the holy one said to him, "Have you not heard the law which says, 'You shall not covet any of your neighbor's possessions: not his house or his field or his livestock or his vineyard or his olive trees'?[24] [. . .] It [says] also '[Woe to those who join] house to house and field to field and take away their neighbors' possessions.'[25] This word 'woe' makes it perfectly clear that severe punishments lie in store for whoever covets his neighbor's things, from the greatest person to the least. Again the Savior cried out, 'Blessed are the merciful, for to them shall mercy be shown.'[26] Then again, 'Mercy shall make a person triumph over judgment.'[27]

112. "Be merciful in this world, my son, that mercy may be shown to you in the other world where you are going. It is good for you to have compassion on the poor, so that the merciless misery and poverty of

24. Ex 20:17; Dt 5:21.
25. Is 5:8; Micah 2:2.
26. Mt. 5:7; 6:14.
27. Js 2:13.

Nineve not be yours, because judgment is without mercy towards him who does not show mercy.[28] Again, 'Mercy shall make a person triumph over judgment.' Haven't you heard about Ahab and what happened to him when he coveted the vineyard of Naboth the Israelite?"[29]

113. Now when the holy man Abba Aaron had said these words to the rich man, the latter answered, saying, "Have mercy on me, righteous and honorable one! Please ask Christ on my behalf that this darkness over my eyes cease, and I will never disobey you in anything." The holy one said to him, "Do you believe that I am able to do this?" The rich man answered, "Oh yes, I do, my holy father! What is more, listen to me, and I will relate to your Charity what happened to me. Now it happened that when the man about whom you have spoken with me had left yesterday, I went up to my house and went to bed. I woke up at night and sensed this great darkness over my eyes. And when morning came, I said to my household, 'I cannot see today.' Now they said to me, 'Clearly this has happened to you through the holy man Abba Aaron. We saw the man with whom you were talking yesterday about money go to him.' As soon as I heard that he had gone to your Holiness, I knew that this had happened to me because of him. I myself have come to you because this I believe: that you have the power to heal me."

114. The holy man said to him, "If you show mercy to the poor man, Christ himself will heal you." The rich man called one of those who had come with him, and he took the loan agreement from him and gave it to the righteous man Abba Aaron. The holy man Abba Aaron said to him, "[If you give wages to the poor man] in this world, God will give you your wages in the world to come." Then he made the sign of the cross over the rich man's eyes. Abba Aaron said to him, "Wash your face in faith." Now as soon as he had washed his face, he was able to see. Those who had accompanied him were amazed and glorified God.

28. In Coptic literature, Nineve is the name given to "Dives," the unnamed rich man in the parable told by Jesus about a beggar named Lazarus (see Lk 16:19–31). For a discussion of a Coptic homily attributed to Saint Peter, bishop of Alexandria (d. 311), which includes an elaborated retelling of the Nineve and Lazarus parable, see Tim Vivian, *St. Peter of Alexandria: Bishop and Martyr* (Philadelphia: Fortress, 1988), 59–62. For the homily itself, see Birger A. Pearson and Tim Vivian, *Two Coptic Homilies Attributed to Saint Peter of Alexandria: On Riches, On the Epiphany* (Rome: Corpus dei Manoscritti Copti Letterari, 1993).

29. 1 Kings 21:13–19, 22:34–38.

115. The rich man rose and prostrated himself before the holy man Abba Aaron, giving thanks both to God and to Abba Aaron because he could see. The holy one gave the loan agreement to the poor man and commanded him, saying, "You too are to be merciful to your neighbor, as mercy has been shown to you. Do not ever say, 'I am a poor man, I'm not able to keep the commandment in the Gospel.' The Gospel will never accept any excuse from you that you make, poor man. But even for something as small as a cup of cold water, God will reward you![30] Do not be like that worthless servant whose lord forgave a debt of many talents. He went and squeezed his fellow servant for the little bit he owed him.[31] No, be like the wise servant who doubled his talent."[32] The poor man answered, "Pray for me, my holy father, and I will keep everything that you require of me." And in this way both men profited, and they left Abba Aaron, glorifying God.

## Abba Aaron Heals a Man's Gout

116. Now when the rich man went home, he told his household everything that had happened to him. There was a man in his house whose feet had for a long time caused him great pain. When he heard the miracles that the holy one had done, he said, "How I wish I were worthy to meet him, so he would have mercy on my misery and I would be healed!" The man with the gout said to the rich man, "Didn't Abba Aaron touch some part of your body?" He said, "Yes, he did; he touched my hands. I had thrown myself at his feet and he raised me up by my hands and I worshiped him. The man with the gout said to [him],[33] "Please come near me." Now when the rich man drew near to him, he took his hand and placed it upon his feet, saying, "I believe [that if the] hand [that touched] the holy man Abba Aaron [touches my feet also, I will be] healed." And so the pain left his feet that very hour, and everyone who heard about it glorified the God of Abba Aaron.

## Abba Aaron and the Miracle of the Donkey

117. Now there was also in Philae a man who owned a donkey that he worked in the mill. When he was getting ready to go home, the don-

---

30. Mk 9:41.
31. Mt 18:28.
32. Mt 25:14–23.
33. Text: "me."

key fell down right there at his feet and died. But he, because of his great faith in the righteous man, left the donkey lying there dead and ran to him and told him about it. Now the righteous one said to him, "He has not died, my son, but has fainted." He gave him a staff and said to him, "Go and strike him with it three times, and he will stand up." And he took the staff and left and struck the donkey with it three times, and it got up on its feet as it usually did. The man came to my father and said to him, "Thank you, my father, for the favor that God has shown me." Now my father admonished him not to tell anyone what had happened, saying, "Do not allow anyone to disbelieve our words. For indeed our Savior said, '[Truly, truly, I say to you, whoever believes in me, the works that I do] he shall do also, and he shall do things greater than these.'"[34]

## Abba Aaron and the Miracle of the Vineyard

118. Now the holy man Abba Aaron would himself do a great deal of work with his hands, for he remembered what is written, "We worked with our hands by day and by night, so that we might not add to the toil of any of you."[35] Sometimes he made grave-clothes and sometimes he plaited rope. And he was never in a hurry to speak unless there was some great urgency. A man came to him one time and bought some cord from him for use in his vineyard. Now that vineyard's [stock][36] was very hard, but when he took the cord from Abba Aaron, he got a very good harvest. And those who heard about it glorified God.

## Abba Aaron and the Miracle of the Fish

119. On another occasion, some fishermen came to him, downhearted, and they entreated him, saying, "Please pray for us. We are being harassed by a certain nobleman about a large quantity of fish, which we have not been able to catch and deliver to him. We're afraid that he will hold us liable and sue us for damages beyond our ability [to pay. . . . "] Abba Aaron replied and said, "Have you not heard that the Lord said to] Peter, 'Cast your net on the right side of the boat, and you will catch something'?[37] He did not say 'on the left side' but 'on the right

34. Jn 14:12.
35. 1 Thess 2:9.
36. Coptic: *čelma*. *Čelma* ("jar") is probably a mistake for *čelm̄* ("dry sticks"), here referring to the root stocks of the vines.
37. Jn 21:6.

side,' which means that when someone abandons himself to evil thoughts, that is to say, to things that are on the left, he does evil. When he does the things of the right hand, that is, things that are good, everything that he asks from God will come to him.

120. "To be sure, the Lord spoke this way to those on the left: 'Depart from me, you accursed, into the everlasting fire that has been prepared for the devil and his angels.'[38] But to those on his right hand he said, 'Come to me, you blessed of my father.'[39] And again he said, 'Come to me, everyone who is weary and burdened, and I will give you rest.'[40] And again, 'You will inherit the kingdom that has been prepared for you from the foundation of the world.'[41] Why? He said, 'I was hungry and you fed me; thirsty, and you gave me something to drink. I was naked, and you clothed me. I was a stranger and you accepted me among [you].[42] I was sick and you visited me; in prison, and you came to see [me].'[43] All this means that if you cast your net on the right side, you yourselves shall catch many fish, according to your need."

121. And they said to him, "We swear by your Salvation, our holy father, it's because of our poverty that we haven't had the leisure to go to church on the Sabbath and on the Lord's day!" He said to them, "Have I said to you, 'You haven't been going to God's church'? If you ask him, he will have mercy on you, and he will not let you be in need of anything, for it is the duty of all Christians to go to the house of God first thing in the morning and to pray to him to make ready the work of their hands."

122. And they prostrated themselves at his feet, saying, "Pray over us, our holy father, and we will obey all your words." And so he prayed over them and gave them a bowl of water, saying, "Sprinkle this over your nets, and you will catch something." Now they left in faith, and they caught a large number of fish. They gave the nobleman as many as he wanted, and they kept the rest for the needs of their households. And they came to the righteous man, and they gave thanks to God and [to him for] his holy prayers [. . .] immediately. Now there was also another

38. Mt 25:41.
39. Mt 25:34.
40. Mt 11:28.
41. Mt 25:34.
42. Text: "us."
43. Text: "him." Mt 25:35–36.

man whose ship was in danger of sinking, and when he called upon God in the name of Abba Aaron, his ship was saved, with all its cargo.

## Abba Aaron and the Miracle of the Man Blind in One Eye

123. Now it happened that one day two Nubians were walking together on their way to Aswan. One of them had only one eye. His friend said to him, "Come on, let's receive a blessing at the hands of this great man." The one-eyed man said, "He isn't a great man. If he really is, let him open my eye," and while the words were still in his mouth, his eye—which had been blind—regained its sight, but his good eye became blind! When his friend saw what had happened, he was utterly amazed, and said to him, "Didn't I tell you that he is a *very* great man?" The one-eyed man said, "It's no great loss, for one eye has been shut, while the other has been opened. However, let's go to him. Perhaps he'll give light to the other eye." So the two of them came to the holy man Abba Aaron. My father said to the Nubian, who was not a believer, "Since you think that it's no great loss, why are you here?" Immediately he became very [fearful] and worshiped him, saying, "[Open my] eye!" and immediately he was able to see with the other eye. And the two believed, and went away joyful, and they proclaimed throughout the whole country the miracle that had taken place.

## Abba Aaron and the Miracle of the Child's Birth

124. And again, there was a certain God-fearing man in the city of Aswan. He was a believer, and came to visit us on numerous occasions. Now one day when he was thinking about coming to see us, his wife said to him, "If you're going to see the holy man Abba Aaron, entreat him to pray to Christ for us to give us a male child. I've heard that when it came time for a certain girl to give birth, she was unable to, but when she called upon Abba Aaron in this matter, she gave birth to a son, but he was dead. Her father went to Abba Aaron and entreated him, and people say that when her father took a little dust from the door of Abba Aaron's house and threw it on the dead infant, he immediately came to life. With you, too, I believe that if you petition Abba Aaron, whatever you ask from him will come to pass."

125. So he came to us and related the story to my father, saying, "I have lived with my wife from the time I was a youth, and [we have

had] no [male] child, [even after all these] years. Now, therefore, [I believe that] God will grant you [whatever you ask] from him." So the righteous one went to the place where he meditated alone, and he prayed in this way, saying, "My Lord, it was you who gave to Sarah our father Isaac when she was barren, and you gave Joseph to Rachel, and you gave Samuel to Hannah.[44] Now therefore, Lord, what you were yesterday you are also today; moreover, you are the same forever. I know your goodness, Lord. Please listen to my prayer and grant the petition of this man who has come to us."

126. When he had finished praying, he went to the man and said to him, "Go, my son, in the name of Christ. I believe that even as God said to our father Abraham, 'I will come. Let it be time for Sarah to have a son,'[45] it will also happen for you." And just as he had said, so it happened, and within a year the man came to us with his small son perched upon his shoulders. He held him out to my father, saying, "Look! The fruit that God has given to me through your holy intercessions." And the holy man Abba Aaron took him in his arms and praised God, saying, "Blessed are you, Lord, in all your works." Then he gave the child to his father, saying, "Behold God's favor which has come to you! May Christ who has graciously given him to you, my son, increase [him and] you, and may he enable us to do his will."

## Abba Aaron and the Miracle
## of the Man Possessed by a Demon

127. Now again, there was a certain man whom a demon was wickedly tormenting. When his parents heard of Abba Aaron's fame, they bound their son hand and foot and set him on a donkey and took him to Abba Aaron. (Now it took four men to hold him.) And when they had brought him, they lifted him off the donkey and set him down by the door. Now the demon was speaking from inside the man, hurling out many disgusting words to my father, saying, "Aren't you some soldier a long ways from the slaughter? Weren't your family noble folk who ate up people with oppressive loans? I remember one day when your father loaned some guy ten oboli, and when the man, because of his poverty, could not come up with the money to pay your father

44. Gen 17:19; 30:22–24; 1 Sam 2:21.
45. Gen 18:10.

back, your father seized his house in lieu of payment. Wasn't what he did a sin? And you—you've come here saying, 'I'm going to heal these sick people.' You're no doctor!"

128. Now my father restrained himself until the demon had finished everything he had to say. He said to him, "As for you, you don't deserve an answer. Now, therefore, I order you in the name of the crucified Christ to leave [this man]." When the demon heard [these words, he tried to] take the man and flee. Then the holy man filled his hand with water and sprinkled it on the man's face three times, saying, "In the name of the Holy Trinity, come out of him!" And the demon came out. The holy one said to him, "Get yourself to Babylon of the Chaldeans, and stay there until the day of judgment, when everyone shall receive according to what he has done. As for you, you will be thrown into the pit of hell."

129. When the demon heard these things, he left in a rage. Now when the man returned to his right state of mind, he glorified God, as did his parents and everyone accompanying them. Then they entreated the holy man to accept something, but he refused, saying that he had never accepted a gift of any kind since he had become a monk. (He was in the habit of telling me often, "Do not set your gaze on the things of this world, which do not profit a person in any way, but as long as we have food and clothing, there will be enough for us. For indeed our Savior said to his apostles, 'Do not acquire for yourselves gold or silver or copper in your belts.'[46] Therefore, it is fitting for a monk to walk in this way and to lead a good life.") As a result, the parents renounced the world and followed the Lord.

## Abba Aaron's Way of Life

130. Now it happened that after these things, the holy man Abba Aaron rose and walked into the valley. As for me, he commanded me, saying, "Stay here. If anyone comes seeking me, say to him, 'He has gone to visit a brother.'" Now this was his ascetic way of life: When winter came he would soak his cloak in water and then put it on and stand in the chilly wet of the evening. He would spend the whole night praying, and when it was morning, he'd go into the crevices of the bitterly cold rocks. He gave himself no rest at all, either day or night. It

46. Mt. 10:9.

was the same during the summer. He'd stand in the burning heat and pray. He spent all of his time in the constant practice of this exacting ascetic way of life.

## Abba Aaron and the Miracle of the Nile

131. Now it happened one year that the Nile did not rise enough to water all our fields, and a multitude of the poor came to him weeping and saying, "Our holy father, we and our children are going to die because the waters have not risen!" He said to them, "Believe [in God and he will deliver you. As it is written,] 'The prayer of the poor man who is downhearted, he pours out entreaty before the Lord.'[47] Again it says, 'The Lord has heard the desires of the poor.'"[48] He quoted them numerous other passages from scripture and explained them to them, and he comforted them, and in this way they departed from him praising God. Now the holy man Abba Aaron was not unconcerned about their distress, and he would go to the river each evening and immerse himself in the water up to his neck and he would pray to God, saying, "My good Christ, compassionate one, have compassion upon your image and likeness." Indeed, he continued this practice until God had compassion for his tears and made the waters of the Nile flow over the face of the whole country.[49]

## Abba Aaron and Another Miracle Concerning the Nile

132. Now it also happened one year that some men came to him filled [. . .] (as the narrative will show us if we continue on). Now they continued to entreat him to petition Christ to send them water [to save] the people. They were terrified because the proper time for the rising of the waters had passed. And they continued to weep [and beg the holy man. He had] compassion [on them and prayed to God,] saying, "God, do not forsake the work of your hands, man and beast. For indeed you created us all from your blood, and you deigned to come into the world. For our salvation you had a human birth. We know that with you nothing is impossible. God, do not forget the lives of the

47. Ps 34:6?
48. Ps 12:5; 69:33.
49. For a comparable story of the raising of the Nile, see the *Life of Pachomius* 100 (Veilleux, trans., 137).

poor, lest they sin with their lips before you. For I remember what the wise man Solomon said, 'Give me neither wealth nor poverty.'[50] Whether God causes the waters to rise or not, it is for our refreshment alone. For God has the power to make all his creatures be in need of their livelihood, but God allows the poor man to ask from the rich, so that when the rich man shows mercy, mercy may be shown to him on the day of reckoning. Now the poor man, for his part, if he bears up under his poverty, he shall go into the kingdom [. . .] the heavenly kingdom.

133. "The merciful person is like the ladder that Jacob saw: Its foot was planted firmly on the earth while its top reached to heaven, and the angels of God supported it, that is to say, the Father of mercy.[51] Consider that the Lord said 'these little ones,' that is to say, those who are of little account.[52] And again, as he said, 'When you prepare a dinner or supper, do not invite your neighbors or your kin, but call the poor and the blind and the lame because they have nothing to offer you in exchange.[53] You will be rewarded at the resurrection of the righteous.'[54] And even if you are not able to climb up to the top of the ladder, that is to say, if we cannot give in abundance, let us find the mercy that is perfect. Therefore, let us show mercy, for mercy allows one to triumph over judgment."[55]

134. Now when the holy man Abba Aaron had said these things, he prayed and dismissed them in peace, saying, "God will make the river fill with water, and he will bring it up to its proper level. Do not be afraid, and do not be unbelieving. You say that the time for the rising of the water has passed. Nevertheless, believe that God has the power to do everything." And they got up and left in peace.

135. Now the following evening, the holy one went to the river and prayed, saying, "Lord, you are the same yesterday and today and forever. It was you who burst open the rock and water flowed forth, and you gave it to the people to drink.[56] And when Samson was thirsty, you caused the jawbone of an ass to bring forth water that quenched his

50. Prov 30:8.
51. See Gen 28:12.
52. Mt 10:42; 18:6, 10, 14.
53. There is a play on words in the text: the Coptic for what is translated as "in exchange" is *toobou*, while "rewarded" is *toboou*.
54. Lk 14:13.
55. Js 2:13.
56. Ex 17:6.

thirst.[57] Therefore, I entreat you today to send the river's water over the entire land so the poor among your people have enough food and bless you and your holy name." And the holy man Abba Aaron spent the whole night praying and calling on God concerning the river's water. And so it was that the water rose and continued to rise, filling the river, and it did not subside for a day, until all of our fields had gotten water. And so there was abundance and plenty that year through the prayers of the holy man, as it is written, "The prayer of a righteous man is powerful and effective."[58]

## Abba Aaron and the Blessing of the Poor Man

136. If we were to narrate all the wonders [that] God worked [through the prayers of the] holy man Abba Aaron, this account would go on too long. Now it happened one day that he was sitting down with some people gathered around him. A poor man with a sack of barley on his back came to him and entreated him, saying, "Bless it for me, holy father, and I will go and make bread from it for my children, for I am a poor man." And the holy man Abba Aaron filled his hand with water and sprinkled it on the sack of barley, saying, "Go, and make bread for your children in the name of Christ." And he took the barley and left and made bread from it and a great blessing took place because of it. He returned to us glorifying God and the holy man Abba Aaron.

## The Death of Abba Aaron

137. You see, my brother Paphnutius, I have told you a few things about the holy man Abba Aaron's way of life. Because I am a tongue of flesh, it is impossible for me to do justice to his virtues. I will tell you the wondrous manner of his death. He was an old man, advanced in years. His body was worn out because of his severe ascetical practices. Now he got sick on the thirteenth of May, and on the following day, which was the fourteenth, I heard the voices of a choir of angels crying out, "Blessed, blessed." I did not know who they were talking about. (Now I, Paphnutius, said to him, "This is his end. They are calling

---

57. Judges 15:19.
58. Js 5:16.

him blessed in heaven just as they blessed him on earth.") Now they continued in this fashion until the great [*sic*] first hour of the seventeenth of May. And at the seventh hour of that day, the holy man Abba Aaron died in very old age.

138. We buried his body with honor and reverence. We laid him beside the bodies of the holy bishops who had been in Philae, that is, Abba Macedonius and Abba Mark and Abba Isaiah.[59] Now, therefore, my brother Paphnutius, pray for me that God will have mercy on me and that he will make my end in this world pleasing to himself. And I said to him, "You are worthy of a great blessing, because from you I have heard of the monastic way of life of these holy men. Moreover, I for my part am going to write them down so that [they][60] may be set down as authoritative models for all future generations." And even so I have written them.

139. Now when we had finished talking with one another, I and Abba Isaac, [concerning] Abba Aaron, he prepared a table, and we ate and drank together. We rose and prayed, and I left him to go visit the brethren to his north.

## Coda

140. This is the life of the holy man and anchorite of Philae, Abba Aaron, who completed his course in the desert to the east of Philae. Glory to the holy Trinity, Father and Son and life-giving and consubstantial Holy Spirit, now and forever.

59. For the stories of these three bishops, see Vivian, *Paphnitius,* 84–114
60. Text: "you."

# 6

# HOLY EXAMPLE AND HEAVENLY INTERCESSOR: SAINT THEOGNIUS

## Introduction
## The "Life of Saint Theognius" and Its Author

"THE LIFE AND ASCETIC PRACTICE OF SAINT THEOGNIUS," AS THIS work is entitled in Greek, is really an encomium, a homily in praise of the life and virtues of Saint Theognius (425–522), addressed, some years after the saint's death, to the monks at the monastery he founded.[1] In his prologue, the speaker, Paul of Elusa, acknowledges "this assembly of your venerable love gathered before me . . . and the holy men gathered here for the sake of remembrance" (chapter 3). The day is a day of "commemoration" (*mneia*), and Paul sets out not only to tell about the saint's life and extol his virtues, but also—and especially—to exhort his listeners, and himself, to repent of their sins and emulate the life of the holy man Theognius. In his brief narrative of the saint's life, Paul says that Theognius left the monastery at Calamon "and occupied this place here" (8) that is, the monastery he founded and that later bore his name.

In order to imagine that feast day, that time, almost 1500 years ago, and to gain a better appreciation for Paul's words, we need to remember that the church in which Paul is speaking to the gathered monks

---

1. J. Van den Gheyn, "Saint Théognius, Évêque de Bételie en Palestine," *Revue des questions historiques* 50 (1891), 564, dates the catastrophes mentioned in paragraphs 23–24, to the years 525–26, and so believes that Paul delivered the encomium not on the first anniversary of the saint's death but in 526, four years after his death.

(24) almost certainly contained the sanctified remains of the monastery's founder, possibly beneath the altar.[2] The monks knew they were standing in a particularly sacred place; saints' relics often had great powers, and throughout the monasteries of Palestine at this time wondrous miracles were known to take place at the tombs of the holy ones. Saint Theognius, then, would have been very much present to the assembled monks, and Paul's words of remembrance and rebuke would have been much more immediate, and touched the heart more deeply, than the words we routinely associate with sermons and preachers today. Theognius, and all the saints, were watching over the assembled brethren, and the words of the holy ones, Paul reminds the monks, are carried to the very throne of God (25).

Can we identify the speaker of the encomium? Paul was known as a citizen of Elusa (present-day El-Khalasa), not far from Bethelia, Theognius's episcopal see. Paul says in his encomium that he came from Greece. When he arrived in Palestine, he met a certain Alexander, "our generation's honored pearl, both the advocate of the Askalonians and counted among the lovers of solitude and the virtuous fathers," who referred him to Theognius (18). Askalon, Bethelia, and Elusa formed a triangle around Gaza, so it is not unlikely that Alexander, Theognius, and Paul knew one another. In *The Spiritual Meadow*, John Moschus mentions a number of Alexanders, but one is of particular interest: Abba Alexander of the laura of Calamon (the monastery Theognius left in order to found, eventually, his own). This Alexander, Moschus says, was with "Abba Paul the Greek at his cave."[3] Where this cave was is not specified, but two clues may point to Elusa. Alexander visits Paul in chapter 163 of *The Spiritual Meadow*, and chapter 164 mentions a monk named Victor who lived at a laura in Elusa. Moschus often groups his stories around locales, so it is not unreasonable to suggest that paragraphs 163 and 164 are concerned with Elusa. Cyril of Scythopolis supplies corroborating evidence: Paul, he says, was "a solitary of

---

2. See, for example, the descriptions of reliquaries in Byzantine monastic churches in Yoram Tsafrir, *Ancient Churches Revealed* (Jerusalem and Washington, D.C.: Israel Exploration Society and Biblical Archaeology Society, 1993), 5 (reliquiary below altar) and 78 (tomb in center hall); and Yizhar Hirschfeld, *The Judean Desert Monasteries in the Byzantine Period* (New Haven and London: Yale University Press, 1992), 124.

3. *Pratum spirituale* 163; John Wortley, trans., *The Spiritual Meadow of John Moschus (Pratum Spirituale)* (Kalamazoo, Mich.: Cistercian Publications, 1992), p. 134.

the city of Elusa."[4] Cyril and John agree, then, that Paul was a solitary. Many solitaries in Palestine lived in caves as members of monastic communities called lauras. Paul was attached to the laura at Elusa
where he was known, because of his homeland, as "Paul the Greek,"
origins to which he himself testifies in the encomium.

Now, however, things get muddier, or perhaps clearer after the mud
settles. John Moschus also refers to an Abba Paul, "higoumen [leader]
of the monastery of Abba Theognius."[5] It seems likely, despite John's
inconveniently not saying so, that these two monks are the same person. Alexander's report is in the first person ("One day when I was
with Abba Paul the Greek at his cave") and may represent a verbatim
account handed down to John. Alexander may have visited Paul when
the latter was a monk at Elusa, or the cave Alexander refers to could be
near the monastery of Theognius, and Alexander visited him there at a
later date (when Paul was higoumen?). In any case, it is reasonable to
suggest that Paul the Greek was a monk at Elusa. Later he moved to
Theognius's monastery, where at some point he became the
monastery's leader (probably as Theognius's successor). It is this Paul,
quite naturally, who is addressing an encomium on the eponymous
founder of the monastery to its gathered monks on the anniversary of
the saint's death.[6]

Rhetorically, Paul begins the encomium very effectively, reminding
the monks of death and of the examples of the apostles. The apostles
are offered as examples par excellence because (1) they "fulfilled blamelessly the duty enjoined upon them" by God and (2) because of that,
after their deaths, "rejoicing before the Creator of the universe, they
stood fearlessly at the kingly and indescribable throne" (chapter 1). But
God's great gifts, Paul reminds his listeners, came also to the disciples,
who have "the crown of righteousness" (2 Tim 4:7) reserved for them.

The figure of the apostles and the disciples allows Paul to segue to a
"modern" disciple, Theognius: "Like an eagle having grown its feathers, he was joyously freed from the shackles of his body and [flew up]

4. *Life of Theognius*, R. M. Price, trans., *Cyril of Scythopolis: The Lives of the Monks of Palestine* (Kalamazoo, Mich.: Cistercian Publications, 1991), 271.

5. Moschus, *Spiritual Meadow* 160 (Wortley, trans., p. 132).

6. For discussions of Paul and his connection with the monastery of Theognius, see J. Van den Gheyn, "Acta Sancti Theognii," *Analecta Bollandiana* 10 (1891), 75–76, and Van den Gheyn, "Saint Théognius," 562–63, from which I have drawn much of the information and argument above.

to heaven, leaving for posterity his own memory like some resplendent monument" (2). Paul forcefully states that Theognius, because of his humility and self-sacrifice, is an example to follow: "How purely and incorruptibly he lived and how humble he was, and how night and day with the greatest suffering of heart and abundant tears he [sacrificed himself] completely for the sake of others" (3). This Theognius, a saint on earth, is now with the saints in heaven, and Paul's prologue reaches its joyful climax as he pictures the rejoicing in heaven on Theognius's feast day, a celebration in which Theognius's heirs also participate: "When the commemoration of Theognius, who is for everyone the dearest of perfumes, is borne upon the lips, let the chorus of heavenly stars be delighted and exult; let the earth be joyous, the air be mirthful, especially when the incorporeal powers rejoice together in the memory of this man of God" (4).

After the prologue (chapters 1–4), the encomium is divided into "The Ascetic Life of Saint Theognius" (5–9) and "Saint Theognius as Bishop of Bethelia" (10–22), followed by the peroration (23–25). The Ascetic Life is sketchy, giving only a bare bones outline of the saint's life (see pp. 147–51, below), supplying very few details about his ascetical life, and almost no information about the monastery he founded (which is natural, given that Paul's audience would have known a great deal about both). When Paul does speak of Theognius's way of life, his descriptions are very general: "holding to his accustomed quiet and gentleness, he benefitted everyone who lived with him" (5); "the man properly administered the place called 'the monastery' and its brotherhood" (5). We can see already that Paul's interest lies not in details but example, the example of the holy man who is model, reproof, and intercessor for those still in the flesh.

This pattern continues in what we might call the historical or biographical details of Theognius's life. But Paul is not interested in history; biographical detail is important to him only insofar as it contributes to his vision of the saint. Theognius's trips to Byzantium when he is bishop clearly show this. The holy man journeys to the imperial capital twice during his episcopacy, once to meet Emperor Anastasius (11) and once to meet Emperor Justin (21). In both cases the reasons for the journey are left vague: the first time he goes "for the purpose of public business," while the second time he is "again compelled by some urgent matter." What matters is not the business of the trip but the great honor and esteem shown Theognius in the Holy

City: he "was honored above all the other bishops that could be found there at that time" (21).

Theognius, Paul wishes to make clear, was a holy man revered throughout the empire. As a holy man, he fits the model of the monastic saint made famous by Saint Antony and scores of holy men after him. Did Paul model his "Life of Theognius" on a received stereotype? Or did Theognius base his own life on the tradition of the holy man as he received it through the stories and sayings of the desert fathers in the monasteries of Palestine (and Egypt)? Probably both. Theognius, like many before him, desired a solitary way of life where he could peacefully pray to God. He, like Antony, and many others, journeys to several different locations seeking solitude. Eventually he inhabits a cave (8), but also like numerous other holy men, he attracts followers and eventually establishes a monastery (9).[7] Like other holy men, Theognius tames wild beasts and lives peacefully with them (7), defeats the devil (9), and performs miracles (11–16, 18). Miracles also occur because of him, even after his death (22).

In giving his readers this picture of Theognius as holy man, Paul establishes what we would call a hagiographical base for his chief—theological and spiritual—concern, which will be the subject of his peroration as he preaches about humility and arrogance, sin and repentance. Paul prepares for his theological theme with an autobiographical piece: When he first came to the Holy Land, he was told by Alexander (see above) to seek out Theognius because he "has preached most often about humility" (17). Paragraph 17, tucked in the middle of Theognius's "Life," is a small sermon by Alexander on humility and arrogance, which prepares us for this theme in the peroration. In chapter 20 Paul emphasizes Theognius's tears of repentance and entreaties to God, and then explicitly urges his audience to follow the example of the holy man: "May we also offer to the Judge a bowl of forgiveness mixed with wailing and inexpressible laments in order that in the future we might share from it in the great rejoicing of the righteous." A powerful and moving description of Theognius both delineates his character and presents him as a model of "unceasing prayer": "After prolonged and intense chanting of psalms, weighed down by sleep, [Theognius] would [still] move his lips and utter the psalms" (20).

---

7. See, for example, in Cyril, *Life of Euthymius* 8–9, 12, 15–17 (Price, trans., 11–13, 18, 20–23) and *Life of Sabas* 16 (Price, 108–9); and see the *Life of Antony*.

Theognius the wonderworker and man of prayer has flown to God, but his example remains. His continuing presence was visibly demonstrated when, on the day he "departed from his body," a miracle of loaves similar to Jesus' feeding of the five thousand took place at the monastery (22). Theognius, like Christ, is now a model and living example by which the monks must measure themselves. At the beginning of his peroration (23) Paul asks: "Shall we be found" at our end like Theognius, "acting holy and just, or in opposition to virtue? Or shall we be seized by the most terrifying angels demanding our soul?" In a wonderfully concrete image, Paul declares that Theognius, "from the foursquare stones of virtue, built for himself a city in heaven," but we who follow after him are building from "four-cornered evil" a "dwelling place here on earth" (23).

This dichotomy between Paul and the present wicked generation is, really, the theme of the encomium. "We," Paul laments, "are idle chatterers and timid folk, grumblers and complainers." We lust after the latest gossip, while we yawn at tales of virtue. God has warned us, Paul insists, with catastrophes and plagues like he visited upon the Egyptians of old, but "remaining incorrigible, we add to our own evil" (23). Paul certainly does not flatter himself or his audience! They are like camels (23) and pigs (24): "We gladly wallow in the mire of meddlesomeness, in self-love and contentiousness, refusing . . . to raise the eye of the soul to heaven or to meditate upon any of the heavenly mysteries, always engrossed instead in earthly things and inclined toward things that are base" (24).

Paul, to his credit, presents *himself* as an example of our inattention to things spiritual as he confesses:

> Now I, worthless slave that I am, when I was praying [in church at the liturgy for Saint Theognius], while I ought to have fearfully and soberly offered up my petition with the greatest humility, instead I counted the suspended candles and the seats in the sanctuary, I calibrated precisely the planks of the roof with the main beams beneath them, and I measured with my fingers the four walls of the building of this house of prayer . . . (24).

After our delight at hearing this preacher own up to what we all have done in church, we might nevertheless smile and gently rebuke Paul for being overly serious. But Paul concludes his confession with themes of the utmost importance to monastic spirituality: "Having given up any benefit from my prayer, I reaped the harm of evil distraction. Who would not bewail, who would not lament, the lethargy of a completely wretched soul?" Distraction was—and remains—one of the chief harms to the soul. Why? Because distractions separate us, pull us away, from God.[8] Now, it is true that Paul undoubtedly idealizes Theognius; such idealizations, utterly human, go back to the beginnings of monasticism. But Paul also believes that Theognius was someone who completely dedicated his life to God and who was, therefore, completely true both to God and to himself. Isn't it just possible that such a person did exist, single-minded in his dedication to God? Our more cynical century has had Gandhi, Thomas Merton, Dorothy Day, and Martin Luther King Jr. Even though we are (sometimes obsessively) aware of their peccadillos and sins, to many they still remain models of the spiritual life, and rightly so.

By contrast, Paul pictures himself (if not rhetorically, then undoubtedly too harshly) as someone weak and failing. Therefore, he believes, he needs an intercessor before God: "Father Theognius, have mercy on me. . ." (25). The encomium, despite its insistence on sin, ends with great hope as all the righteous in heaven, Theognius among them, intercede "with the compassionate King" on behalf of all humanity. There *is* judgment, Paul insists: "for sinners, those who refused to repent until their death," God will "pour out like rain cataclysms and streams of fire." For the devout, "God comes with a multitude of angels to judge the just judgment and open the gates of his kingdom" (25). It is a familiar vision of heaven and hell—nothing original here. But Paul would not have wanted originality, and our squeamishness at God's judgment would have surprised him. To God "belongs authority over everything."

What makes Paul's encomium spiritually valuable, I believe, is his rock-solid belief in the communion of saints, in the community of God's saints living and dead, and his belief, often deemed old-fashioned now, in sanctity, in holiness of purpose, and in the purposefulness of prayer—and his willingness to call a spade a spade, not a "manual digging utensil." For Paul, sinful thoughts and actions are just that—sinful—not inadvertencies to be wished away or blamed on others. Paul's vision, finally, is a moral and ethical one, common in early monasticism, for those striving to live in godly community: Look to God first,

---

8. On distraction, see pp. 9–12 above.

not to yourself; honor your neighbor, not your own incessant whims and desires, your self-love; avoid gossip and slander and hubris; heed God's signs of displeasure. And look to God's holy ones in your midst. They are there, if you'll only see them.

Good preaching—for his day and for ours.

## The Life of Theognius[9]

Theognius is known to us primarily from the encomium by Paul and from a brief "Life of Theognius" included by Cyril of Scythopolis in *The Lives of the Monks of Palestine*. Although Cyril preserves a few details not given by Paul, his account of Theognius's life is drawn mostly from Paul's encomium.[10] Cyril in fact cuts short his narrative because Paul "has preceded me in writing the life of the same blessed Theognius both accurately and comprehensively."[11] From Cyril and Paul we can construct an outline of Theognius's life that appears to be reliable, if somewhat lacking in detail.

Theognius was born in 425 in Cappadocia; Cyril adds that he came from Ararathia. While still "a young man" Theognius "put on the monastic habit" and lived for a number of years—perhaps ten—"in solitude and quiet and in conduct proper to monks." Then, like Saint Antony, he heard "God speaking" in the scriptures: Antony heard Jesus speaking in the gospels; Theognius heard God telling Abraham to leave his homeland and go to a land that God would show him (Gen 12:1). "And immediately, as though he himself had been commanded to do this, he took himself away from his homeland and sought Jerusalem, in order to pray in the holy places . . ." (5). Cyril says that this was in the fifth year of Marcian's reign,[12] so in 454–55 Theognius became one of the many pilgrims journeying to the Holy Land.[13]

9. For an earlier summary of Theognius's life, see Van den Gheyn, "Saint Théognius," 566–76.

10. Cyril similarly epitomizes Theodore of Petra's encomium on the famous monk Theodosius, given on the first anniversary of Theodosius' death. See Van den Gheyn, "Saint Théognius," 559. Van den Gheyn, 565, believes that Paul and Cyril have independent sources. I would prefer to say that Cyril is dependent on Paul but has some independent information.

11. Cyril, *Life of Theognius* (Price, trans., 271).

12. Ibid., 269.

13. On this theme, see E. D. Hunt, *Holy Land Pilgrimage in the Later Roman Empire A.D. 312–460* (Oxford: Oxford University Press, 1982).

While in the Holy Land, Cyril says, Theognius "attached himself to a virtuous lady, protected by the Holy Spirit, called Flavia, who at this time was founding near the Mount of Olives a monastery and church of the saintly martyr Julian."[14] Melania the Elder, along with Rufinus of Aquileia, had founded a double monastery for men and women on the Mount of Olives around the year 379. Paul terms Flavia's new establishment some 75 years later as "the monastery of Flavia," although apparently nothing more is known about it, or her.[15] According to Cyril, at this time the monasteries in the Holy City were "in the control" of the Aposchists, that is, the Monophysites who opposed the Council of Chalcedon. (In Cyril's view, they had "cut themselves off" the meaning of "aposchist" from the church.) Juvenal had been restored as the Chalcedonian bishop in 453, a year or two before Theognius's arrival, but we learn from Cyril that Gerontius, the head of Melania's monasteries, was at this time strongly opposed to the Chalcedonian settlement.[16] Perhaps this is why Flavia founded a new monastery, "down the slope" from Melania's on the Mount of Olives, "in the region of Gethsemane."[17] Theognius apparently found both theological and spiritual refuge in Flavia's monastery.[18]

Cyril and Paul disagree about what happened next. Cyril states that Flavia left for her homeland on an expedition to raise funds for the monastery, and died there. After her death, Theognius, forced into becoming superior, "fled to the desert."[19] Paul says nothing about Flavia's departure or death but explains that she persuades Theognius to accept the administration of the monastery (5). Later, Theognius realizes that he has made a mistake: the "pressing business" of the monastery is distracting him from his life of prayer, and "the many praises of those honoring him" are becoming a temptation. (Cyril shifts this latter problem to the time when Theognius is at the monastery of Theodosius.) So he leaves for the desert.

Theognius travels to the monastery Theodosius had founded near

---

14. Cyril, *Life of Theognius* (Price, trans., 269).

15. Hirschfeld, *Judean Desert Monasteries,* does not mention her or the monastery.

16. Cyril, *Life of Euthymius* 27 and 30 (Price, trans., 38, 40, 46).

17. Derwas J. Chitty, *The Desert a City* (Crestwood, N.Y.: St. Vladimir's, n.d.), 93.

18. On the theological warfare in Palestine at this time and the involvement of the monks in it, see Chitty, 86–97

19. Cyril, *Life of Theognius* (Price, trans., 269).

Jerusalem.[20] Theodosius was five years younger than Theognius and had come to Jerusalem around 451. He too was from Cappadocia, and perhaps this drew Theognius to him. Around 479 Theodosius established the largest cenobium in the Judean desert "on the southern bank of the Kidron valley," three to four miles southeast of Jerusalem.[21] After staying with Theodosius awhile, Theognius once again leaves—and once again Cyril and Paul disagree as to why. According to Cyril, Theognius was "afraid of the harm his soul would naturally suffer from praise and human glory"—and besides, the monastery was getting too big.[22] Paul offers a less ascetically minded reason: because of some "growths" on his fingers, Theognius is advised to go to the Jordan region for the warm weather, and so he goes to the monastery of Calamon east of Jericho and near the Jordan River. "Afterwards," for unstated reasons, he returns to the area around the monastery of Theodosius (7).

Both sources now agree that Theognius withdraws to a cave and lives as an anchorite. Paul describes his regimen and says he "believes" that Theognius was about fifty at this time. This date (475) fits roughly, though a bit early, with the establishment of Theodosius's monastery. Perhaps Theognius came to live with Theodosius before 475 when his "monastery" was a loosely organized group of hermits attached to a master.[23] As the number of monks increased, Theodosius needed to found a cenobium. This took place around 479, and Theognius, because of this change, moved to his own cave about this time. Whatever the chronology, our sources have Theognius withdrawing to his cave around 475–80. In a pattern common in the Judean desert,[24] Theognius lives alone for awhile and then attracts disciples. Like his own master Theodosius, he too eventually founds a cenobium. Unfortunately, little is known about Theognius's monastery, and references to it are rare.[25]

20. On this monastery, see Hirschfeld, *Desert Monasteries*, 59–60, 69–70, 159–61, 198–99, and the index, 304.

21. Ibid., 15.

22. Cyril, *Life of Theognius* (Price, trans., 269).

23. Van den Gheyn, "Saint Théognius," 569, suggests that Theognius came to the monastery of Theodosius around 456, but admits that our imprecise sources forbid an exact dating.

24. See Hirschfeld, *Desert Monasteries*, 69–70.

25. Virgilio Corbo believes he has identified Theognius's monastery at Khirbet Makhrum, about one and a half miles southwest of the site of Theodosius's monastery. It was a medium-sized monastery, with an area of 1,500 square meters. See Corbo, *Gli Scavi di*

Some twenty years later when Theognius was around 70, Elias, archbishop of Jerusalem, heard about the famous monk and ordained him bishop.[26] In western Europe, Cassian warned his monks to flee women and bishops, but among those monks who later revered his writings in Gaul, many accepted the episcopacy.[27] In Palestine in the fifth and sixth centuries, although the earlier tradition of monks refusing ordination continued, many monks were ordained and a number of them became bishops.[28]

Theognius, according to our accounts, apparently accepted his episcopal calling with equanimity, becoming bishop of Bethelia on the Gaza coast, "a small seaside town ninety miles distant from the Holy City."[29] Neither source offers many details about Theognius's episcopate, which is surprising since the Monophysite controversy was raging throughout Palestine during Theognius's episcopacy.[30] According to Paul, Theognius travels to Constantinople during the reign of Emperor Anastasius (491–518), perhaps to plea for a reduction in the city's taxes,[31] and again at the beginning of the reign of Emperor Justin, in 518 (11, 21).[32] At the end of his life, both sources agree, Theognius returned to his monastery. (Cyril says that "after a short illness," he died there.)[33] Paul places his death "on the eighth day of February, in the fifteenth indiction": February 8, 522 (21).[34] He was ninety-seven years old. "He returned dust for dust," Paul states simply, "but his spirit, like pure gold, he placed in the hands of the Savior . . ." (21).

---

*Kh. Siyar El-Ghanam (Campo dei Pastori) e i Monasteri dei Dintorni* (Jerusalem: Tipografia dei PP Francescani, 1955), 151–55, esp. 155, and Hirschfeld, 260 n. 5. John Moschus refers to "Abba Paul, higoumen of the monastery of Abba Theognius." See *The Spiritual Meadow* 160 (Wortley, trans., p. 132).

26. Elias was archbishop from 494–518, so Theognius became bishop after 494. Van den Gheyn, "Saint Théognius," 572, dates his episcopacy from 494/5–522.

27. See Robert Markus, *The End of Ancient Christianity* (Cambridge: Cambridge University Press, 1990), esp. 199–202.

28. Juvenal, bishop of Jerusalem, tried to ordain Peter the Iberian, but Peter, after finding out about the plan, jumped from a roof and escaped. He was later ordained but refused to celebrate the Eucharist. See Chitty, *The Desert*, 87–88. Conversely, "Archbishop Juvenal ordained Stephen of Melitene bishop of Jamnia; Cosmas the Cappadocian he ordained priest and made guardian of the cross" (Cyril, *Life of Euthymius* 20 [Price, trans., 29]). Antipatrus ordained Gaianus bishop of Medaba (*Euthymius* 34 [Price, trans., 49]). Monks also became bishops of the Encampments and Scythopolis.

29. Cyril, *Life of Theognius* (Price, trans., 270). Bethelia has a wide variety of spellings, ancient and modern. See Van den Gheyn, "Saint Théognius," 571–72.

30. For brief treatments of the controversy, see Van den Gheyn, "Saint Théognius," 573–74; M. Simonetti, "Monophysism—Monophysites," *Encyclopedia of the Early Church*, ed. Angelo Di Berardino (New York: Oxford University Press, 1992), 569–70; W. H. C. Frend,

# AN ENCOMIUM ON THE LIFE OF
# SAINT THEOGNIUS,
# BISHOP OF BETHELIA[1]

## Translated with William Morison

*The life and ascetic practice of our father Theognius,*
*the ascetic and anchorite, who became bishop of Bethelia,*
*and who is among the saints.*
*Bless us, father.*[2]

## I. Prologue[3]

1. "Let your light shine before others, so that they may see your good works and give glory to your father in heaven,"[4] Christ, the glorious king, commanded his disciples. Because these men gladly received the divine command, they gloriously illuminated all that is under the sun with the brightness of their own accomplishments. Having fulfilled blamelessly the duty enjoined upon them, they departed their own

---

*The Rise of Christianity* (Philadelphia: Fortress Press, 1984), 837–40; and John Meyendorff, *Imperial Unity and Christian Divisions: The Church 450–680* (Crestwood, N.Y.: St. Vladimir's, 1989), 202–6. For more detailed discussion, see Frend, *The Rise of the Monophysite Movement* (Cambridge: Cambridge University Press, 1972).

31. See Cyril, *Life of Sabas* 54 (Price, trans., 155), where Sabas goes on such a mission to see Anastasius. See also Van den Gheyn, "Saint Théognius," 573.

32. For a discussion of a council held in Jerusalem at this time, and the curious absence of Theognius as a signatory to it, see Van den Gheyn, "Saint Théognius," 573–74.

33. Cyril, *Life of Theognius* (Price, trans., 271).

34. On the date, see Van den Gheyn, "Saint Théognius," 574.

1. The translation is based on the text published by J. Van den Gheyn, "Acta Sancti Theognii," *Analecta Bollandiana* 10 (1891): 73–113, and his corrections in *Analecta Bollandiana* 11 (1892): 476–77, supplemented by the text edited by M. Papadopoulos-Kerameus (with a Russian translation by M. G. Destouni) in *Pravoslavnyi Palestinskii Sbornik* 32 (1891): 1–21.

2. This is the Greek title, but since the work is clearly an Encomium and not a "life," for our title we have decided to follow Van den Gheyn, who titles the piece in Latin, "An Encomium Concerning Saint Theognius Given by Paul, a Monk of Elusa."

3. Section titles are those of Van den Gheyn; however, we have used "Peroration" instead of "Epilogue" for chapters 23–25. Paragraph titles are the present translators'.

4. Mt 5:16.

honored bodies—God-made works, the very ones that the ancient law called "rams' skins dyed red"[5]—and like the fire-breathing prophet Elijah, left their mantle upon the ground.[6] Rejoicing before the Creator of the universe, they stood fearlessly at the kingly and indescribable throne.

But indeed not to the apostles alone has faith in God been given and the keeping of his commandments and the rewards for personal struggles and toils that are reaped at the right hand of the omnipotent, but also to the disciples after them and to those who have become imitators of the Word. Paul, of course, the great herald of Christ, having watered the churches with streams of godly teaching flowing with honey, wishing to demonstrate this said, "I have fought the good fight," and then, "From now on there is reserved for me the crown of righteousness, which the Lord, the righteous judge, will give me on that day, and not only to me, but also to all who have longed for his appearing."[7]

2. So it was also for Theognius, the Cappadocian: Clasped by gentle talons with desire for the Lord and fulfilling the saying of Jeremiah, "As for me, I have not grown weary following after you,"[8] having adorned himself with good works, both with celibacy and everything else pleasing to God, and having made fragrant his own soul and all who knew him, he "renewed his strength,"[9] as Isaiah says, and, like an eagle having grown its feathers, he was joyously freed from the shackles of his body and [flew up] to heaven, leaving for posterity his own memory like some resplendent monument.

3. I, therefore, reckoning what has been said about this remarkable man, both how purely and incorruptibly he lived and how humble he was, and how night and day with the greatest suffering of heart and abundant tears he [sacrificed himself] completely for the sake of sinners, and reflecting on what sort of ineffable, eternal tabernacles and indestructible kingdoms he now resides in with the angels, knowing my own indolence and the abyss of unquenchable fire and those unceasing torments into which I think I shall be delivered, I wished just now to be silent before you (for the law decreed that one wounded

---

5. Ex 25:5; 26:14.
6. 2 Kings 2:11–14.
7. 2 Tim 4:7, 8.
8. Jer 17:16 (LXX).
9. Is 41:1.

by sin shut his mouth with a cover of silence), to seal myself in a dark cave, and to weep unceasingly and beat my breast. For I know, I know, and I am reproved by my conscience, that I have traveled carelessly the path of my present life, having despised the saying advising me to turn my foot from the difficult path and to traverse the easy one.[10] But lest I cause this assembly of your venerable love gathered before me to grow sad and the holy men gathered here for the sake of remembrance to be disappointed, I shall attempt to speak concisely and briefly, with the deepest sorrow at spreading about a cloud of faintheartedness.

4. Moreover, when the commemoration of Theognius, who is for everyone the dearest of perfumes, is borne upon the lips, let the chorus of heavenly stars be delighted and exult. Let the earth be joyous, the air be mirthful, especially when the incorporeal powers rejoice together in the memory of this man of God. Those, moreover, who saw this man contending like an athlete during his life were amazed how one bearing a bodily frame could be arrayed in battle against disembodied enemies and how this lowly man, pitiful and penniless, beat, bound hand and foot, trampled beneath him, and took captive the rulers and authorities, both the cosmic powers of darkness and the spiritual forces of evil.[11]

## II. The Ascetic Life of Saint Theognius
### Theognius Becomes Head of the "Monastery of Flavia"

5. Theognius was raised in his homeland, Cappadocia. In that land, while he was a young man, he put on the monastic habit. Then, having spent some time in solitude and quiet[12] and in conduct proper to monks, he heard God speaking to the patriarch Abraham in the scripture: "Go out from your country and from your kindred, and go to the land that I will show you."[13] And immediately, as though he himself had been commanded to do this, he took himself away from his homeland and sought Jerusalem, in order to pray in the holy places,[14] and

---

10. Is 40:4; Jer 2:25.
11. Eph 6:12.
12. "Solitude and quiet": Greek *hēsuchia*.
13. Gen 12:1.
14. On the gradual sanctifying of the holy places in Palestine and the important role of the monks in that process, see Robert L. Wilken, *The Land Called Holy* (New Haven and London: Yale Univ. Press, 1992), esp. 149–92.

there he was received by pious men in the place called "the monastery of Flavia."[15] Having lived in that place and holding to his accustomed quiet and gentleness, he benefited everyone who lived with him, and he resolved to give offense to no one, not even once. Then, within a short time, the Christ-loving woman who founded the monastery through her entreaties persuaded him to be in charge of the administration of the place, the very monastery that is outside the Holy City in the place called Gethsemane. Afterwards, the man properly administered the place called "the monastery" and its brotherhood.

## An Old Man Advises Theognius to Seek the Desert

6. Afterwards, having reflected that he was being distracted, and that he had quickly turned away from peaceful prayer to God and instruction in Holy Scripture, both on account of a plentiful abundance of duties and because the monks were always coming to visit and the laity were disturbing him (at that time the monastery was located near the city), he was afraid that at some point his way of life would be weakened by the incessant uproar and amount of pressing business—and not only by these but also because of the many praises of those honoring him—and that he would do or consider something unworthy of his high calling. And so, appealing to one of the highly regarded old men to consider his concerns, he revealed his secrets. The old man then gave an answer such as follows: "Those who want to keep their own soul blameless before the Almighty—as you seem to me to want to do—do not entangle themselves with business affairs. Even if possessions should seem a concern for monks, nevertheless leave these things to indifferent people, those able to be distracted without harm. Even those who have possessed the virtue of being free from business still desire to avoid the circumstances of the multitude, so that the lamp is not hidden by the shadow of the bed or of the basket[16]—if indeed a bed and a bushel basket are evidence of laziness and the love of business. But often the shining light is extinguished when some strong gust suddenly comes upon it. If, therefore, you obey me, you will leave this place and dwell in the desert." Theognius replied to this:

---

15. Cyril of Scythopolis, *Life of Theognius* (Price, trans., 269), says that this took place in the fifth year of the reign of Marcian or 454/5.

16. See Mt 5:15.

"I completely accept the advice of your holy soul, but I'm afraid of suffering and hard work." And the old man said to him, "If you are being led by love for God himself, and not by empty glory, you will seek the desert. Seek suffering, and you will find relief; but if you seek rest, you will be defeated by sufferings."

## Theognius Goes to the Caves of Calamon

7. Having heard this, the blessed man embraced the old man and went out into the desert, and having attached himself to the most God-loving and holy archimandrite Theodosius, a famous man, he lived with him a certain number of years. Then, a certain trial came upon him: some growths appeared on Theognius's finger and, becoming seriously inflamed, burst, so that each day a great deal of blood poured from that area. While he was suffering from this, then, a certain person experienced in such matters gave him this advice: "Since the hill country is very cold, but the suffering gripping you needs warmer airs, go into the Jordanian regions, and there within a few days, you will be healed." And so having gone down there, he lived in the laura of Calamon,[17] and he was freed very quickly from the suffering. And he lovingly devoted himself to solitude and to his prayers.

## Theognius and the Serpent

Now a most fearsome serpent was accustomed, before the arrival of Theognius, to lurk in that cave[18] and slither out into the desert from that place after sleeping and to come back again from the desert into it. The serpent had gone outside on the day when the blessed man first received the cell from his superior at the monastery, and it saw him sitting inside holding his baskets and working on them.[19] (For, indeed, he did not cease working until the end of his life, but would work—unless someone disturbed him—and he steeped his entire handicraft with tears.) When the beast put its head within the entryway but kept the

---

17. For the location of the monasteries of Theodosius and of Calamon, see the map in Hirschfeld, *Desert Monasteries,* xviii–xix. For further information on these monasteries, see Hirschfeld's index.

18. For a description of the remains of some caves at Calamon, see Hirschfeld, *Desert Monasteries,* 180.

19. For a discussion of the practice of basket-weaving and its place in the monastery of Theodosius, see Hirschfeld, *Desert Monasteries,* 105.

rest of its body outside of the cell and, waiting without moving, saw Theognius all alone, the blessed man said to it, "If you are accustomed to stay inside, come on in; I won't bother you." And, to be sure, it slithered its whole body inside and coiled itself into one corner and was quiet. From that day on, then, it continued this practice: It entered whenever it wanted to, and the holy man remained undaunted until the day he departed from there.

## Theognius Leaves Calamon and Inhabits a Cave

8. Afterwards, by the grace of Providence, he left Calamon and occupied this place here. And having found a cave, he lived in it by himself, satisfying his hunger with a small piece of bread and a few carob and quenching the natural compulsion of thirst with a cup of water,[20] waging war continuously against demons who were fighting against him by means of impure thoughts. And truly, like a shining star come to earth, he was attending to his quiet contemplation and asceticism in the cave, persevering in his fasts with prostrations and wailing, with vigils and numerous genuflections, and by prayerfully reciting the utterances[21] of the Spirit. I believe he had reached at that time the fiftieth year of his life. Many came to him, wishing to be helped, for his fame had traveled. And each of those who came on account of a variety of sufferings, having found comfort for his soul and sufficient relief, departed with joy.

## After Defeating the Devil
## Theognius Builds a Tower There

9. One night the deceitful one cast upon him fearful thoughts, and after this, when darkness is deepest, in very truth made a Saracen appear, who, with sword drawn, threatened that if Theognius did not quickly leave the cave, he would immediately cut off his head. As a result, having become filled with fear, the man fled from the cave and beseeched God to give him aid. And, indeed, immediately an angel appeared to him and said to him with a very stern voice: "You seem to

20. Hirschfeld, *Desert Monasteries,* 87, provides a brief discussion of this passage within the context of monastic diet; see 96 for a discussion of the cup.

21. Greek *logioi,* that is, scriptures.

me to be completely terrified. Enter the cave. You've been afraid over nothing at all, for he is not, as you think, a Saracen, but is an unclean spirit who has transformed himself into the guise of a Saracen."

Suddenly the fear left him. He gained boldness and a certain inexpressible joy, and the demon took to his feet. As a result, the man became famous for his noble way of life, and certain Christ-loving men came and, vigorously entreating him, persuaded him to build a suitable little tower,[22] which very thing happened. And although many wished to remain with him, never did he allow himself to mix with a large crowd, but having received a certain few, he spent his time with them, performing the offices[23] required by ascetics with the fear of God.

## III. Saint Theognius as Bishop of Bethelia
### Theognius Becomes Bishop of Bethelia

10. And after a period of time elapsed, at the prompting of some and the force and compulsion imposed upon him by the order of the one holding the patriarchal throne in Jerusalem[24] at that time, he became the bishop of the church in Bethelia.[25] The city itself was very small, ninety miles distant from here.[26] Thus, he spent a certain amount of time in that city, and a certain amount of time coming here and living happily with his own children. The church itself had already been founded and, indeed, was small at first, but later, about ten years before the death of the holy man, had become larger. For this reason, the number of pious monks also increased at that time by the will of God. This blessed man was accustomed to inhabit the smallest cell

---

22. Sabas built a tower that served as his cell. See Cyril, *Life of Sabas* 18 (Price, trans., 111–12), in a passage similar to the one here: "Above the church built by God there is an extremely high and abrupt crag; on this our father Sabas built himself a tower. . . . Here he would stay for the office and the rest of the administration. Since his fame spread everywhere, many came to him bringing plentiful offerings. . . ." There was a "laura of the towers," so named because its cells "may have been two or even three stories high, in contrast to the simpler cells in other lauras, which had only a single story" (Hirschfeld, *Desert Monasteries*, 173).

23. Greek *leitourgias*.

24. That is, Elias (patriarch from 494–518), a defender of the Council of Chalcedon. See Cyril, *Life of Theognius* (Price, trans., 270). See Chitty, *The Desert*, 110–11 and 113–16 for a discussion of his role in the political and theological battles of the time.

25. Thus, Theognius was sixty-nine or seventy when he became bishop. On the name "Bethelia," see note 29 above.

26. Ninety Roman miles.

when he came from Bethelia to spend some time here, and it was built so low that unless the one entering it paid attention, he would bump his head against the roof.

So, having come up here from the plain, and having entered the place called "the cell," he would raise his hands and give thanks to the Lord, and afterwards he would say: "Greetings, my kingdom; for truly, truly I think that this old and little dwelling of mine is a kingdom. And like someone having been storm-tossed on the great sea and so having been saved from the surf, I flee into the harbor of the little cell so I can return to my former state of mind." But a certain one of the brothers, having spoken freely, said to him once, "You, father, at such an old age and after having overcome all the adverse passions, should not still hold before your eyes, as I think you do, that which is spiritually harmful, but both in your city and here you should keep to the same sensible conditions." The noble old man said to him, "Believe, son, that until the time my soul departs from my body, I have no security, courage is not at hand; for we clothe ourselves in flesh, and making our way among the various traps, we are afraid of getting ensnared."

## Theognius Meets the Emperor in Byzantium

11. At the time when Anastasius was emperor,[27] the inhabitants of Bethelia decided that the great man, for the purpose of public business, should sail to the royal city of cities.[28] And so, being of good courage and in the company of certain brothers, he sailed to Byzantium. When he arrived at the great city and met the emperor, after the customary address he presented three gifts to him, placing them in a little napkin. And the emperor said, "Do you wish me to take only the presents or this napkin also, which has been spread under them?"[29] He replied to the emperor, "If the napkin pleases you," he said, "I gladly offer it to you as a gift." At this the emperor smiled and embraced him and gladly received the things presented to him, and he inquired about all of his business, an annoyance that the old man

27. That is, 491–518.
28. Ibid.
29. This statement was far less strange to its contemporary audience than it most likely is to us. Giving napkins as gifts has literary antecedents at least as far back as the Roman poet Catullus (first century B.C.E.).

patiently endured. And soon, having handled himself well, within a few days with every honor and full provisions for the journey, he sailed back to Bethelia. The many cures and marvels, however, that God, who loves humanity, demonstrated through him at that time in Constantinople (for most of those living there came to knowledge) I omit by silence, leaving these for others to relate.

## Theognius and the Miracle of the Ships

12. Keeping silent about most of what happened in Caesarea, Askalon, and Gaza, I shall now reveal a very few things. At Maiouma in Gaza[30] two ships were being built by men who were believers, and these ships were made ready on the beach the way they should have been. But when their captains wished the ships to be dragged down into the sea and commanded an innumerable multitude for this purpose, the men were unable to move them at all because the hulls were being interfered with by the plotting of evil people with certain incantations. As a result, having battled vigorously for many days with the aid of the multitude and having met with uncountable losses and, finally, having driven themselves to dejection and despair, they did not know what they should do. But after a certain good man offered his opinion to those who were suffering, the blessed one was persuaded and came to the place, and with the weapons of prayer against the sorcery of the foul ones, stood in battle array. Circling the merchant ships a second and a third time and calling upon the name of Christ, he commanded that the ships be launched into the sea, with each of them employing only thirty laborers. But one owner contradicted him: "Every day these past days I've furnished two hundred able men, and I haven't helped at all; and now how can a ship be launched by only thirty men?" The old man said to him, "Do what I have told you, and quit talking so much." And having said this, he went in silence to his own cell. Then the captains of the ships did what had been commanded. With a few tugs they easily and quickly dragged the ships down to the sea. And immediately amazement gripped those present, and racing up to the old man's dwelling, they were embracing him reverently, like one of the glorious apostles, and bringing gifts.

---

30. See Van den Gheyn, "Acta Sancti Theognii," 91 n.2, for a discussion of this site and the various other sites named Maiouma in ancient times.

## Two Healing Miracles

13. Among these people was a certain God-loving woman. Having buried a certain member of her family long before, while grieving at the grave of the dead man with an inconsolate heart, she had clouded her eyes and saw nothing at all of visible things. Having learned of his righteousness and having acquired a guide, she hastily came to him and, grasping his head, with a cry she began to rub her eyes against the forehead of the old man. The cloudiness dissipated, and all of a sudden she could see. She cried out to the astounded multitude because of the unexpectedness of the miracle, "Glory to you, Lord, the worker of wonders!" So many fell upon him, from his head to his feet, kissing every part of the righteous man's body, that he was very nearly suffocated, except, having quickly recovered himself, he stripped off his cloak and left it behind for the mob. Rushing into the chapel of a certain martyr's shrine, he escaped from the danger. Back in Caesarea, the governor's wife's breast had become swollen, like a wine sack, because of some condition. All the doctors there had tried countless remedies and had been unable to heal her, and this condition the blessed Theognius healed by genuflecting three times and by a stream of tears and the anointing of consecrated oil.[31]

## The Miracle of the Sea [32]

14. A miracle he performed in Bethelia became known not only on the coast but also in nearly all of Egypt and Cilicia and Cappadocia, and Byzantium itself rejoiced at the news. The neighboring sea, having passed beyond its boundaries, dashed against the little city with an army of the roughest waves, threatening to root out and obliterate it by its violent pounding. But this happened entirely through divine dispensation, in order that even sinners might be chastened by fear and the grace given by justice might be glorified all the more. Thus, all the inhabitants of those places fell into a trembling of the hands and a weakening of the knees when they saw such wrath being unleashed upon them more and more, about to crest. Because of this, with

---

31. See van den Gheyn, "Acta Sancti Theognii," 93 n.1, for a discussion of other stories of miraculous cures through the use of consecrated oil, and for examples, Vivian and Athanassakis, *The Life of Saint George of Choziba*, 102-3.

32. Cyril, *Life of Theognius* (Price, trans., 270), repeats this story.

numerous lamentations they entreated the servant of Christ to check the onslaught of the sea through prayer. So the old man rose and went down with them. He proceeded up to a certain place, and extending those holy hands in prayer and placing his faith in God who said, "Look, even while you are still speaking, here I am,"[33] he planted a cross in that place and proclaimed words like these to those present: "We enjoy unceasingly the aid of the master of the universe; however much the sea might rage, it will come only as far as this cross. Therefore, my children, proceed fearlessly in the future, fearing only the act of sinning but dreading not at all the threat of the sea." For this very reason, from that time up to the present the great man's word, made firm by the power of the Almighty, has stood uncorrupted, indissoluble, undiminished.

## The Miracle of Theognius's Broken Foot

15. Again one time, having resolved to visit us and make clear his counsel to his followers (at that time he was in the Holy City), he saw Satan speaking to him in a dream: "Because you plan to visit your own monastery[34] after being away awhile and are happy about this, I will turn your joy into sorrow."[35] Thus, at daybreak, seated upon an ass, he left the city with two acolytes, and, indeed, when they had come as far as the place immediately opposite the monastery of the blessed Abba Eustathius,[36] the right foot of the beast slipped, and it happened that he rolled off and fell into the drainage ditch running alongside the road and the noble old man's foot was immediately fractured. When the brothers climbed down there, they found that the ass had gotten up and was standing, but the old man was lying in agony and breathing hard because of the pain of the fracture. Immediately one of the attendants, having a small linen cloth in his hands, bound up the old man's foot, and they put him on the animal and with sad faces brought him home to us.

As it turned out, because he was in pain and was groaning steadily, all of us embraced sorrow instead of joy. We then summoned from the city a man knowledgeable in the treatment of fractures. That man

33. Is 58:9.
34. Literally "sheepfold" (Greek *mandra*), used in patristic Greek of monasteries (here and in paragraph 16) and of the church.
35. See Prov 14:13 (LXX).
36. This monastery is apparently unknown.

came and did all the proper things correctly, remaining a day and a half. He returned to the city, having first bound the fractured foot with certain reeds and ordering Theognius not to move at all until many days had passed. And he ordered a clay pot put beneath the bed, which had a hole bored through it, so that whenever Theognius had the need, lying in bed without moving he might relieve his bowels.[37] (Now why God, the ruler of all, at the appropriate time permits Satan to strike his chosen, let this be sought out another time.) A second day, then, he remained motionless in bitter pain, and the third night an angel stood beside him in silence and removed the sheet covering him (since it was summer) and said to the old man in a gentle voice: "Your pain has ceased. Fear nothing; you are well." And having said this, he drove the pains from him and departed. Immediately the great man called out and related these things to us and tested whether he could now move his foot, and he was fully able to. So he sat up and took a cane and walked unhindered and without pain, except that the fearful memory of his previous suffering made him limp a little. After a few days he traveled to Bethelia, and all of us, together with the doctor, who, indeed, had tended to the fracture, raised our voices full of thanks to the all powerful Lord Christ for the unexpected and swift recovery of the great man.

## The Wondrous Appearance of a Dove

16. And there was a certain other miracle that should be told presently. For from the day when the doctor forbade him to walk until the appearance of the angel, a beautiful dove was seen one time by everyone as it flew in the air above the monastery and another time as it was sitting quietly in the eastern window at the feet of the holy man until the great man was relieved of his pains. And after this the above-mentioned dove disappeared. Thus, the great man said about it: "Don't be surprised, my children, that it has disappeared, for evidently it has gone to aid others also."

## Concerning Arrogance and Humility

17. Alexander, our generation's honored pearl, both the advocate of the Askalonians and counted among the lovers of solitude and the virtu-

---

37. For a discussion of this passage and the use of beds and chamber pots in the daily lives of the monks, see Hirschfeld, *Desert Monasteries*, 94–97.

ous fathers, was truly beloved not only by believers because of the great nobility of his own character and works and his deep love of the good, but also by unbelievers. When, a long time ago, I left Greece and arrived in Palestine, when I met the man, I asked where I needed to bind myself in order to gain spiritual benefits. He said to me, "Join lord Theognius, and you will benefit from it in every way; and if you should choose to remain in his monastery, you will be indebted to me for the good advice. Join Theognius, and you will know God, being led to life by such a great man as he. Aemilianus, a good pastor, as I have heard, more than adequately anointed your soul with the fear of God. But if now you see lord Theognius, you will be more secure, for the man has preached most often about humility. Moreover, since the human race, being self-important, is easily dragged into false pretension, we need not the empty words of teachers but works of the cultivators[38] of humility, which is the best fruit. That man Jacob, the vanquisher of the passions,[39] circumcised the flesh of the foreskin,[40] just as his ancestors. We too ought to emulate the patriarch according to the spirit, cutting off our own pleasures of the flesh with the sharp blade of self-control. Or again, at another time someone touched the flat part of his thigh, and immediately this was sufficient.[41] We, therefore, also benefit by always accepting, in the manner of a touch, the word of humility—that which has been fixed and perfectly joined together in its interior disposition—in order that through it, the breadth[42] and diffusion of foolish conceit might be emptied out within, and the mind, drawn together into itself, might be enabled to apprehend its own limits and advance like Christ, who humbled himself for us[43] and served his own servants and redeemed the sons of humanity from shameful servitude to the demons. And if, servant of God, you flee to him, desiring both exile and poverty, he will gladly open the doors of compassion for you."[44]

38. Greek *geōrgountōn* (*geōrgein*) is a common metaphor in patristic literature for Christian teachers and ascetics.

39. "Vanquisher": Greek *pternistēs*, literally "one who trips up," an epithet applied especially to Jacob in patristic writing (see Gen 35:25).

40. Gen 17:11.

41. Although "his" is as ambiguous in the Greek as in the English, the reference is undoubtedly to Gen 32:35 (LXX 32:36), when the man wrestling with Jacob "touched the flat part of his thigh."

42. There is a play on words crucial to this exegesis of Gen 32:25 (LXX: 32:26): "breadth" translates *to platos*, the same word used when the man touched the flat part (*tou platous*) of Jacob's thigh.

43. Phil 2:8.

44. See Mt 7:7.

## Wondrous Acts of Theognius

18. Theognius, who by himself with the help of the Almighty cut away pleasure and empty glory, the roots and nurturers of all sins, as though cutting off the heads of two serpents doing harm to many, this lord Theognius, the unguent of monks, relieved my brother Andronicus from the disease of dysentery and its unspeakable stench. He also against all hopes raised the son of Aelian, a lover of Christ and an advocate at Gaza, who had been completely despaired of. He is the one who through prayer granted childbirth to sterile women. Certain evil men once broke into the house of a virtuous person in the middle of the night and, more than that, planned to carry off the goods that they found. Theognius, who is equal to the angels, appeared and roused the master of the house from his deep sleep, and they thwarted the robbery and delivered the housebreakers, bound, into the hands of pious men.

Again, a certain ascetic, a marvelous man who possessed not a little of the higher knowledge, was a guest at my house when he was gripped by some abominable suffering. I brought to him at various times all the doctors of the city and procured a number of things for the sake of a cure but was unable to help the man at all, and I suffered terribly listening to those inflamed cries and the constant wailing of the ascetic. Certain luminaries of the city and those Greeks who offer sacrifices and libations at Askalon came to visit him (they already knew the ascetic), but they were unable to effect anything through their medicine. They could only weep together in sympathy with the suffering man. A little later, when the great man was present at Bethelia, I summoned him and entreated [. . . .][45] they were brought under control. For he was emphatically not a lover of money, but was compassionate, if anyone is, both sympathetic and charitable.

## Theognius Frees a Clergyman from the Dux Antipater

19. Antipater,[46] just now entrusted with the office of *dux*, you know well. He possessed great severity and insolence, as the people of that

---

45. Van den Gheyn, "Acta Sancti Theognii," 101 n.1, believes that a folio has fallen out of the manuscript here and thus a page of our text is missing. A lacuna also exists here in Papadopoulos-Kerameus's text.

46. This Antipater, governor of Palestine, is mentioned nowhere else. See Van den Gheyn, "Acta Sancti Theognii," 101 n.2.

time used to affirm who saw him in the city (for I myself was living in the desert and did not see the man's face). A clergyman from Bethelia was brought up on a certain charge and was remanded to the *dux*, and by that man's order he remained in jail, expecting to face even the danger of death. All of his friends stayed away out of fear, and no one could help—or would. But the blessed Theognius by himself took the trouble to go to the *dux* on behalf of this fellow. And though a number of people were hindering him and saying to him, "Please take care of yourself, father, and stay here; if, on his account, you go to Antipater, you will be undeservedly insulted and driven away, since it is the man's habit always to dishonor men who are lovers of virtue," the noble old man replied, "I have not desired honor from people up to now; I will hasten, therefore, through the compassion of Christ, to free this man, seized by an unforeseen misfortune, from affliction; and if because of this I should come to dishonor and abuse, I will not be pained at all, but will be joyous."

After saying these things, he went to the *dux*. When that man saw from a distance that the great man was coming, he came running up to meet him and embraced him and affectionately kissed him. The old man immediately addressed the *dux* on behalf of the man locked up in prison, and Antipater said, "Wait, father, first let a meal be made ready for us, and I will receive a blessing from your hands at the table, and afterwards I will give an answer that will please you." And so it was, and they reclined together, Antipater at one end, and Theognius at this end of the couch, and they shared the meal. And while they were eating, Antipater swore a truly awe-inspiring oath as follows: "Many days ago Christ revealed to me the sight of your honorable person. And now, as a result, I see you dining with me and speaking to me! For this reason I was passionately seeking from that time to see you with my own eyes. And now, look—my desire has been fulfilled, and I have gained your blessing. Therefore, let your clergyman be freed from prison from now on. Nor, from this time and in perpetuity may he be suspected of a single charge." And so, taking the clergyman from Antipater, the blessed man returned to his own church, glorifying the Lord.

## Tears Lead One to Love

20. I often saw that blessed man drenched in tears and beseeching God on behalf of the entire world. May we also offer to the Judge a

bowl[47] of forgiveness mixed with wailing and inexpressible laments in order that in the future we might share from it in the great rejoicing of the righteous. For we see in the Gospels that those who are laughing are considered wretched while those who suffer are blessed.[48] Again, I observed that the aforementioned man, after prolonged and intense chanting of psalms, weighed down by sleep, would move his lips and utter the psalms. He would praise and marvel at all the virtues, but especially poverty and temperance[49] in eating. He constantly admonished those obedient to him to oppose foolish chatter and to keep the mind fixed on the holy teachings in order that through them, one could each day possess tears, for unless one desired, through the burning of these tears I mentioned earlier, to oppose the soul's passions, he would not be able to possess love, the very thing which is the fulfillment of the law.[50]

## Theognius Is Honored in Byzantium; His Death

21. At the beginning of the reign of the emperor Justin,[51] again compelled by some urgent matter, he went down to Constantinople and was honored above all the other bishops that could be found there at that time. It happened that the emperor himself learned about the virtues of the man from certain members of the senate who especially revered Theognius. The emperor granted the petition for which he had come to Byzantium, and with the greatest honors, along with the entire senate he reverently honored the holy man and dismissed him.

He sailed healthy and happy to Bethelia and came up here and embraced his children and once again eagerly returned to his own city. Then, after a short time, he came up to us, and when the length of his life was completed, having sailed the fearsome sea of this transient life, like a good helmsman and captain on it, he brought the ship of his prosperous soul, laden with virtues, safely into the port of Christ. He returned dust for dust, but his spirit, like pure gold, he placed in the hands of the Savior, having completed a course of ninety-seven years on the eighth day of February, in the fifteenth indiction.[52]

47. Greek *phialē*, an interesting term, since a *phialē* was a bowl used to offer libations to the gods.

48. Lk 6:21, 25.

49. Greek *enkrateia*, so possibly "abstinence."

50. Rom 13:10.

51. That is, probably in 518.

52. Thus, Theognius died on February 8, 522.

## Wonders Concerning the Holy Man

22. A drought occurred at the time of the death of the holy man, and when the cistern[53] that held the rain water was about to give out and the brothers were seeking to leave because of the lack of drinking water, one week after the mortal end of the great man a cloud full of rain raced in from the west. It had sprinkled with very small drops the regions through which it had passed, but when it came here and stood above the mountain, it poured out so great an abundance of rainwater that it burst the canals through which the water was accustomed to run because they could not contain the violent deluge. An amount sufficient for our needs had flowed into the cistern, and the excess was diverted away by the hands of the brothers from the walls and dispersed here and there, for they were afraid that that great mass of water, if it collected within the buildings, might undermine the foundations of the monastery.[54]

These things took place, then, seven days after the repose of the holy man. But on the very day in which the servant of God departed from his body, an enormous multitude rushed together here. But the cellarer had only the bread from two ovens, which would have been sufficient for fourteen days' sustenance for our ascetics alone, but when the entire crowd that had come here had dined and everyone was full, the pieces of bread that remained were gathered by us, and they miraculously sufficed another two weeks for the fathers with us.[55]

Not long afterwards, a certain merchant who briefly went up to the Holy City for prayer reported to its inhabitants that two months earlier he had been sailing along the shore when he saw a spout rising from the sea and with his sailors heard a voice saying, "Draw the water quickly, and carry it to the monastery of Theognius." When the citizens heard what was said, they realized that the water that had been given to us earlier through the ministrations of the cloud was what was being referred to by the man; and quickly rushing here, they recounted what had been said.

53. For a description of cisterns, see Hirschfeld, *Desert Monasteries*, 156–61.
54. For a brief discussion of this passage in the context of the maintenance of the water systems in monasteries, see Hirschfeld, *Desert Monasteries*, 149.
55. See Mt 14:13–21 and parallels.

## IV. Peroration

23. Thus, father Theognius, now that you have left behind the toiling sea filled with shipwrecks and anxieties and have come within to that undisturbed life, may you rest from now on for all eternity in pure joy and unceasing delight. We, however, still sailing the sea of human life, experience daily the disturbance, agitation, and bitterness of such great waves and, in the meantime, do not know what sort of end we shall find to our life. Shall we be found, at that time, acting holy and just, or in opposition to virtue? Or shall we be seized by the most terrifying angels demanding our soul? Oh, the vain work of the present age! Oh, the pleasure filled with every kind of woe! Oh, the treachery and great derision! We neglect virtue, which is wholly blessed and glorious, and gaping at those things that have lost their mooring, we wander about among things unstable. Theognius, from the foursquare stones of virtue, built for himself a city in heaven, but we, through the wicked agency of the enemy, are making from four-cornered evil and completely unalterable calculations a generally accommodating and unshakable dwelling place[56] here on earth. For, those who love wealth and the applause of their fellow citizens and eloquent activities have made themselves foreigners and strangers to the holy love of the Almighty.

We are idle chatterers and timid folk, grumblers and complainers. If someone relates worldly and shameful stories not at all beneficial to the soul but rather harmful to it, all of us, agape, eagerly accept the report with its wicked words, alert[57] for what is evil. Oftentimes someone will offer a story of conversion and salvation and we, having yawned four or five times while emitting a roar from our mouth just like camels, and having picked at our beards with our nails, give ourselves over to a deep and deathlike sleep. We have without a doubt plugged the ears of the heart, so that a story beneficial to the soul never sneaks through and enters into the storeroom of our understanding.

---

56. Greek *katagōgion*, "dwelling place," but the word was also used more specifically to indicate a monastic dwelling, a cell, whose smallness is being contrasted with the city built by Theognius.

57. Greek *nēphontes* (*nēphein*). There is a real reversal of meaning here in this heavily ironic phrasing. *Nēphein* usually means "to be sober, sober-minded, vigilant" (1 Th 5:6, 8), but here the vigilance is for evil hearsay and gossip. *Nēpsis*, its cognate noun, "vigilance, alertness," was considered an important monastic virtue.

God teaches us through attacks, even if we wish to ignore them. Barbarian incursions taking place throughout the region were announced to us, but we pretended we did not know. There occurred reversals to wealthy and famous men who were nearly equals in glory to the emperor, catastrophes, and destruction, earthquakes and burnings, eruptions, and the destructions of different cities.[58] Through those who suffered these things, God wanted us who are foolish to be afraid, and we became all the more ill with our lack of fear. Remaining incorrigible, we add to our own evil. Let us not, I exhort and beseech you, let us not die in such a state! Let us not persevere up to the end in this useless practice and in the weakening of our dispositions. Let us instead change and turn our life to the most beautiful and solid way of life,[59] one that is pleasing to God who is calling us, so that we, while others fly angelically into heaven, will not be dragged down pitifully into the fiery abyss.

24. Let us examine carefully the past and the present and the future. Such a great host of locusts and their offspring have voraciously devastated the fruits of the earth that whether we are fearful or ashamed, let us kneel in repentance and heal our wounds. Springs are giving out and the rains stay away. Famines and pestilences and the deaths of people and livestock and, in order that I might speak succinctly, countless types of plagues sent by God have come upon us, as they once came upon the Egyptians. But we, being hard-hearted, do not wish to have our consciences pricked, not even a little, nor to change for the better the evil habits in which we are bound. No, in three ways we imitate pigs. Now first, having closed the eyes of the heart and having violated the boundary of the divine commandments, we are judged transgressors, desiring the present while we refuse to entertain a thought for the future. Now second, we gladly wallow in the mire of meddlesomeness, in self-love and contentiousness, refusing our whole lives to raise the eye of the soul to heaven or to meditate upon any of the heavenly mysteries, always engrossed instead in earthly things and inclined toward things that are base.[60]

Soon we shall appear more wretched and pitiful than the aforementioned pigs! To be sure, they will neither obtain resurrection after

---

58. Van den Gheyn, "Saint Théognius," 564, suggests that catastrophes such as these took place in Cilicia and Edessa, and in Antioch.

59. The Greek makes an important distinction between the two "lives": the first "life" translates *bios*; "way of life" translates *poluteia*, which often connotes an ascetic, monastic, or spiritual life.

60. Greek *chamaizēla*, literally "seeking the ground," like a pig rooting in the dirt.

death nor will they come into judgment. But woe to us honored with reason—who have received great promises and have been called to eternity and to the life of angels—who are eager to appear more dishonorable than [the most dishonorable of irrational beasts]![61] We despise God, we are heartless, we scorn the troubled, we neglect continual prayers and psalmody. We are called the faithful and commit the acts of the faithless. Whenever you hear that some people are afflicted with unbearable misfortunes, do not say that they alone have sinned and because of this they have been punished, but rather know that they are often chastised for your sake so that you, having heard of their calamities, might become wise without receiving a blow.[62] But you yourself refuse to lament in any way at all!

I sit in solitude,[63] and my mind watches over the cities and reflects upon some of its business and affairs and roams from street to street having chance conversations. I came to this church to offer through my address supplication for sins, but he that approaches God through prayer should think nothing at all of worldly matters. Now I, worthless slave that I am, when I was praying, while I ought to have fearfully and soberly offered up my petition with the greatest humility, instead I counted the suspended candles and the seats in the sanctuary, I calibrated precisely the planks of the roof with the main beams beneath them, and I measured with my fingers the four walls of the building of this house of prayer, and having given up any benefit from my prayer, I reaped the harm of evil distraction. Who would not bewail, who would not lament the lethargy of a completely wretched soul!

25. But having extended the present narrative excessively, in order not to perhaps also annoy those who are here, I shall cease from the public discussion of those things that distract the soul, first allowing myself and those listening to me to be reproved by individual conscience. After that, I shall turn this speech to you, the most noble of shepherds, O garlanded and God-bearing Theognius.

I have often heard in scripture some rich man pitifully saying: "Father Abraham, have mercy on me, and send Lazarus to dip his finger in water and cool my burning tongue."[64] But there was no way for him to attain his request for, already having passed away, he had

---

61. For the lacuna here, Van den Gheyn, "Acta Sancti Theognii," 110 n.1, prints the conjecture of Usener, which we have used, with modifications.

62. In Greek the words for "blow" and "calamities" are related.

63. Greek *en erēmōi*, which also means "desert, wilderness."

64. Lk 16:24.

departed from the human condition, and after one departs this life, repentance is futile because the door of compassion is closed immediately for those who refuse to repent here. Meanwhile, during the time that my spirit is not being demanded back,[65] and while my soul still inhabits this perishable tent and I let loose a voice of lamentation, I believe that I am pitied.

Father Theognius, have mercy on me,[66] who even before the coming wrath has been burnt sufficiently by the flame of my errors. Have mercy on me and beseech the Lord on my behalf, for I believe that you will obtain what you seek from the one who always proclaims and says: "Ask and it will be given you, knock and it will be opened for you."[67] But if you dare not approach the Master alone, take with you, father, all the holy ones who love you and, together with them, intercede on our behalf with the compassionate King, for the righteous are compassionate and fully compassionate towards those encompassed in flesh, since they themselves were also once mortal.

You see us continually, father Theognius, you consider us always. Immaterial and spiritual now, having put away the gloom and burden of the flesh, cross over the chasm stretched between the living and the dead! Come to us flying upon the wings of that virtue that you long ago achieved. Bearing to us divine gifts, strip us from our wealth of evil, clothe us invisibly in robes that flash like lightning, the very ones that the all-powerful grace of the Almighty, sought by us, weaves. One spark of your prayer will be able to incinerate untold heaps of sins! May we be purified from the filthiness of sin. May we be set aright and saved by your prayers, both those of the saints and of all the elect, in order that we might have a defense on that fearful day when God comes with a multitude of angels to judge the just judgment and to open the gates of his kingdom for the devout, but for sinners, those who refused to repent until their death, to pour out like rain cataclysms and streams of fire, because to him belongs authority over everything and to him worship is due and owed by all, to the Father, Son, and Holy Spirit, now and forever.

65. Wisd 15:8 (LXX).
66. "Have mercy" and "pity" both translate Greek *eleein*.
67. Mt 7:7.

# 7

# PARADISE REGAINED:
# SAINT ONNOPHRIUS

## Introduction

ATHANASIUS, IN THE LIFE OF ANTONY, THOUGHT THE MONKS HAD made the desert a city (Greek *Life*, chapter 14)—but that is the vision of a city-dweller. The monks believed with a different metaphor: God will make the desert paradise.[1] Adam and Eve are nowhere mentioned in the *Life of Onnophrius,* but the ghost of their fall and the angel of their restoration nevertheless live on the land in the realized eschatology of the desert monks. To Cyril of Scythopolis, later biographer of monks in the Judean desert, the life of Saint Euthymius was a "tale of the restoration of a pristine state in which human beings were no longer subject to the hegemony of sin. Euthymius is a second Adam and an image of the new creation."[2]

The *Life of Onnophrius* is a story, once again, of journeying, farther and farther into the desert—until God makes the desert paradise: in

---

1. The theme of finding paradise on earth occurs frequently in early monastic sources. In the *Life of Antony* 44, the first monks "were of one mind (see Acts 2:44–47), given to virtue, so that someone who saw them would say, 'Good are your dwellings, Jacob, and your tents, Israel; like shady groves and like gardens beside the rivers, and like the fruit beside the waters' (see Num 24:5–6)." See also Paul B. Harvey, trans., "Jerome: Life of Paul, the First Hermit," in Vincent L. Wimbush, ed., *Ascetic Behavior in Greco-Roman Antiquity: A Sourcebook* (Minneapolis: Fortress Press, 1990). For a discussion of this theme in the *Apophthegmata,* or *Sayings* of the desert fathers and mothers, see Douglas Burton-Christie, *The Word in the Desert* (New York and Oxford: Oxford University Press, 1993), 231–33. See also Peter Brown, *The Body and Society: Men, Women and Sexual Renunciation in Early Christianity* (New York, 1988), 218–24.

2. Robert L. Wilken, *The Land Called Holy: Palestine in Christian History and Thought* (New Haven: Yale University Press, 1992), 160. See *Cyril of Scythopolis: The Lives of the Monks of Palestine,* trans. R. M. Price (Kalamazoo, Mich.: Cistercian Publications, 1991), 1–92.

a final rebuke to the devil and all his demons, God *does* change stone into bread (see Mt 4:2–4), sand into water, the arid landscape into every kind of fruit-bearing tree, until we can only exclaim with the monks at the seemingly impossible: "Is this God's paradise?" (chapter 29).

In the *Life of Onnophrius,* Paphnutius, like Antony and Pambo, journeys into "the further desert" looking for "servants of Christ Jesus." The first servant he comes upon disintegrates in his hands, "like salt":

> I looked up and I saw a short-sleeved tunic hanging up, and when I touched it, this also fell apart [in my hands] and turned into dust. I, your brother, stood up, and I prayed and wept. I took off the robe I was wearing and wrapped him in it. I dug in the earth with my hands, and I buried him. I left that place (2).

The desert, Paphnutius discovers, is a serious place. Like the monastic life, like the Christian faith deliberately lived, it's not for Sunday visitors. Death is its doorkeeper.

Paphnutius, though, walks on "into the mountain of the desert" (3) where, on the other side of death, he catches his first glimpse of paradise: "Afterwards, when the sun was setting, I looked up, and I saw a herd of antelope coming from a distance—with the brother running with them, naked. Now when he came near me, I saw that he was naked and that his hair covered his entire body, serving as clothing." Abba Timothy, the solitary whom Paphnutius discovers, is Adam restored to paradise, naked and living in innocence with the animals.[3] Theognius lived peaceably with a snake in his cave;[4] fourteen hundred years later, monks on Mt. Athos still believed that such restoration was possible. Elder Isaac of Dionysiou had a snake as

> his inseparable friend. It was a huge, venomous asp, about a meter and a half long.
>
> During the two years that Fr. Isaac spent in the Monastery bakery, the snake never left his side. He would prepare good meals for him of paste and flour, and would care for the snake fearlessly. . . . He became so familiar with Fr. Isaac that he would climb up and sleep on his wooden bed. There he would coil up and quietly rest. . .

3. On the theme of the monks living peaceably with animals, see Burton-Christie, *The Word,* 231.

4. See pp. 149–50 above.

> All of this confirms the fact that many men of God, through their
> great virtues, are worthy to attain the state of Adam before the Fall,
> and to consort with the beasts.[5]

Timothy had been living quietly as a monk when God called him into the desert to be an anchorite. Timothy defines the anchoritic life in classic monastic terms: he will remain by himself, leading a life of "quiet contemplation" (*hesychia*), showing hospitality to strangers, and earning enough through the work of his hands to feed himself and help those in need (5–6). But the snake has entered the garden: Timothy gives in to sexual temptation and the need for human intercourse ("When we had become accustomed to talk freely with one another, we ate bread together") and has sexual relations with a female monk (6). The narrative in these two short paragraphs wonderfully captures both the ideal and the difficulty of devoting oneself completely to God. Monasticism, more often than not, is honest with itself.

Afraid of "the outer darkness and the gnashing of teeth and the fire that cannot be quenched and the worm that never sleeps and devours the soul," Timothy flees his sin. In archetypal monastic terms, he has overcome sexual distraction, the final temptation that draws one away from God.[6] Saint Antony believed that human beings could, through prayer and discipline, and—most importantly—guided by the Holy Spirit, return to their "original condition" of goodness.[7] The *Life of Onnophrius* visualizes this belief and gives it a setting: In the desert Timothy finds a spring of water, a cave, and a date palm tree that supplies all his food. The tree bears fruit year-round, as the trees must have done for Adam and Eve. Thus fed, Timothy eats no bread and clothes himself with his hair grown long, in a land of "uniform temperature." He tells Paphnutius that he has been there thirty years. It is paradise regained—except that Timothy is aware that his nakedness "should be respectfully covered" (see Gen 2:25; 3:7, and 21) (7).

Timothy's awareness runs deep, like a subterranean stream beneath paradise: paradise is not gained without a fierce, ongoing struggle with

5. Archimandrite Cherubim, *Contemporary Ascetics of Mount Athos*, vol. 1, (Platina, Calif.: St. Herman of Alaska Brotherhood, 1992), 355–56.

6. See Tim Vivian, "'Everything Made by God Is Good': A Letter Concerning Sexuality from St. Athanasius to the Monk Amoun," *Église et Théologie* 24 (1993): 75–108.

7. Vivian, 83.

the demons, especially the demons of the self. When Paphnutius begs Timothy to stay with him, he refuses, saying, "You are not strong enough to resist the attacks of the demons" (9). So Paphnutius takes himself even further into the desert, into his fears ("where this race of barbarians lives"), faces and overcomes death ("I allowed death into my presence"), and finally comes upon Onnophrius (9a).

Onnophrius, like a pillar of the more ancient desert, is "completely fire," an image the monks understood well.[8] Like Timothy, Onnophrius had lived in a monastic community, the monastery of Erēte "in the Shmoun area of the Thebaid." But when he heard the elders speak of the great Elijah and the even greater John the Baptist, both of whom had lived in the desert, he realized that the desert was the more perfect way. Unfortunately, the devil knows this, too, and wages even fiercer war against the monks in the desert. But if they endure, God rewards them with a taste of paradise: "They will journey and not grow weary, they will journey and not be hungry" (Is 40:31 [LXX]). God "brings them water from a rock. He makes the grass that grows in the desert sweet in their mouths, sweeter than honey (Is 48:21)" (12).

Paphnutius—and who can blame him?—cannot easily accept this vision, and so, like Pambo, he must ask Onnophrius: "My good father, did you suffer when you first came to this place in the desert?" (16) .The old man replies with the truth that Paphnutius, like us, is afraid to hear: "I suffered a great deal, my son. Believe me, my beloved son, I came close to dying many times on account of hunger and thirst and on account of the burning fire during the day and the frost at night" (16). But Onnophrius perseveres, and crucifixion—crucifixion of the self—becomes resurrection; Gethsemane becomes paradise regained:

> When God saw me, that I patiently endured in the fight of fasting and that I devoted myself to ascetic practice, he had the holy angels serve me my daily food, giving it to me every night and a little water every night in order to strengthen my body. And this palm tree pro-

8. "Abba Lot went to see Abba Joseph and said to him, 'Abba, as far as I can, I say my little office, I fast a little, I pray and meditate, I live in peace and as far as I can, I purify my thoughts. What else can I do?' Then the old man stood up and stretched his hands towards heaven. His fingers became like ten lamps of fire and he said to him, 'If you will, you can become all flame.'" *Apophthegmata* Joseph of Panephysis 7, *The Sayings of the Desert Fathers: The Alphabetical Collection*, trans. Benedicta Ward, rev. ed. (Kalamazoo, Mich.: Cistercian Publications, 1984), 103.

duced for me twelve bunches of dates each year, one each month, and I would eat it. And he made the other plants that grow in the desert places sweet in my mouth, sweeter than honey in my mouth. For it is written, "A person shall not live by bread alone, but he will live by every word that proceeds from the mouth of God"(Mt 4:4) (16).

God feeds Onnophrius, and we realize from the scripture Onnophrius cites that the food God offers is sacramental: Onnophrius, like Timothy, does not live "by bread alone" but by the word of God. Those who live by this word, this bread, receive the Eucharist directly from the hand of God. They are also granted visions of "the heavenly heights" (17). Paphnutius has now been vouchsafed a taste of paradise and a vision of heaven, but his journeying is not yet over. He stays with Onnophrius until the old man's death, at which time he travels further into the desert and comes upon four men who have seen no one for sixty years (25).

Now the story repeats itself: Timothy, Onnophrius, the four men—the same story, but it deepens the vision of paradise. The four men, like Timothy and Onnophrius, are fed by God, but the first two monks Paphnutius encounters eat fruit supplied year-round by date palm trees. The four eat bread baked by God:

> And suddenly some loaves of bread were brought forth, warm as though brought straight from a hot oven, and in addition other good dishes were brought in to eat. And we sat down and ate together. They said to me, "See, it has been sixty years since we came here. Four loaves of bread have been allotted to us each day; from God they come to us. Now since you have come to us today, look, yours too has been brought for us today and we have never known where they came from, but when we come in we find them sitting here all by themselves" (26).

With Timothy, Paphnutius glimpses paradise; with Onnophrius, he sees the paradise of another. But now, after leaving the four, he journeys on and comes to his own:

> I journeyed, and I came upon a well of water. I sat down and rested myself for a little on account of the hardships of the journey. Now there were great trees growing by that well, and when I had rested a

bit I rose and set about walking among the trees, looking at the fruits on them and saying, "Who was it that planted these trees here?" Indeed, there were date palms growing there laden with fruit. There were citron and pomegranate and fig trees and apple trees and grapes and nectarine trees and other trees with their beautiful fruits sweet as honey, with some myrtle trees growing in their midst and other trees that gave off a sweet fragrance. The well produced water and watered all the trees growing there (28).

Paphnutius, "standing in awe of the trees," can only exclaim, "Is this God's paradise?" (29). It is, because now four young men come—clearly a doublet of the earlier story of the four—and tell Paphnutius of their encounter with an angel. While they are speaking to Paphnutius, he smells "a powerful and sweet fragrance whose like I had never smelled" (33). As he prepares to leave the next day, the Lord's day, "the fragrance returned, very sweet." An angel of the Lord comes and kindles their hearts. When Paphnutius receives Communion from the angel, God's messenger proclaims to him, "Life eternal shall be yours, and imperishable food."

We know now, if we have not realized it fully before, that Paphnutius's journey, like Pambo's, is really an interior one: the path he travels is the way to God; the bread he is searching for is the imperishable food offered by and in Christ (Jn 6:58); the monks he meets have perfectly realized the monastic calling—they have regained paradise. What marks this paradise? An abundance of food, as we have seen, but it is food shared, fresh bread heaven sent and fruits of every description, eaten by the monks together. Such sharing is a foretaste, quite literally, of the great banquet to come, which Christ will share with all believers (Mt 26:26–29). The monks in the desert practice what a friend of mine calls "banquet theology," anticipating while experiencing in the present the eucharistic kingdom, *Babette's Feast* in the desert. The main action of the *Life of Onnophrius* is not fasting but feasting.

And so the journeying ends—and continues—in the kingdom and towards the kingdom. T. S. Eliot wisely observed that "in my end is my beginning," and the desert monks knew that wisdom gained brought one full circle to humility. The *Sayings of the Desert Fathers* preserves a condensed variant on the *Life of Onnophrius*. In a story told about Macarius the Great, Macarius journeys into the interior desert where he meets two naked men. They are living in peace with the animals on an island surrounded by water in the middle of the desert. The experience of meeting these monks, this experience of paradise, has such a profound effect on Macarius that when, years later, renowned for his wisdom, he is asked to say a word to the brethren, he can only reply, "I have not yet become a monk myself, but I have seen monks."[9]

# THE LIFE OF ONNOPHRIUS[1]

*The life and monastic practice and ascetical habits
of the holy Abba Onnophrius the Anchorite,
who wandered in the desert on account of God,
resting himself from his labors on the tenth of June.
He ascended to Christ Jesus who loved him.
In the peace of God, Amen.*

1. A certain brother, an anchorite whose name was Abba Paphnutius, narrated a story to some God-loving brethren. These were the words that he spoke.

## Paphnutius Journeys into the Farther Desert

2. I, your brother, was thinking one day. He [*sic*] said that I should flee to the further desert so I could see whether there were any brother monks in the farthest reaches of the desert living as servants of Christ Jesus. So I walked four days and four nights without eating bread or drinking water. I continued walking into the farther desert, and on the fourth day I came upon a cave. When I approached it, I knocked at the mouth of the cave according to the monastic custom in order that a brother might come out and I might greet him. Now although I continued knocking at the mouth of the cave, no one answered me. I said to myself, "Perhaps there's no brother monk inside." I went inside the cave, calling out before me, "Bless me." Now I saw a brother sitting

---

9. *Apophthegmata* Macarius the Great 2 (Ward, trans., 125–26).

1. The translation is based on the unpublished text of Codex Pierpont Morgan M. 580, folios 1v–19v, found in the Coptic manuscript collection of the J. Pierpont Morgan Library in New York. I wish to thank the Morgan Library for permission to publish this translation. Paragraphing and chapter headings are the translator's.

silently inside. I stretched out my hands and took hold of both his shoulders, and they disintegrated in my hands like salt. I felt his body all over and found that he had been dead a long time. I looked up and I saw a short-sleeved tunic hanging up, and when I touched it, this also fell apart in [my hands] and turned into dust. I, your brother, stood up, and I prayed and wept. I took off the robe I was wearing and wrapped him in it. I dug in the earth with my hands, and I buried him. I left that place.

## Paphnutius Meets Timothy the Hermit

3. I walked on into the mountain of the desert. I found a cave, and I found some human footprints inside at the mouth of the cave. I summoned up my courage and knocked at the mouth of the cave. No one answered me, so I took counsel with myself, saying, "This is where the servant of God lives. He usually comes here." So I stayed there praying until late in the day, reciting scripture I had learned by heart. Afterwards, when the sun was setting, I looked up and I saw a herd of antelope coming from a distance—with the brother running with them, naked. Now when he came near to me, I saw that he was naked and that his hair covered his entire body, serving as his clothing. Now when he came near me and saw me, he got very scared, thinking that I was a spirit. He stopped and prayed, for numerous spirits would tempt him, as he told me later.

4. Now I perceived [that he was afraid]. I went up to him. I said to him, "Why are you afraid, servant of Christ Jesus who is God? Look, and you'll see by my footprints that I am a man. Touch me, and see that I am flesh and blood." He gazed at me and recited the Lord's Prayer. Now I urged him to take me into the cave, and when I had gone into the cave he said to me, "Why have you come into this desert place, servant of God?" I said to him, "I have come to see the servants of God who live in this desert, and God has not refused me what I was seeking." Now I asked him in turn, "How is it that you came to this place? And how long has it been since you came here? What do you eat and drink? Why aren't you wearing any clothes?"

## The Story of Abba Timothy

5. Now he began to speak with me in this fashion: "I was a monk living in a community of monks in the district of the Thebaid, working as a basket weaver. There came into my heart a thought of this kind:

'Rise and go away into this desert. Remain by yourself in your dwelling, and you will lead a life of quiet contemplation[2] as an anchorite, and you will show hospitality to the stranger, and you will earn more than enough through the work of your hands.' Now I—that which I thought, I did, and I departed from my brother monks. I built myself a small dwelling, and I stayed in it. Numerous people gave me work to do, and I profited from my life as an anchorite, and what I earned each day I would give to strangers in charity.

6. "Now the enemy, who hates all that is good, was jealous of me at that time because of the wages I was going to receive from God on account of what I was doing for strangers and for others who were in need. Seeing the work of my hands, how diligent I was and how I gave it to God, he was jealous of me on account of what I was doing. He went to a female monk. She came to me and employed me to do a little work, and when I got everything done I gave it to her. Now she in turn gave me some more small jobs to do, and when it had become a regular thing for us to meet with one another, the enemy put it into her heart to take more work from me. When we had become accustomed to talk freely with one another, we ate bread together. [The affair continued to grow] until finally we conceived suffering and gave birth to wickedness. Now when I had fallen into folly with her, we persisted in wickedness with each other for six months. After a while, I was reflecting in my heart about what I had done. I deeply regretted it and was sorry for what I had done. I wept bitterly and groaned in my heart, saying, 'If today or tomorrow I were to die, I would be punished with a severe punishment for what I have done.' I reflected on the outer darkness and the gnashing of teeth and the fire that cannot be quenched and the worm that never sleeps and devours the souls of the ungodly.[2a] I wept for myself, all alone, saying, 'Woe is me! Arise, my soul! Let us leave this place and go into the desert.'

7. "Now I was glad to flee from my sin with the woman. I rose and I came to the desert, and I renounced everything between myself and that woman. I found this spring of water and this cave and date palm tree. And my life was fixed like this: This palm tree produces twelve bunches of dates each year, one each month, and this bunch from a single palm tree lasts me for thirty days at a time, and after the thirty days another bunch grows in its place. I have no bread for food and my hair has con-

2. Coptic *esychia* = Greek *hesychia*.
2a. Mk 9:48 and Mt 22:13

tinued to grow and my clothes have completely worn out. Now I clothe with the hair of my head what should be respectfully covered. And look! It has been thirty years today since I came here. The weather offers me a uniform temperature and I eat no bread at all."

## The Man of Light

8. Now I asked him, saying, "When you first came here, did you suffer a great deal or not?" He said to me: "I suffered a great deal when I came here, so much that I threw myself to the ground on account of the pain I had in my heart and was unable to do my appointed prayers. I would stand up but then fall to the ground because of the pain I had in my heart, crying out to God on account of my many sins. I suffered greatly from a great infirmity.[3] Now it happened one day while I was sitting down because this pain was afflicting me more than usual that I looked and saw a man radiant with glory. He came and stood before me. He said to me, 'Show me where you are sick,' and I showed him my diseased liver. He stretched out his hand over me, and with his fingers joined together, he cut open my side as with a knife. He brought out my liver and showed me the wounds on it. He healed them and bound them up. He put my liver back as it was. He smoothed over my body with his hand and rejoined the place that he had cut apart. He said to me, 'See, you are healed. Do not sin again, that no worse evil happen to you.[4] But be a servant of the Lord now and forever.' Since that day the pain in my liver has ceased, and I have lived in this desert without pain since that day. And he taught me about the bindings with which he treated me."

## Paphnutius Leaves Timothy

9. I begged him to let me stay in the cave where he lived. He said to me, "You are not strong enough to resist the attacks of the demons." I entreated him to tell me his name, and he said to me, "My name is Timothy. Remember me, my brother, so that the Lord will allow me to finish my good work." I knelt down at his feet so that he might bless me and remember me. He blessed me, saying, "May my Lord Jesus bless you and guard you and watch over you and keep you from all

---

3. Or: ". . . crying out to God. On account of my many sins I suffered. . . ."
4. Jn 5:14.

snares of the devil, and may he always set you on paths of righteousness so that you always flee to his holy ones."

## The Man of Light Returns

9a. Now when he had blessed me, I immediately left him, and I gave glory to God. I was not concerned about my life, but I took myself into the further desert where this race of barbarians lives. I fled to that place, saying, "Perhaps I will find one of the anchorites who live there, a servant of Christ Jesus." Now I took a little bread with me and a little water, enough for four days' journey. I rose and I journeyed. When four days had passed, I ran out of the little bit of bread and water I had. I was so worn out that I thought I was going to die, but at the same time my heart was strengthened. I allowed death in my presence. I journeyed on another four days without eating or drinking. I was in great distress on account of withering thirst and the hardships of the road. I was close to death, and my soul was close to leaving my body. I threw myself down to the ground, thinking that I was going to die. Suddenly, a man of light touched my lips as a physician touches a person's eyes. Immediately my strength returned, and I did not feel hungry or thirsty. Now when I saw this great wonder that had happened to me, I rose and I journeyed into the desert.

## Paphnutius Meets Onnophrius

10. Now when four days had passed, I was worn out. I rose and stretched out my hands and I prayed, and suddenly a man of light came to me, the one who had come to me the first time. And when he came, he stood over me and he strengthened me as he had done the first time. In short, seventeen days passed while I journeyed in this manner. Suddenly I looked in the distance. I saw a man coming who was completely fire, his hair spread out over his body like a leopard's. Indeed, he was naked, and leaves from a plant covered his shameful parts. Now when he came close to me, I climbed up on a mountain ledge, thinking that he was a mountain man. Now when he came closer, he threw himself under the mountain ledge in the shade because he was exhausted and because of his hunger and thirst. Indeed, he was in grave danger of dying. He raised his eyes to the mountain ledge and called to me, saying, "Paphnutius, come down to me, man of God. I,

too, am a man of the desert, like yourself. I live in this desert on account of God." Now when I heard these things, I went down. I fell on my face and worshiped him. He said to me, "Rise, my son, you are a friend; you too are a servant of God." And when I had sat down in front of him, I began to entreat him to tell me his name and to teach me his way of life.

## The Story of Onnophrius

11. He said: "My name is Onnophrius, and for sixty years I have lived in this solitary place and desert. I walk in the mountains like the wild beasts, and I live on the plants and trees, and I have not seen anyone I know. I lived in a monastic community in the Shmoun area of the Thebaid, and the name of that monastery was Erete.[5] There we were gathered together, all of one mind, living with each other and eating together, with the peace of God dwelling in our midst. We lived a life of quiet contemplation, glorifying God. Now I was a youth, receiving spiritual formation from these great and perfect ones for the service of God. For many times I heard them speaking of the life of Elijah the Tishbite, how he was powerful in God in every way. There lived in the desert also John the Baptist: Of those born of woman, none has arisen greater than he.[6] He lived in the desert until the day of his manifestation to Israel. I said to them, 'My fathers, aren't those who live in the desert more glorious than we before God?' They said to me, 'Indeed we gather together every day, and we eagerly gather together for worship. When we are hungry, we find food prepared for us; when we are thirsty, we find water to drink. When we are weak, the brothers help us, and when we want something to eat, we serve one another. But how will those who live in the desert find things like this? Or if they are hungry, how will they find food so they can eat?

12. "Indeed, when they begin their lives as anchorites, they suffer on account of hunger and thirst and the difficulties of the anchoritic life and the difficulties of the war against them. Therefore, the devil knows that there is a great reward for them before God. Only when they [endure] do the mercies of God establish them. He sends his angel and he serves them. For it is written in the prophet: "Those who wait for

---

5. Shmoun was the Egyptian Khemenu, the Hermopolis Magna of the Greeks, and the Ashmunen of the Arabs.

6. Mt 11:11.

the Lord will renew their strength, they will spread their wings like an eagle. They will journey and not grow weary, they will journey and not be hungry,"[7] and he "brings them water from a rock."[8] He makes the grass that grows in the desert sweet in their mouths, sweeter than honey. If trouble overtakes them or temptation comes upon them, immediately they stretch out their hands and pray to Jesus the true King. He causes his help to come speedily and he saves them because of the uprightness of their hearts. Haven't you heard that "the Lord will not ever forsake the poor man; the patient endurance of the poor man will not perish utterly"?[9] And again, "This is the poor man who has cried out. The Lord has heard him and rescued him from all his afflictions."[10] God gives to each person according to his heart. Blessed is he who will do the will of God on earth, for the angels serve him and continue to comfort him at all times.'

13. "Now I, my beloved and God-loving brother, when I heard these things from these great and perfect ones, it was as if I had traveled to another world. I got up at night. I took with me a little bread to eat, enough for a journey of four days, until I reached the place that the Lord would determine for me. Now when I had left my little cell at night, I set out on the road. And when I had gone up into the mountain, I looked and I saw the form of a man before me. I was very afraid. I was thinking in my heart that I would turn back and remain where I first was. He said to me, 'Do not be afraid. I am the angel who has walked with you since you were a child. Indeed, you shall complete this stewardship.'

14. "Now as I walked he walked with me, and when I had gone up into the mountain, I journeyed on into the desert six or seven miles. I saw a small cave. I turned towards it to see whether or not there was a brother monk inside. And I called in front of the cave according to the custom of the brethren, 'Bless me.' Suddenly a great and perfect one of God came out to me; there was a great glory upon his face and his form was very beautiful. Now when I saw him, I fell on my face and worshiped him, and immediately he raised me up and greeted me. He said to me, 'You are Onnophrius, my fellow worker in the Lord. Come

7. Is 40:31 (LXX).
8. Is 48:21 (Num 20:11).
9. Ps 9:9–12?
10. Ps 34:6.

in. The Lord be with you. You have succeeded in the good work that was appointed for you.'

15. "I went in, and I stayed with him a few days, and he taught me how to do the works of the desert. Now when he saw that I was enlightened in mind and that I understood the fighting that takes place in the desert, he said to me, 'Rise, come with me, and I will take you to a desolate place in the further desert, and you will remain there practicing asceticism for the sake of God because the Lord has determined that you will do work of this sort.' Now he rose and walked with me into the desert a four days' journey. We came upon a hut and a date palm growing alongside the hut. He said to me, 'This is the place where the Lord has determined you will remain.' Now he stayed with me for a month of days until I knew how to do the good work that it was right for me to do. Afterwards he left me, and we did not see each other for a year, until the day that blessed old man laid his body down. I buried him where he had lived."

## Paphnutius Learns of the Ascetic Life

16. I said to him, "My good father, did you suffer when you first came to this place in the desert?" The blessed old man said: "I suffered a great deal, my son. Believe me, my beloved son, I came close to dying many times on account of hunger and thirst and on account of the burning fire during the day and the frost at night. My members were soaked by the dew of the sky. When God saw me, that I patiently endured in the fight of fasting and that I devoted myself to ascetic practice, he had the holy angels serve me my daily food, giving it to me every night and a little water every night in order to strengthen my body. And this palm tree produced for me twelve bunches of dates each year, one each month, and I would eat it. And he made the other plants that grow in the desert places sweet in my mouth, sweeter than honey in my mouth. For it is written, 'A person shall not live by bread alone, but he will live by every word that proceeds from the mouth of God.'[11] For if you do the will of God, wherever you are he will care for you, because your Father in heaven knows what all your needs are, what you will eat or what you will drink. But rather 'seek first his kingdom and his righteousness, and all these things will be added unto you.'"

11. Mt 4:4; Lk 4:4.

17. Now when I heard these things from him I was greatly amazed. I said to him, "My sweet and good father, where do you receive the Eucharist on the Sabbath and the Lord's day?" He said to me: "Every Sabbath and every Lord's day, an angel comes to me and gives me the Eucharist on the Sabbath and the Lord's day. And blessed is every one who lives as a citizen in the desert on account of God and sees no human being—he brings the Eucharist to them and comforts them. If they desire to see anyone, they are taken up to the heavenly heights and they see them. They greet them[12] and their hearts are filled with light. They rejoice in the Spirit and are glad in the good things they will never lack. When they see them, they are comforted, and they completely forget the afflictions that have been theirs. Afterwards they return to their places, and they are comforted for a long time, as though they had been removed to another world. Because of the great joy they have seen, they do not remember that this world even exists."

## Paphnutius Goes to Live with Onnophrius

18. When I heard these things from him, I greatly rejoiced, and I forgot all the sufferings I had experienced while I journeyed in the mountains; the hunger and thirst were as nothing to me. The strength returned to my body, and youthful vigor returned to my soul. I said to him, "Blessed am I, my father, that I have been worthy to see you and that I have been worthy to listen to your comforting words." He said to me, "Rise, my good brother, and let us journey to where we will live." Now the two of us rose and journeyed together two or three miles. (I marvelled at the strength of that blessed old man and anchorite!) Now we walked together and came to a hut with a date palm growing beside the hut. He stood and prayed with me, and when he had finished praying, he gave the "Amen." We sat together and continued to talk with each other about the greatness of God.

19. When evening had come and the sun was about to set, I saw a loaf of bread lying there and a jar of water. He said to me, "Rise, my brother, and eat this bread lying here and this little bit of water, for you are exhausted from hunger and thirst and the hardships of the journey." I said to him, "As my Savior lives, I will not eat nor will I drink unless we stretch out our hands together and eat together, the

---

12. Or "They are greeted. . . ."

two of us." Now when I continued to entreat him, with difficulty and after a long time I caused him to change his mind. Afterwards we stretched out our hands and ate together from the bread. We drank and left some water, and then we drank some more water and left some. Afterwards, we spent the whole night praying until morning.

## Onnophrius Commissions Paphnutius

20. When morning came, while he was praying, he turned around and came towards me. I looked and I saw that his face had been transformed and changed. He had become a different person, as though he had changed into fire, and his appearance greatly frightened me. But he said to me, "Do not be afraid, my God-loving brother, for it is the Lord who has sent you to care for my body and place earth upon earth, for this very day I shall complete my stewardship and go to the place of my everlasting rest." (Now that day was the tenth of June.) He said to me, "My brother Paphnutius, when you go to Egypt, proclaim my name as fragrant incense in the midst of the brethren. For whoever at worship makes an offering in my name and in memory of me, the Lord will bring him first at the hour of the glorious thousand years. And whoever feeds a poor brother on my feast day, the Lord will bring him first at the hour of the thousand years." But I said to him, "My father, if he is poor, he will not be able to make an offering at worship on your feast day or feed a brother on account of his need of bread." He said to me, "Let him offer a little incense in my name." I said to him, "If [he] has no incense on account of [his] complete destitution and poverty, will you not bring him first at the hour of the thousand years? Come, my father, let your grace rest upon these other ones, for whatever you ask from God, he will grant it to you." He said to me, "Let him recite the prayer three times in my name if he is poor. I will cause the Lord to bring him first at the hour of the thousand years, and he will receive an inheritance with all the saints."

21. Now I said to him, "My holy father, what if [he is] ill and unable to stand and recite three of the six prayers?" He said to me, "Let him eat bread with some of the brothers on my feast day—for I will still approach the Lord in this manner—and I will ask the Lord to bring him first at the hour of the thousand years." Now I said to him, "My father, if I am worthy, I wish to remain here when you depart from this place." He said to me, "My son, you have not been appointed to this

task. Rather, the Lord has appointed you to profit and comfort his holy ones who live in the desert, to proclaim their memory and sweet fragrance among the brethren as a benefit to those who listen. Now go to Egypt, my son, and persevere in the good work." I fell on my face and said to him, "Bless me, then, my holy father, that I may stand before God, and as I have been worthy to see you in this world, so may I be worthy to see you in the other world before my Lord Jesus Christ."

22. Now he said to me, "May the Lord not cause you to grieve about anything, my son. May he strengthen you in this [. . .],[13] for surely your eyes will see the light of his divinity; that you neither turn away nor fall, my son; that you succeed in the good work that you have undertaken. May the angels of God shelter you and deliver you from all plottings of the evil one, and may no accusation find you when you come to meet God."

## The Death of Onnophrius

23. When he had finished blessing me, he praised God with great sighs and many tears. Afterwards, he lay down on the ground and gave his spirit into the hands of God. And I heard great angelic voices singing hymns before the blessed Abba Onnophrius, and there was great gladness when he came to meet God.

24. Now I took off the cloak I was wearing (and) tore it in two. I put one piece on his form as a burial shroud; with the other piece I covered myself so I would not stay naked. I set his body down in a depth of rock. I heaped upon him a great gathering of rocks, and I stood and prayed and suddenly the palm tree fell down and the hut fell down too. Now I was greatly amazed at what had so suddenly happened, and I ate what was left of the bread and I drank the water that remained in the jug.

## Paphnutius Meets the Four Men

25. Now when I saw that it was not God's will that I remain there, I stretched out my hands, and I cried out to my Lord, and suddenly the man whom I had seen the first time came to me again. He strength-

---

13. A word is missing in the text. Another manuscript of the Coptic *Life* has "in his love."

ened me as he had done the first time. Now I journeyed on from that place, very sorrowful about the blessed old man, but at the same time there was great joy in my heart because I had been worthy of the blessing of the holy one, Abba Onnophrius. Now I walked on another three days and three nights, and I came upon a small monastic cell all by itself in the desert. I went in but I did not find anyone inside. Now after I had sat for a little bit, I was thinking and I said, "Why isn't there anyone in this cave?" Just as I thought this to myself, all of a sudden a man beautiful in appearance came inside to me with palm leaves partly covering him in the shape of a garment. When he saw me he said to me, "You are Paphnutius, the one who watched over the body of the blessed Abba Onnophrius." Now I immediately threw myself on the ground and worshiped him. He said to me, "Rise, my brother. The Lord has given you to me as a fellow servant, for I was shown that you were coming to me today, my beloved brother. Indeed, I have been here for sixty years, and I have not seen another person except for the other brothers who are here with me." While he was speaking with me, three other brothers joined the one. They said to me, "You are Paphnutius, our fellow servant. Indeed, our Lord informed us that you were coming here to us today. You're the first person we've seen in sixty years." Now when they had spent some time talking with me, finally they said to me, "Strengthen yourself with a little bread, for you have come a great distance. Indeed, the wish of the Lord is that we remain together for a few days and that we rejoice with you, our beloved brother."

26. And suddenly some loaves of bread were brought forth, warm as though brought straight from a hot oven, and in addition other good dishes were brought in to eat. And we sat down and ate together. They said to me, "See, it has been sixty years since we came here. Four loaves of bread have been allotted to us each day; from God they come to us. Now since you have come to us today, look, yours too has been brought for us today, and we have never known where they came from, but when we come in we find them sitting here all by themselves."

## The Four Send Paphnutius to Egypt

27. We passed the whole night in worship and prayer until dawn. Now when dawn came, I entreated them to let me stay with them until the day of my death. They said to me, "Our brother, God has deter-

mined that your work is not to remain here. Rather, rise and leave this mountain for Egypt and tell those of the brethren whom you see to keep us in their thoughts, and it will profit those who listen." I entreated them to tell me their names, but they refused to tell them to me. Now I tried all the more to force them, but they would not tell them to me. They answered and said to me, "The one who has given names to everything and who knows them, he is the one who knows our names. Now, then, our brother, remember us until we see you in the house of God. Be careful now that you not allow the world to deceive you as it has done to so many." Now when they finished speaking with me, they blessed me and I left them in peace.

## Paphnutius Makes His Discovery

28. Now they showed me some other things that would happen to me, and when I left them, I journeyed, and I came upon a well of water. I sat down and rested myself for a little on account of the hardships of the journey. Now there were great trees growing by that well, and when I had rested a bit, I rose and set about walking among the trees, looking at the fruits on them and saying, "Who was it that planted these trees here?" Indeed, there were date palms growing there laden with fruit. There were citron and pomegranate and fig trees and apple trees and grapes and nectarine trees and other trees with their beautiful fruits sweet as honey, with some myrtle trees growing in their midst and other trees that gave off a sweet fragrance. The well produced water and watered all the trees growing there.

## The Four Young Men

29. While I was saying to myself, "Is this God's paradise?" and while I was standing in awe of the trees, four young men appeared in the distance, handsome in their appearance. They were dressed in expensive sheepskin clothing that they wore wrapped around them. When they came up to me, they said to me, "Greetings, our brother Paphnutius!" I prostrated myself and greeted them, but they raised me up and embraced me. We sat down and spoke with each other. Now they were very glorious and youthful, as though they had gone from this world to another world of light, so much comfort and joy did they bring to me. They set about gathering fruit from the trees, placing them in my

mouth. And as for me, I rejoiced because of the affection and loving-kindness that they showed toward me. I spent seven days with them, eating fruit from the trees.

## The Story of the Four Monks

30. Now I responded [*sic*] and said to them, "How is it that you've come here?" and "Where are you from?" They said to me, "Since God has sent you to us, we will tell you our whole manner of life. We are natives of a city called Pemjē[14] in Egypt. Indeed, our fathers were magistrates of the city of Pemjē, and they sent us to school to have us educated. Now we were in school, the four of us, friends with each other, and the four of us were like-minded fellows. When we had finished our education in the school, we were sent on to college to be well educated. Now it happened one day that we were alone together, and we said, 'Look, we've been well educated in the wisdom of this world. We also want to be well educated in the wisdom of God.' Now on the day when we were talking with each other in these words, a good inspiration stirred us to action. We rose, the four of us, and set off into the desert to see if we could find a little place and find shelter for ourselves inside it for a few [days] until we saw what the Lord had determined for us. We took with us a few loaves of bread and a little water, enough for a journey of four days.

31. "And suddenly an ecstatic vision from the Lord came upon us: A man of light stood over us; he took us and brought us to this place. (Indeed, this is the sixth year since we came here). Now when we had come here, we found a great and holy one of God and the angel of the Lord entrusted us to him. We stayed with him for a year of days, and he taught us to be servants of the Lord. Now when the year was finished, the blessed old man died, and we remained alone here. Believe us, our brother, for six years we have not known the taste of bread nor any other kind of food except for these trees alone, and we live on their fruit. Indeed, we see each other once each week. This is the place where we customarily gather, seeing each other on the Sabbath and the Lord's day for worship. Afterwards each one of us goes home and lives the life of God according to his ability."

14. Oxyrhynchus.

## Paphnutius Learns about Their Asceticism

32. I said to them, "Where do you gather for the Eucharist?" They said to me, "We assemble right here for that purpose, since every Sabbath and every Lord's day an angel of God comes to us and gives us Communion." Now I stayed with them and rejoiced greatly. On the seventh day—which is the Sabbath—they said to me, "Prepare yourself, our good brother, for the angel of the Lord comes and gives Communion to us—and to you, too. The one who receives Communion from the hand of the angel will be washed clean from all sin, and the adversary will in no way have power over him."

33. While they were talking with me, I smelled a powerful and sweet fragrance whose like I had never smelled. Immediately we rose and stood and sang praises to our King. Afterwards the angel of the Lord came and gave Communion to us. Now because of the fearful sight I had seen, I became like those who are asleep. He blessed me and ascended into heaven, while we all watched him with our eyes. And when the angel had gone, they brought me to my senses and said to me, "Be a person of determination." I rose, like those overcome by wine. We spent the whole night of the Lord's day standing and praising God.

## Paphnutius Is Sent by the Angel to Egypt

34. Now when dawn came and daybreak of the Lord's day, the fragrance returned, very sweet. We took delight in the fragrance like those in the other world of light. Afterwards the angel came and gave Communion to us and kindled our hearts. I too received from the hand of the angel, and he was saying, "Life eternal shall be yours and imperishable food." We in turn cried out, "Amen!" Afterwards he turned to me and said, "Rise and journey. Go to Egypt and tell what you have seen to the God-loving brethren, that they may emulate the good way of life. Behold, God has chosen you and counted you among the number of his holy ones on earth." I entreated him to let me remain longer with them, but he said to me, "Let each person walk according to what God has appointed for him, for all the things of the Holy Spirit are good. Indeed, God assigns to each person what he can bear. Now, then, rise and go." And after he had spoken to me, he ascended to heaven in glory.

## Paphnutius Leaves the Four

35. Now they brought a large quantity of plums, and we ate together. I left them, and they accompanied me about a mile. Now I entreated them to tell me their names. The first was John, the second was Andrew, the third was Hēraklamōn, and the fourth was Theophilus. And they commanded me to tell their names to the brethren so they would remember them. I made my journey and was very sad, but at the same time there was great rejoicing in my heart because of the blessings that the holy ones had spoken to me.

## Paphnutius Comes to Scetis

36. Now I left and set out on a journey of seven days. And when I stayed with the brethren, they were fearful of God. I rested myself with them for ten days. I told them what I had seen and what had happened to me. They said to me, "Truly you have been worthy to see God's great and perfect ones."

## Coda and Doxology

37. Now these brethren were [kind] and they lived in Scetis. They hurriedly wrote down all the words that they heard from me. They took the book to Scetis and placed it in the church for the benefit of every one who heard it read. And it was the topic of conversation in their mouths all the time as they glorified God and his holy ones. Glory to the Father and to the Son and to the life-giving Holy Spirit, now and at all times, forever and ever. Amen.

## Colophon

38. The life of the holy one, Abba Onnophrius, which he completed in peace on the sixteenth of Paone. Amen.

# BIBLIOGRAPHY

Albrecht, Ruth. "Women in the time of the church fathers." *Theology Digest* 36; no. 1 (Spring 1989): 3–7.

Blackman, Winifred S. *The Fellāhīn of Upper Egypt: Their Religious, Social, and Industrial Life To-day, with Special Reference to Survivals from Ancient Times.* London: G. G. Harrap, 1927.

Binns, John. *Ascetics and Ambassadors of Christ: The Monasteries of Palestine, 314–631.* Oxford: Clarendon, 1994.

——————. "The Distinctiveness of Palestinian Monasticism, 450–550 A.D." In *Monastic Studies: The Continuity of Tradition*, edited by J. Loades, 11–20. Bangor, Wales: Headstart History, 1990.

Brakke, David. *Athanasius and the Politics of Asceticism.* Oxford: Clarendon, 1995.

Brown, Peter. *The Body and Society: Men, Women and Sexual Renunciation in Early Christianity.* New York: Columbia Univ. Press, 1988.

——————. "The Rise and Function of the Holy Man in Late Antiquity." *Journal of Roman Studies* 61 (1971): 80–101.

——————. "The Saint as Exemplar in Late Antiquity." In *Saints and Virtues*, edited by John Stratton Hawley. Berkeley: University of California Press, 1987.

Brueggemann, Walter. *Interpretation and Obedience: From Faithful Reading to Faithful Living.* Minneapolis: Fortress Press, 1991.

Budge, E. A. Wallis, ed. and trans. "[Histories of the Monks in the Upper Egyptian Desert by Paphnutius]." In *Coptic Texts*, vol. 5, part 1 of *Miscellaneous Coptic Texts.* London, 1915.

——————. "The Life of Apa Cyrus." In *Coptic Texts*, vol. 4 of *Coptic Martyrdoms Etc.* Oxford: Oxford Univ. Press, 1914.

Burton-Christie, Douglas. *The Word in the Desert: Scripture and the Quest for Holiness in Early Christian Monasticism.* New York and Oxford: Oxford Univ. Press, 1993.

Caddell, H., and R. Rémondon, "Sens et emplois de *to oros* dans les documents papyrologiques." *Revue des études grecques* 80 (1967): 343–49.

Castelli, Elizabeth. "Virginity and its Meaning for Women's Sexuality in Early Christianity," *Journal of Feminist Studies in Religion* 2, no. 1 (1986): 62–63.

Cherubim, Archimandrite. *Contemporary Ascetics of Mount Athos.* 2 vols. Platina, Calif.: St. Herman of Alaska Brotherhood, 1992.

Chevillat, Alaine and Evelyne. *Moines du Désert D'Égypte.* Lyon: Terre du Ciel, 1990.

Chitty, Derwas J. *The Desert A City.* Crestwood, N.Y.: St. Vladimir's, n.d.

Clark, Elizabeth A. "Ascetic Renunciation and Feminine Advancement: A Paradox of Late Ancient Christianity." *Anglican Theological Review* 63 (1981): 240-57.

—————., trans. *The Life of Melania the Younger.* Studies in Women and Religion 14. New York and Toronto: The Edwin Mellen Press, 1984.

Conder, C. R. and H. H. Kitchener, et al. *The Survey of Western Palestine.* Vol. 3 of *Judea.* London: The Committee of the Palestine Exploration Fund, 1883.

Corbo, Virgilio. *Gli Scavi di Kh. Siyar El-Ghanam (Campo dei Pastori) e i Monasteri dei Dintorni.* Jerusalem: Tipografia dei PP Francescani, 1955.

Corrigan, Kevin. *The Life of Saint Macrina by Gregory, Bishop of Nyssa.* Saskatoon, Saskatchawan: Peregrina Publishing Co., 1987.

Deferrari, Roy J., trans. *Saint Basil: The Letters,* 4 vols., Loeb Classical Library: Cambridge, Mass.: Harvard Univ. Press, 1953.

Dembinsvka, M. "Diet: A Comparison of Food Consumption between Some Eastern and Western Monasteries in the 4th–12th Centuries." *Byzantion* 55 (1985): 431–62.

Doran, Robert. *The Lives of Simeon Stylites.* Kalamazoo: Cistercian Publications, 1992.

Elm, Susanna K. "The Organization and Institutions of Female Asceticism in Fourth-century Cappadocia and Egypt." Ph.D. diss., Oxford University, 1986.

—————. *"Virgins of God": The Making of Asceticism in Late Antiquity.* Oxford: Clarendon, 1994.

Emmett, Alanna M. "An Early Fourth-century Female Monastic Community in Egypt?" In *Maistor: Classical, Byzantine and Renaissance Studies for Robert Browning,* edited by Ann Moffatt, 77–83. Byzantiana Australiensia 5. Canberra: The Australian Association for Byzantine Studies, 1984.

Flusin, Bernard, and Joseph Paramelle, "De Syncletica in Deserto Jordanis (BHG 1318w)." *Analecta Bollandiana* 100 (1982): 291–317.

Friedan, Betty. *The Fountain of Age.* New York: Simon & Schuster, 1994.

Frend, W. H. C. *The Rise of Christianity.* Philadelphia: Fortress Press, 1984.

—————. *The Rise of the Monophysite Movement.* Cambridge: Cambridge Univ. Press, 1972.

Goehring, James E. "The Encroaching Desert: Literary Production and Ascetic Space in Early Christian Egypt." *Journal of Early Christian Studies* 1, no. 3 (Fall 1993): 281–96.

—————. "The Origins of Monasticism," In *Eusebius, Judaism and Christianity,* edited by Harold W. Attridge and Gohei Hata, 235–55. Detroit: Wayne State Univ. Press, 1992.

Gregg, Robert C., trans. *Athanasius: The Life of Antony and the Letter to Marcellinus.* New York: Paulist Press, 1980.

Harvey, Susan Ashbrook. *Asceticism and Society in Crisis: John of Ephesus and The Lives of the Eastern Saints.* Berkeley: Univ. of California Press, 1990.

Hirschfeld, Yizhar. *The Judean Desert Monasteries in the Byzantine Period.* New Haven and London: Yale Univ. Press, 1992.

[House, C.] "Nota in Vitam Sancti Georgii Chozibitae." *Analecta Bollandiana* 8 (1889): 209–10.

——————. "Vita sancti Georgii Chozibitae auctore Antonio Chozibita." *Analecta Bollandiana* 7 (1888): 95–144.

Hunt, E. D. *Holy Land Pilgrimage in the Later Roman Empire* A.D. *312–460.* Oxford: Clarendon Press, 1984.

Huxley, Aldous. "Distractions—I." In *Vedanta for the Western World,* edited by Christopher Isherwood, Hollywood: Vedanta Press, 1946.

Jones, A. H. M. *The Later Roman Empire 284–602: A Social, Economic, and Administrative Survey.* Norman, Okla.: University of Oklahoma Press, 1964.

Judge, E. A. "The Earliest Use of Monachos for 'Monk' (P. Coll. Youtie 77) and the Origins of Monasticism." *Jahrbuch für Antike und Christentum* 20 (1977): 72–89.

Leech, Kenneth. *Experiencing God: Theology as Spirituality.* San Francisco: Harper and Row, 1985.

Leipoldt, J. *Schenute von Atripe. Texte und Untersuchungen* 25.1. N.F. 10.1; Leipzig: J. C. Hinrichs, 1903.

Luibhéid, Colm. "Antony and the Renunciation of Society." *Irish Theological Quarterly* 52 (1986): 304–14.

Luibhéid, Colm, and Norman Russell, trans. *John Climacus: The Ladder of Divine Ascent.* New York: Paulist, 1982.

Markus, Robert. *The End of Ancient Christianity.* Cambridge: Cambridge University Press, 1990.

McNamara, JoAnn. "Muffled Voices: The Lives of Consecrated Women in the Fourth Century." In *Medieval Religious Women,* edited by John A. Nichols and Lillian Thomas Shanks. Vol. 1, *Distant Echoes,* 11–29. Kalamazoo, Mich.: Cistercian Publications, 1984.

Meinardus, Otto F. A. "Anachorétes modernes en Palestine." *Revue Biblique* 73 (1966): 119–27.

Meimaris, Yiannia E. "The Hermitage of St. John the Chozebite, Deir Wady El-Qilt." *Studii Biblici Franciscani Liber Annuus* 28 (1978): 171–92.

Meyendorff, John. *Imperial Unity and Christian Divisions: The Church 450–680.* Crestwood, N.Y.: St. Vladimir's, 1989.

Meyer, Robert T., trans. *Palladius: The Lausiac History.* Ancient Christian Writers No. 34. New York and Ramsey, N.J.: Newman Press, 1964.

O Murchu, Diarmuid. "St. Antony of Egypt: The Man and the Myth." *Cistercian Studies* 20, no. 2 (1985): 88–97.

O'Neill, J. C. "The Origins of Monasticism." In *The Making of Orthodoxy: Essays in Honour of Henry Chadwick,* edited by Rowan Willams, 270–87. Cambridge: Cambridge Univ. Press, 1989.

Ovadiah, Asher. *Corpus of the Byzantine Churches in the Holy Land.* Bonn: Peter Hanstein, 1970.

Ovadiah, Asher and Carla Gomez de Silva. "Supplement to the Corpus of the

Byzantine Churches in the Holy Land." *Levant* 13 (1981): 200–61.

Papadopoulos-Kerameus, M. "[An Encomium on the Life of Saint Theognius]." *Pravoslavnyi Palestinskii Sbornik* 32 (1891): 1–21

Patrich, J. "The Cells (*ta kellia*) of Choziba, Wadi el-Qilt." *Christian Archaeology in the Holy Land: New Discoveries. Archaeological Essays in Honour of V. C. Corbo*, edited by G.C. Bottini, et al., 205–25. Jerusalem: Franciscan Publishing Co., 1990.

Pearson, Birger A., and Tim Vivian. *Two Coptic Homilies Attributed to Saint Peter of Alexandria*. Rome: Corpus dei Manoscritti Copti Letterari, 1993.

Price, R. M., trans. *Cyril of Scythopolis: The Lives of the Monks of Palestine*. Kalamazoo, Mich.: Cistercian Publications, 1991.

——————. *Theodoret of Cyrrhus: A History of the Monks of Syria*. Kalamazoo, Mich.: Cistercian Publications, 1985.

Regnault, Lucien. *La vie quotidienne des pères du désert en Égypte au IVe siècle*. Paris: Hachette, 1990.

Rubenson, Samuel. *The Letters of St. Antony: Origenist Theology, Monastic Tradition and the Making of a Saint*. Lund: Lund Univ. Press, 1990.

Russell, Norman, trans. *The Lives of the Desert Fathers*. Kalamazoo, Mich.: Cistercian Publications, 1981.

Schneider, Alfons Maria. "Das Kloster der Theotokos zu Choziba im Wadi el Kelt." *Romische Quartalschrift* 39 (1931): 297–332.

Tsafrir, Yoram, ed. *Ancient Churches Revealed*. Jerusalem and Washington, D.C.: Israel Exploration Society and Biblical Archaeology Society, 1993.

Vailhé, S. "Les premiers monastères de la Palestine." *Bessarione* 3 (1897–98): 39–58, 209–25, 334–56.

——————. "Répertoire alphabétique des monastères de Palestine." *Revue de l'Orient chrétien* 4 (1899): 512–42.

Van den Gheyn, J. "Acta Sancti Theognii Episcopi Beteliae." *Analecta Bollandiana* 10 (1891): 73–118.

——————. "Saint Théognius, Évêque de Bétélie en Palestine," *Revue des questions historiques* 50 (1891): 559-74.

Veilleux, Armand. "Monasticism and Gnosis in Egypt." In *The Roots of Egyptian Christianity*, Birger A. Pearson and James E. Goehring, 271–306. Philadelphia: Fortress Press, 1986.

——————. ed. and trans., *Pachomian Koinonia*. 3 vols. Kalamazoo, Mich.: Cistercian Publications, 1980–82.

Vivian, Tim. "'Everything Made by God is Good': A Letter Concerning Sexuality from St. Athanasius to the Monk Amoun," *Église et Théologie* 24 (1993): 75–108.

——————. "Mountain and Desert: The Geographies of Early Coptic Monasticism." *Coptic Church Review* 12, no. 1 (Spring 1991): 15–21.

——————. *St. Peter of Alexandria: Bishop and Martyr*. Philadelphia: Fortress, 1988.

——————, trans. *Histories of the Monks of Upper Egypt and the Life of Onnophrius*. Kalamazoo, Mich.: Cistercian Publications, 1993.

—————— and Apostolos N. Athanassakis, trans. *Antony of Choziba: The Life of Saint George of Choziba and The Miracles of the Most Holy Mother of God at*

*Choziba*. San Francisco: Catholic Scholars Press, 1994.

Ward, Benedicta. "Apophthegmata Matrum," *Studia Patristica* 16, no. 2 (1985): 63–66.

——————, trans. *The Sayings of the Desert Fathers: The Alphabetical Collection*. Rev. ed. Kalamazoo, Mich.: Cistercian Publications, 1984.

Wilken, Robert L. *The Land Called Holy: Palestine in Christian History and Thought* (New Haven and London: Yale Univ. Press, 1992.

Wimbush, Vincent L., ed. *Ascetic Behavior in Greco–Roman Antiquity: A Sourcebook*. Minneapolis: Fortress Press, 1990.

Wortley, John, trans. *The Spiritual Meadow of John Moschus*. Kalamazoo, Mich.: Cistercian Publications, 1992.

Yarbrough, Anne. "Christianization in the Fourth Century: The Example of Roman Women." *Church History* 45 (1976): 149–65.

# SUGGESTIONS FOR
# FURTHER READING

We do not go into the desert to escape people but to learn how to find them; we do not leave them in order to have nothing more to do with them, but to find out the way to do them the most good.

—Thomas Merton
*New Seeds of Contemplation*

## I. Ancient Texts

(For a full bibliography, see Tim Vivian, "Reading the Saints: Early Monastic Texts and Resources Available in English." *Cistercian Studies Quarterly* 28, no. 1 (1993): 17–58.)

*Athanasius: The Life of Antony and the Letter to Marcellinus*, translated by Robert C. Gregg. New York: Paulist, 1980.

*John Cassian: Conferences*, translated by Colm Luibheid. New York: Paulist, 1985.

*The Coptic Life of Antony*, translated by Tim Vivian. San Francisco: Catholic Scholars Press, 1994.

*Cyril of Scythopolis: The Lives of the Monks of Palestine*, translated by R. M. Price. Kalamazoo, Mich.: Cistercian, 1991.

*Holy Women of the Syrian Orient*, translated by Sebastian P. Brock and Susan Ashbrook Harvey. Berkeley: Univ. of California, 1987.

*The Life of Saint George of Choziba and the Miracles of the Most Holy Mother of God at Choziba*, translated by Apostolos N. Athanassakis and Tim Vivian. San Francisco: Catholic Scholars Press, 1994.

*The Life of Shenoute by Besa*, translated by David N. Bell. Kalamazoo, Mich.: Cistercian, 1983.

*The Lives of the Desert Fathers: The Historia Monachorum in Aegypto*, translated by Norman Russell. Kalamazoo, Mich.: Cistercian, 1981.

*The Lives of Simeon Stylites*, translated by Robert Doran. Kalamazoo, Mich.: Cistercian, 1992.

*John Moschus: The Spiritual Meadow (Pratum Spirituale)*, translated by John Wortley. Kalamazoo, Mich.: Cistercian, 1992.

*Pachomian Koinonia*, translated by Armand Veilleux. 3 vols. Kalamazoo, Mich.: Cistercian, 1980.

*Palladius: The Lausiac History*, translated by Robert T. Meyer. New York: Newman Press, 1964.

*Paphnutius: Histories of the Monks of Egypt and the Life of Onnophrius*, translated by Tim Vivian. Kalamazoo, Mich.: Cistercian, 1993.

*The Sayings of the Desert Fathers: The Alphabetical Collection*, translated by Benedicta Ward. Kalamazoo, Mich.: Cistercian, 1975.

*Theodoret: A History of the Monks of Syria*, translated by R.M. Price. Kalamazoo, Mich., Cistercian, 1985.

*The Wisdom of the Desert: Sayings from the Desert Fathers of the Fourth Century*, translated by Thomas Merton. New York: New Directions, 1960.

## II. Modern Reflections

Binns, John. *Ascetics and Ambassadors of Christ: The Monasteries of Palestine, 314–631*. Oxford: Clarendon, 1994.

Bondi, Roberta C. *To Love as God Loves: Conversations with the Early Church*. Philadelphia: Fortress, 1987.

—————. *To Pray and to Love: Conversations on Prayer with the Early Church*. Minneapolis: Fortress, 1991.

Boulding, Maria, ed. *A Touch of God: Eight Monastic Journeys*. Still River, Mass.: St. Bede's, 1982.

Boyer, Ernest Jr., *Finding God at Home: Family Life as Spiritual Discipline*. San Francisco: Harper and Row, 1988.

Cherubim, Archimandrite *Contemporary Ascetics of Mount Athos*. 2 vols. Platina, Calif.: Saint Herman of Alaska Brotherhood, 1992.

Chittister, Joan *The Rule of Benedict: Insights for the Ages*. New York: Crossroad, 1992.

—————, *Wisdom Distilled from the Daily: Living the Rule of Saint Benedict Today*. San Francisco: Harper, 1991.

Davis, Bruce *Monastery Without Walls: Daily Life in the Silence*. Berkeley: Celestial Arts, 1990.

de Waal, Esther *Living with Contradiction: Reflections on the Rule of Saint Benedict*. San Francisco: Harper, 1989.

—————. *Seeking God: The Way of Saint Benedict*. Collegeville, Minn.: The Liturgical Press, 1984.

Elm, Susanna *"Virgins of God": The Making of Asceticism in Late Antiquity*. Oxford: Clarendon, 1994.

Jones, Alan *Soul Making: The Desert Way of Spirituality*. San Francisco: Harper and Row, 1985.

Leech, Kenneth *"God of the Desert,"* chapter 5 of *Experiencing God: Theology as Spirituality*. San Francisco: Harper, 1985.

Meninger, William *1012 Monastery Road: A Spiritual Journey.* Petersham, Mass.: St. Bede's, 1989.

Merton, Thomas *Contemplation in a World of Action.* New York: Image Books, 1973.

—————. *The Monastic Journey.* Kalamazoo, Mich.: Cistercian, 1992.

—————. *New Seeds of Contemplation.* New York: New Directions, 1961.

—————. *The Sign of Jonas.* New York: Image Books, 1956.

—————. *The Silent Life.* New York: Farrar, Straus & Giroux, 1957, 1989.

—————. *Thoughts in Solitude.* New York: The Noonday Press, 1956, 1988.

Nouwen, Henri *The Genesee Diary: Report from a Trappist Monastery.* New York: Doubleday, 1976.

—————. *The Way of the Heart: Desert Spirituality and Contemporary Ministry.* San Francisco: Harper, 1981.

Patrich, Joseph *Sabas, Leader of Palestinian Monasticism: A Comparative Study in Eastern Monasticism, Fourth to Seventh Centuries.* Washington, D.C.: Dumbarton Oaks, 1995.

# SCRIPTURE INDEX

## OLD TESTAMENT

*Genesis*
2:25    168
3:7     168
3:21    168
12:1    147
17:11   157
17:19   128
18:10   128
19      85
25:27   12
28:12   131
29:3    33
30:22-24  128
32:25   157
32:35   157
35:25   157
37:3    31

*Exodus*
17:6    131
19      27
20:17   122
24      27
25:5    146
26:14   146
32      26

*Numbers*
20:11   178
24:5-6  166

*Deuteronomy*
5:21    122

*Judges*
15:19   132

*1 Samuel*
2       99
2:21    128
17:36   113

*1 Kings*
18:15   18
21:13-19  123
21-22:40  99
22:34-38  123

*2 Kings*
2:11-14  146
5:27    121

*Job*
15:15   98
40:16(LXX)  15

*Psalms*

| | |
|---|---|
| 9:9-12 (?) | 178 |
| 12:5 | 130 |
| 17:12 | 17 |
| 27:3 | 19 |
| 34:6 | 179 |
| 34:6 (?) | 130 |
| 54:22 | 51 |
| 57:7 | 77 |
| 60:12 | 116 |
| 68:1 | 117 |
| 68:1-2 | 23 |
| 69:33 | 130 |
| 115:6 (LXX) | 103 |
| 118:7 | 17 |
| 118:11 | 23 |
| 119 | 86 |

*Proverbs*

| | |
|---|---|
| 9:10 | 100 |
| 14:13 (LXX) | 155 |
| 26:11 | 84 |
| 30:8 | 131 |

*Wisdom*

| | |
|---|---|
| 15:8 (LXX) | 165 |

*Bel and the Dragon*

| | |
|---|---|
| 33-39 | 32 |

*Isaiah*

| | |
|---|---|
| 5:8 | 122 |
| 6:2 (?) | 80 |
| 14:13-14 | 99 |
| 40:4 | 147 |
| 40:31 (LXX) | 169, 178 |
| 41:1 | 146 |
| 48:21 | 169, 178 |
| 58:9 | 155 |

*Jeremiah*

| | |
|---|---|
| 2:25 | 147 |
| 17:16 (LXX) | 146 |

*Hosea*

| | |
|---|---|
| 4:12 | 17 |

*Micah*

| | |
|---|---|
| 2:2 | 122 |

NEW TESTAMENT

*Matthew*

| | |
|---|---|
| 1:12 | 26 |
| 4:1-11 | 1 |
| 4:2-4 | 167 |
| 4:4 | 179 |
| 4:10 | 87 |
| 4:20 | 9, 13 |
| 5 | 27 |
| 5:7 | 122 |
| 5:15 | 148 |
| 5:16 | 145 |
| 5:22 | 99 |
| 6:7 | 81 |
| 6:14 | 122 |
| 6:29 (?) | 113 |
| 6:34 | 13 |
| 7:3 | 98 |
| 7:7 | 157, 165 |
| 9:48 | 175 |
| 10:1 | 121 |
| 10:9 | 129 |
| 10:37 | 114 |
| 10:42 | 131 |
| 11:11 | 177 |
| 11:23 | 82 |
| 11:28 | 115, 126 |
| 11:28-29 | 99 |
| 11:29 | 82 |
| 14:13-21 | 161 |
| 16:17 | 35 |
| 18:6 | 131 |
| 18:10 | 131 |
| 18:14 | 131 |
| 18:28 | 124 |
| 19:21 | 9, 13 |
| 22:13 | 175 |
| 23:12 | 82 |
| 25:14-23 | 124 |
| 25:34 | 126 (twice) |
| 25:35-36 | 126 |
| 25:41 | 126 |

26:26-29    171

Mark
1:6         51
2:19-20     104
5:43        75
7:36        75
9:41        124
9:48        16

Luke
3:16        30
4:3-13      26
4:4         179
6:21        160
6:25        160
7:1-10      121
9:23        94
9:28-36     27
10:15       82
12:25       81
12:27       28
13:6-9      74
14:11       82
14:13       131
14:26       94
14:33       9
16:19-31    123
16:24       164
18:14       99

John
1:3         29
5:14        175
6:58        171
11          29
14:2        35
14:12       111, 125
21:6        125

Acts
4:32        12, 15
4:34        13
4:34-35     9
7:54        16
8:20        10, 21, 121

Romans
2:6         94
8:3-4       17
8:32        23
8:35        19
13:10       160
14:4        98

1 Corinthians
3:13        35
6:10        99
7:24        94
9:27        17
14:34       43
15:10       16

2 Corinthians
6:15        84
12:10       18

Ephesians
6:12        147

Philippians
2:8         65, 82, 157
3:13        18
3:20        82

Colossians
1:5         13
3:16        103

1 Thessalonians
2:9         125
5:6         162
5:8         162
5:17        11, 14

2 Thessaalonians
3:10        14

1 Timothy
6:10        121
6:12        103

2 Timothy

4:7        146
4:8        146

*Hebrews*
12:23      24

*James*
2:13       122, 131
2:24       94
5:16       132

*1 Peter*
2:12       116
5:7        51
5:8        17

*2 Peter*
2:21       85
2:22       84
3:13       99

*1 John*
1:9        99
3:8        17

# INDEX OF
# NAMES AND SUBJECTS

Aaron, Abba, 2, 4, 107–33.

Abbas, 37, 74 n. 15.

Abraham, 26, 141, 147, 164.

Action, 108, 140.

Acts of the Apostles, 9, 13, 106.

Adam and Eve, 166–67.

Aelian, 158.

Aemilianus, 157.

Aeneas, 26.

Agape, 76.

Ahab, 99.

Alexander, 135–36, 138, 156.

Alexandria, 37.

Anastasius, Emperor, 137, 144, 152.

Andrew, 187.

Angels, 5, 25, 29, 31, 35, 126, 132, 140, 146, 150, 156, 158, 162, 164, 166, 171, 177–78, 180, 182, 186.

Animals, 20, 82, 87, 91, 171.

Antipater, 158–59.

Antony of Choziba, 53, 59, 65, 68–69, 93–97, 100–2.

Antony, St., 2, 4, 8–11, 13–24, 38, 45, 108–9, 138, 141, 167–68.

Ants, 81.

Aphrahat, 111.

Apollo (monk), 107.

*Apophthegmata* (*Sayings*), 11, 43, 171.

Aposchists, 142.

Apostle (St. Paul), 94, 120.

Apostles, 8, 13, 29–30, 35, 106, 136, 153.

Arabia, 1, 65, 89, 93, 95.

Ararathia, 141.

Arcadius, 33.

Archimandrite, 34 n. 11.

Arrogance, 17, 63–64, 80–82, 82 n. 38, 99.

Arsinoë, 24.

Asceticism, 2, 8, 11, 14–15, 17, 22–24, 64, 67, 74, 76, 86, 129–30, 132, 137, 145, 147, 150, 179.

Asia Minor, 1.

Askalon, 135, 153, 156, 158.

Aswan, 110, 118, 121, 127.

Augustine, St., 39.

*Babette's Feast*, 171.

Babylon, 129.

Bakery, 69, 88.

Balkans, 5.

Banquet Theology, 171.

Baptism, 4, 26, 109.

Basil, St., 39.

Belial, 84.

Benedict, St., 5.

Bethelia, 144–45, 151–54, 156, 158–59.

Bible, 44.

Bishops, 4, 5, 108, 113, 137–38, 144, 160.

Books, 14.

Bostra, 92.

Bread, 14, 18–19, 22, 46, 54, 60, 66, 78, 88, 113, 122, 132, 139, 150,

167–68, 170, 172, 174–76, 179–80, 183, 185.
Brueggemann, Walter, 3, 8.
Burial, 179, 182.
Byzantium (see Constantinople)

Caesarea, 56, 153–54.
Calamon, 44, 46, 62, 71–72, 78, 93, 134, 143, 149–50.
Capers, 101, 101 n. 92, 102.
Cappadocia, 141, 143, 146–47, 154.
Cassian, St., 5, 144.
Castelli, Elizabeth, 39, 44.
Castellium, 58.
Cave, 4, 47, 51–52, 56, 95, 136, 143, 147, 149–50, 167–68, 172–74, 178.
Celibacy, 146.
Cell (monastic), 24, 27, 29–33, 35–36, 52, 55–56, 58, 60–62, 67, 72, 78–80, 92, 101–2, 149–52, 178, 183.
Cell–dwellers, 58, 66, 79, 79 n. 30.
Cellarer, 78, 88, 97.
Chalcedon (Council), 142.
Chariton, 55.
Charity, 6, 65.
Cherubim, 64, 80.
Choziba, 53–58, 62–63, 65, 72, 78, 83, 93–94.
"Cells of Choziba," 56, 58, 60–61.
five Syrian monks of, 55–56, 58, 73, 86.
monastery of, 54, 56, 58, 73, 86.
Christ, 1, 3–4, 7, 16, 19–20, 23, 26–30, 33–35, 39, 52, 65, 71, 82, 84–85, 87, 94, 100, 103, 105, 109–11, 113, 117, 119, 121, 123, 127, 129, 145, 148, 151, 153, 155–60, 167, 171–73, 175–76, 178, 182.
Christians, 1, 12, 42, 57, 83–84, 107.
Church, 8, 12–14, 30–33, 36, 53, 67, 95, 101, 134, 139, 151, 187.
Church, the, 44.
Cilicia, 83, 154.
Clark, Elizabeth, 42, 45.
Cloak, 46, 72, 129.
Communion (see Eucharist)

Compassion, 65, 103, 107, 119, 122, 130, 140, 157–59, 165.
Constantinople, 3, 5, 39–41, 44, 48, 60, 66, 83, 137, 144, 152–53, 160.
Contemplation, 108, 150, 168.
quiet contemplation (see hesychia)
Control, 4.
Coprotha, 49.
Counsel, 67–68, 83, 90, 155.
Cowl, 72, 76.
Crocodiles, 24, 109, 118.
Cross, the, 65, 91, 155.
sign of the cross, 22, 82, 119.
Crucifixion, 169.
Cyprus, 71, 104.
Cyril of Scythopolis, 1 n. 1, 56, 135–36, 141–44, 166.
Cyrus, Abba, 28, 32, 36.

Damascus, 91–93.
Daniel, 32, 45.
Dates (food), 31, 86, 168–69, 174.
David, 113.
Day, Dorothy, 140.
Death, 28–29, 32, 35, 76, 82, 86, 95, 102, 109, 132, 136, 140, 160, 165, 167, 169, 173, 176, 182–83, 185.
Demons, 2, 5, 8–12, 19–20, 22–23, 68, 85, 116–17, 128–29, 150–51, 167–68.
Desert, 1, 2, 4–5, 21, 26, 29, 31, 33, 37–38, 40, 52–53, 55–56, 58, 65, 114–15, 142–43, 148–49, 159, 166–69, 171–74, 176–77, 179–80, 182.
Devil, the, 4, 10, 15–17, 20–21, 26, 34, 68–69, 79, 85, 95, 126, 150, 155–56, 167, 169, 174, 176–77.
Diospolis, 95.
Disciples, 136, 145–46.
Distractions, 9–10, 76, 140, 164, 168.
Divine Office, 79.
Doorkeeper, 74, 87, 89–91.
Dorotheus, Abba, 83, 94.
Dove, 156.
Dux, 158–59.

Earthquakes, 163.
Easter, 46.
Ecclesiastes, 64.
Egypt, 1, 5, 12, 14, 26, 56, 138, 154,
    184–86.
    Upper Egypt, 106–7.
Eli, 99.
Elias, 144.
Elijah, 18, 27, 109, 146, 169.
Eliot, T.S., 171.
Elisha, 109.
Elusa, 135–36.
Emperor, 33, 91, 152, 160, 163.
Enemy, the (see Devil)
England, 1, 5.
Epiphanius (monk of Choziba),
    66–68, 83–85.
Epiphany, 1.
Erete, 169, 177.
Esau, 33.
Eucharist, 60, 73, 97, 171, 180, 186.
Eunuch, 43, 47–50.
Eustathius, Abba, 155.
Euthymius, St., 1, 4, 166.
    *Life of Euthymius*, 1 n. 1.
Evil, 121, 126, 139, 147, 153, 158, 165.

Faith, 16, 70, 75–76, 83, 85, 111.
Fasting, 15–16, 23.
Fear, 34–35, 70, 77, 98, 100, 110, 116,
    151, 163, 173, 187.
Flavia, 142, 148.
Food, 12, 18, 31–32, 44, 51–52, 66, 74,
    74 n. 14, 76, 78–79, 86, 116,
    170–71, 173–74, 177, 179, 185–86.
Footpaths, 60–62, 68, 87.
Forgiveness, 63, 160.
Fornication, 17.
    demon of fornication, 16.
Forts, 23, 74, 74 n. 13.
Fundamentalists, 7.

Galatia, 101, 101 n. 91.
Gandhi, 108, 140.
Gardens, 54, 62.
Gaul, 5, 144.
Gaza, 135, 144, 153, 158.

George of Choziba, St., 3–5, 53, 56,
    58, 61–105.
Gerasimus, St., 58.
Gerontius, 142.
Gethsemane, 142, 148.
God, 2, 4, 6, 9–10, 13, 16, 18–19, 21,
    23, 26–28, 30–35, 41, 43–45, 47–49,
    51, 54, 64,71, 75, 77, 82–85, 87–88,
    91–93, 98, 100, 102, 104, 107, 112,
    116–17, 119–21, 123–28, 130–31, 133,
    136–41, 146–49, 151, 153–59, 161,
    163–64, 167–70, 172–73, 175–81,
    183–87.
Golgotha, 50.
Gospel, the, 1, 4–5, 8, 11, 13, 29,
    53–54, 114, 124.
Grace, 14, 93.
Greece, 1, 5, 135, 157.
Greeks, 159.
Gregory of Nazianzus, St., 43.
Gregory of Nyssa, St., 39, 43.
Guardian of the Cross, 83, 83 n. 44.
Guestmaster, 73,
Guests, 78, 78 n. 28, 80, 80 n. 34, 88,
    90, 97, 102–3.

Habakkuk, 32.
Hagia Sophia, 5.
Hagiography, 6, 8, 67.
Healing, 23, 63, 82, 106, 109–11, 114,
    123, 154, 158.
Heaven, 13, 24, 137, 145–46, 163, 180,
    186.
Hell, 81, 129, 146, 163.
Heracleides, 63–64, 70–72, 74–76.
Heraklamon, 187.
Hermopolis, 107.
Hesychasm, 5.
*Hesychia* (solitude), 4, 147, 147 n. 12,
    168, 174, 177.
Hierama, 46.
Hierax, Abba, 27–28, 30–31, 36.
Hillaria, 30.
History, 6, 40.
*History of the Monks of Egypt*, 106.
Holiness, 3, 38, 69–71.
Holy City (see Jerusalem)

Holy Land, 3, 5, 39, 44, 49–50, 54, 138, 141–42.
Holy man, 106–10, 112, 119–22, 124, 127, 132–34, 138, 160.
Holy Sepulchre, 50.
Holy Spirit, 26, 32, 48, 103, 117, 120, 120 n. 17, 142, 150, 180, 186.
Holy woman, 107.
Honorius, 33.
Hospitality, 59, 65, 69, 84.
Huck Finn, 26.
Humankind, 23, 75, 82–83.
Humility, 5, 63–65, 82, 99–100, 105, 137, 146, 164, 171.
Hunger, 169, 176–77.
Huxley, Aldous, 9–11.

Idols, 4, 107.
Illusions, 4.
Incarnation, 3, 29, 65.
India, 1.
Indians, 92.
Isaac, Abba, 2, 109, 113–14, 133.
Isaac of Dionysiou, 167.
Isaiah, 146.
Isaiah, Abba, 133.
Italy, 1, 5.

Jacob, 33–34, 157.
Jeremiah, 146.
Jericho, 50, 54, 56, 59–60, 63, 65, 69, 75, 88–89, 91–93, 96, 143.
Jerome, St., 37 n. 4, 39, 54.
Jerusalem, 1, 5, 39–40, 54–57, 59–60, 63, 65, 71–72, 83, 89, 91–93, 96, 137, 141, 143–44, 147–48, 151, 155, 161.
Jesus (see Christ)
Jews, 95.
John (*Life of Onnophrius*), 187.
John the Baptist, 169.
John of Choziba (John of Thebes), 56, 58.
John the Hesychast, 58.
John of Lycopolis, 111.
Jordan, 40, 59, 71, 76, 83, 93, 149.
Joseph, 31.

Journeying, 1, 26, 28–30, 43–44, 52, 166, 170–71, 176, 178–80, 183–87.
Judea, 1, 53, 55–56, 58, 65, 143, 166.
Judging, 35, 146, 159, 165.
Judgment, 32, 36, 82, 131, 138, 140, 163–64.
Julian, 142.
Juvenal, 142.
Justice, 108.
Justin, Emperor, 137, 144, 160.

Kallinikos, 57.
*Kelliotai* (see cell–dwellers),
Kidron Valley, 143.
King, Martin Luther, Jr., 140.
Kingdom of God, 99, 105, 126, 171, 179.
Kitchen, 58.
Krou(s)ma (signal), 86, 86 n. 53.
Ktema, 71.

Laban, 33.
Lazarus, 29.
Lent, 4.
Leontius of Choziba, 63, 69, 78.
Leopards, 87, 88, 176.
*Life of Antony*, 1, 7–10, 12–24, 37 n. 4, 166.
*Life of Melania the Younger, The*, 40.
*Life of Pachomius*, 111.
*Life of Sabas*, 56.
*Life of St. George of Choziba*, 53, 55, 58–59, 62–63, 68, 70.
Lions, 20, 32, 77, 113, 116.
*Lives of the Monks of Palestine*, 141.
Lord, the (Christ), 5, 8, 13, 17–21, 23, 31, 34, 70, 77, 85–86, 88, 92, 103, 108–9, 119, 125, 128–30, 146, 152, 159, 165, 175, 178–79, 181–83, 185–86.
Lord's day (Sunday), 34, 67, 84, 86–87, 126, 180, 186–86.
Lord's Prayer, 173.
Love, 5, 7, 18, 23, 29, 65, 98, 100, 109, 147, 162.

Macarius the Great, St., 171–72.

Macedonius, 108, 133.
Macrina, St., 43.
Magicians, 100.
Maiouma, 153.
Man of light, 119, 175–76, 182.
*Manouthion*, 66, 80, 80 n. 33, 81, 86,
  88–89.
Marcian, 141.
Mark, Abba, 133.
Mary, St., 17, 34, 60, 63, 68–69, 72,
  89–91, 95.
Meditation, 86.
Melania the Elder, 142.
Melania the Younger, St., 44–45.
Mercy, 107–8, 122, 131, 165, 177.
Merton, Thomas, 140.
Mesopotamia, 33, 72.
Minister, 77, 77 n. 20, 86, 86 n. 56.
Ministry, 59, 87–88, 95–96, 101–3,
  114.
Miracles, 6, 63, 68, 91, 106, 108–10,
  118, 127, 132, 135, 139, 153–55, 161.
*Miracles of the Most Holy Mother of*
  *God at Choziba*, 68.
Modestus, 83, 83 n. 45.
Monastery, 5, 14, 24, 36, 53, 55,
  57–60, 71, 77–78, 83–84, 87–88,
  90–91, 93, 101, 134–38, 143,
  148–49, 155, 169.
  cenobia, 4, 58–60, 80, 84, 86, 97,
    102, 143.
  hermitages, 143.
  laurae, 4, 58–60, 71, 71 n. 4, 72,
    77, 149.
Monasticism, 4, 7, 10–11, 24, 37, 45,
  168.
  anchoritic, 4, 41–42, 46, 136, 143,
    145, 168, 177.
  cenobitic, 4, 58.
  Coptic, 25.
  eremitic (see anchoritic),
  origins, 38, 108.
Monk/Monks, 1, 4–7, 9, 19, 21, 24,
  27–28, 33, 37, 37 n. 4, 38, 43, 45,
  51, 64–65, 71–72, 79–80, 86, 95,
  106, 108, 134–35, 144, 166–69, 172.
  dress, 43, 51, 173.

monastic habit, 43, 51, 65, 105,
  113–15, 147.
  way of life, 61–67, 116, 133.
Monophysites, 142, 144.
Moschus, John, 135–36.
*The Spiritual Meadow*, 135.
Moses, 26–27.
Mother of God (Mary), 63, 69, 72,
  78, 88–89, 91.
Mountain, 2, 10, 21–22, 24, 26, 29,
  34, 77, 117, 167, 173, 176, 184.
Mt. Athos, 5, 167.
Mt. of Olives, 44, 142.
Muledrivers, 90.
Muslims, 5, 56.
Mystery, 2, 26–27, 29, 79.

Nile, the, 24, 37–39, 107–8, 116, 130.
Nineve, 123, 123 n. 28.
Novices, 58.
Nubians, 108–10, 116, 116 n. 11,
  117–18, 127.

Odysseus, 26.
Oil (annointing), 18, 111–12, 154.
Oil (food), 78, 97, 97 n. 75.
Onnophrius, St., 4, 169–70, 172,
  176–87.
Oratory, 83.
Origenism, 101 n. 91.
Ovens, 54, 66, 89, 183.

Pachomius, 45, 112.
*Pachomian Koinonia*, 38–39.
Palestine, 3, 5, 40, 44, 56, 135–36, 138,
  144, 157.
Palladius, 37.
Palm Sunday, 1.
Palm trees, 31, 119, 169, 174, 182, 184.
Pambo, Abba, 2, 4, 25–36, 167, 169.
Pamoun, Abba, 28, 31–32, 36.
Paphnutius, 2, 4, 107, 109, 112–14,
  132–33, 167–87.
*Histories of the Monks of Upper*
  *Egypt*, 107–8.
"Life of Abba Aaron," 2, 112, 113
  n. 1.

*Life of Onnophrius*, 2, 4, 166–68, 171.
Paradise, 166–72, 184.
Passions, 98–100, 157.
Patient endurance, 15, 104.
Paul, Abba, 30.
Paul of Elusa, 134–41, 143–44, 157–59.
Paul, St., 82, 146.
Paula, 44.
Paulinus of Nola, St., 39.
Peace, 82, 105, 107, 131, 171, 184.
Pemje (Oxyrhynchus), 185.
Perfect, 9.
Persians, 53, 56, 79, 91, 91 n. 62, 92–93, 95–97, 102.
Peter, St., 29, 35, 82, 85, 106, 125.
Pharan, 46, 55.
Philae, 108, 113, 118, 120, 124, 133.
Piety, 62, 71–72, 75, 82.
Pilgrimage, 3.
Pilgrims, 3, 54, 58, 60, 63.
Poemen, Abba, 62.
*Politeia* (way of life), 8, 109.
Poor, the, 13–14, 33, 63, 90, 108, 114, 122, 131–32.
Possessions, 2, 7, 9, 12, 13, 15.
Power, 4, 20, 64, 106, 110, 135.
Prayer, 2–3, 5, 11, 14–15, 19, 24, 26, 34, 47, 51, 59, 62–63, 72, 75, 86–87, 95, 104–5, 108, 110, 124, 126, 132, 139–40, 142, 149, 161, 164, 173, 175, 181, 183.
Priests, 31, 34, 47, 58, 96, 115.
Prophets, 16, 34.
Proverbs, 64.
Providence, 84, 150.
Psalms, 3, 64, 67, 103, 138, 160.
Punishment, 34, 83.

Raïthos, 94, 94 n. 66, 101.
Reason (*logos*), 23, 164.
Regnault, Lucien, 37.
Relics, 135.
Repentance, 73, 85.
Reptiles, 72.
Resurrection, 28–29, 34, 109, 163, 169.

Rich, 111, 121, 124, 131.
Righteous, 35, 82, 99, 119, 126, 132, 136, 138, 154, 160, 179.
Roman Empire, 4, 56.
Rule (monastic), 77.
Russell, Jeffrey Burton, 6.
Russia, 5, 57.

Sabas, St., 56.
Sabbath, 67, 79, 115, 126, 180, 185–86.
Sackcloth, 49–50.
Saints, 6, 13, 17, 73, 84, 91, 103, 135, 140, 145.
Samson, 108, 131.
Saracens, 94–95, 150–51.
Sarah, Amma, 43, 128.
Satan (see Devil)
Savior, the (Christ), 8, 13, 17, 35–36, 106, 111, 115, 125, 144, 160, 180.
*Sayings* (see *Apophthegmata*)
Scetis (Wadi Natrun), 4, 30–33, 36, 114, 187.
Schneider, Alfons Maria, 54.
Scripture, 8–9, 14, 17, 44, 77, 89, 94, 130, 141, 147–48, 173.
Self–centeredness, 4.
Self–denial, 59.
Self–sacrifice, 5.
Shenoute, St., 34–35, 38.
Shmoun, 177.
Silas, Abba, 39–40, 43, 45–52.
Simplicity of heart, 86.
Sin, 17, 33, 35, 85, 93, 131, 134, 147, 158, 165–66, 168, 175.
Sinners, 34–35, 75, 87, 104, 140, 146, 165.
Slander, 63, 141.
Slaves, 42, 49–50.
Snakes, 20, 87–88, 91, 149–50, 167.
Social justice, 5.
Sodom and Gomorrha, 85.
Soldiers, 91–92, 128.
Solitude, 4, 52, 149, 164, 168.
Solomon, 28.
Sorcerers, 83–84.
Soviet Union, 5.

Soul, 18, 20, 53, 82, 84–86, 95, 140, 148, 150, 152, 162–63, 165, 174.
Spirit (see Holy Spirit), evil spirit, 68, 83, 87.
Spirituality, 5, 8, 11, 25, 41, 45, 53, 62–65, 68, 139–40.
Stephen, St. church and oratory of, 56.
Stephen the Syrian, Abba, 93.
Suffering, 33, 112, 146, 149–50, 158, 160, 169, 175, 180.
Suluh, 107.
Superior (monastic), 72, 77–78, 89, 93–96, 149.
*Synaxis*, 78 n. 27.
Syncletica, Amma, 3–5, 38–52.
Syria, 56, 111.

Tears, 35, 64, 75, 85, 92, 104, 149, 182.
Temptation, 17, 75, 95, 104.
Thebaid, 107, 169, 173.
Theodosius (monk), 142–43, 149.
Theodosius, Emperor, 33.
Theognius, St., 3, 4, 26, 134–65, 167.
Theophilus, 187.
Timothy, Abba, 167–70, 173–76.
Tombs, 19, 73, 86.
Tower, 150–51, 151 n. 22.
Transvestitism, 43.
Trinity, the, 27, 36, 84, 129, 133, 165, 187.

Tunic, 32, 78, 114, 167.

United States, The, 7.

Veilleux, Armand, 9.
Vigils, 14, 18.
Virginity, 8, 14, 41–42.
Virgins, 8, 14, 38, 42, 44, 48.
Visions, 22, 28–30, 77–78, 170, 185.
Visitors (see Guests)

Wadi Qilt, 54–55, 57, 62.
*Wall Street Journal, The*, 11.
Washington, George, 7.
Washington, D.C., 57.
Way of life, 3, 8, 24, 61–67, 76, 86, 108–9, 116, 133, 137, 148, 174–75, 177.
Widows, 38, 44.
Wine, 74, 78, 81.
Women, 8, 37, 60, 120.
  as monks, 8, 14, 37–38, 42–43, 47–48.
  as temptations, 16, 38, 51, 168, 174.
  in Roman society, 40–42, 45, 48.
Work, 14, 29, 65–67, 101, 108, 149, 174, 179, 184.
Worship, 21, 67, 183, 185.

Zeno, 30.
Zenon, 60.